Daniel Defoe and Middle-Class Gentility

Coat of arms from Defoe's frontispiece portrait
in *Jure Divino*, 1706

Daniel Defoe and Middle-Class Gentility

MICHAEL SHINAGEL

HARVARD UNIVERSITY PRESS

CAMBRIDGE, MASSACHUSETTS 1968

© Copyright 1968 by the President and Fellows of Harvard College

All rights reserved

Distributed in Great Britain by Oxford University Press, London

Publication of this volume has been aided by a grant
from the Hyder Edward Rollins Fund

Library of Congress Catalog Card Number 68-14273

Printed in the United States of America

To My Parents

Preface

In a recent book entitled *The English Gentleman,* the author began his work with a frank admission: "I myself am not a gentleman. If I were, I would almost certainly not be writing this book, for one of the marks of a gentleman is that he seldom mentions the question of gentility, whether in application to others or to himself." [1] The author who is the subject of this study was born just about three hundred years before this recent book on the English gentleman was published, and he also was not born a gentleman. But unlike this candid modern commentator on English gentility, Daniel Defoe was determined to claim for himself the status of a gentleman, and he wrote with disarming frequency and passion on "the question of gentility" to persuade the world — and perhaps himself as well — that he merited the title.

The aim of this work is to examine the significance of the theme of middle-class gentility in Defoe's life, works, and age. As a careful survey of Defoe's life will reveal, the quest for status and security, specifically his determined efforts to establish himself in society as a gentleman, beginning with his decision to become a London merchant, played a profound and intensely personal role in his mature life. Similarly a close examination of Defoe's works, both fiction and nonfiction, will disclose how consistently he gave expression to his ideas on the subject of gentility, sometimes incidentally but often prominently and personally; in fact, his treatment of the theme will be seen to span virtually his entire career as a writer, from *The True-Born Englishman* (1701) to *The Compleat English Gentleman* (1729). Finally the impact of Defoe's writings on his age was of far-reaching importance, for the turbulent years of the first three decades of the eighteenth century witnessed nothing less momentous than a cultural revolution in England, with the Whigs, largely middle-class and commercial, assuming the ascendancy over the Tories, largely upper-class and landed. From this shift in power, as Bonamy Dobrée has noted, "there emerges a new concept of culture, that is of values, and the relationships of people towards each other." [2]

[1] Simon Raven, *The English Gentleman* (London, 1961), p. 9.
[2] *English Literature in the Early Eighteenth Century, 1700–1740* (Oxford: Oxford University Press, 1959), p. 9.

Preface

Such a broad tripartite approach to Defoe's significant role as exemplar and exponent of middle-class gentility seems best suited to this kind of a study. If we are to arrive at a proper understanding of Defoe's unique place in his times, we must see him both as a remarkable person in his own right and as a representative product of his background and age. Professor Dobrée has summed up well Defoe's importance: "The most sanguine optimist could not hope for a more perfect representative of the changing, seething society of the time than Daniel Defoe, embodying as he does the essence of the new middle class." [3] In his richly varied career he became not only the celebrated author of *Robinson Crusoe*, for which he is still largely remembered and esteemed today, but also the vigorous spokesman for the trading middle class, with which he identified his interests most closely and which during the eventful period of his life was rising — as it ever rises — to a new and assertive national prominence. By focusing on Defoe as spokesman for this middle class we can gain a valuable perspective on those changing times, and by studying Defoe in the light of his personal interest in gentility perhaps arrive at a better understanding of him as well.

In the more than five years that I have worked on this project, I have benefited from the assistance of many persons, more than I can name here. But I would like to acknowledge my thanks to Professors W. J. Bate and John M. Bullitt, Dean John U. Monro, and Dr. Richard G. King, all of Harvard University, for their kindnesses and encouragement in the early stages of this study; to Professor Arthur Gold of Wellesley College for fruitful discussions on Defoe; to Professor Paul J. Korshin of the University of Pennsylvania for a close reading of a preliminary draft of this manuscript; and to Professor George H. Healey of Cornell University for generously sharing with me his extensive holdings of Defoe materials and his equally extensive knowledge of Defoe. I have profited from the research of many Defoe scholars, notably Professors John Robert Moore, Maximillian E. Novak, and James Sutherland, among others; I hope I have made my indebtedness to them all clear in my notes.

I have also been assisted in my research by the staffs of the Widener and Houghton Libraries at Harvard, the Boston Public

[3] *Ibid.*, p. 34.

Library, the Olin Library at Cornell, and the British Museum. A summer research grant from the Clark Fund of the Department of English at Cornell enabled me to complete my research and a supplementary grant from the same source enabled me to have this manuscript prepared for the press.

Finally I think it only fitting to mention my children, Mark and Victoria, in spite of whose affectionate interruptions my work somehow got done, and my wife Ann, largely because of whose devotion and good cheer it was brought to completion.

Ithaca, New York   M. S.
May 1967

Contents

Part I. The Making of a Middle-Class Gentleman

Chapter 1. A Crucial Decision: Minister or Merchant?

His parents dedicated him, by vow,
To serve the Church, and early taught him how.
  — Defoe, *The Character of the Late Dr. Samuel Annesley,*
    By way of Elegy (1697)

The central fact about Daniel Defoe's life from the time of his birth in the autumn of 1660 until his application for a marriage license as a "marchant" at the end of 1683 is that he was, by his own admission, designated for a career in the nonconformist ministry. The knowledge that he was being prepared for the high calling of the clergy underlay and informed his life as he was growing up in and around London during the Restoration. Later in life Defoe was to record, with some apparent misgiving, "It is not often that I trouble you with any of my divinity: I acknowledge the pulpit is none of my office. It was my disaster first to be set apart for, and then to be set apart from, the honour of that sacred employ." [1] This candid comment on his early life, and the subsequent course of his career, is our key to an understanding of the young Defoe. For how was he "set apart for" the ministry? Why did he come to consider himself "set apart from" an office he obviously held in high esteem? And what was the "disaster" connected with the altered course his life took? These questions bear so directly on an understanding of Defoe that they must be explored in some detail.

As far back as Defoe could conceivably have remembered, he and his family and their friends had been persecuted for their religious beliefs. In 1662, when Daniel Foe — as he was then called — was hardly two years old, the notorious Act of Uniformity was passed and put into effect. This act was to alter radically the lives of James Foe, a tallow-chandler, his wife, two daughters and his son Daniel, then living in the parish of St. Giles, Cripplegate, in London.

The Making of a Middle-Class Gentleman

The Act of Uniformity was an attempt to settle finally and completely the ecclesiastical problems created by the Puritan Interregnum. At the close of 1660 the King had approved the Act for Confirming and Restoring of Ministers, a preliminary attempt at restoring the disenfranchised Loyalist clergy who had been clamoring for repossession of their benefices forfeited under Cromwell. The final settlement fell to a Cavalier Parliament hostile to the Puritan interests and eager to redress the balance in favor of the Church of England. The resultant Act of Uniformity, which received royal assent in July 1662, required of all ministers three basic conditions: first, formal acceptance of everything in the Prayer Book of the Church of England (newly revised with a decided anti-Puritan bias by a national synod under the Bishop of London); second, a signed declaration abjuring any opposition to the Crown or the Church of England; and third, ordination by a bishop. The act was aimed at purifying the clergy of suspected radical elements, both ecclesiastical and political.

All clergy were given until Sunday, August 24, 1662 — St. Bartholomew's Day — to comply with the terms set forth in the act or forfeit their benefices and, in turn, their livelihoods. If they persisted in preaching after St. Bartholomew's Day, they faced a penalty of three months in prison. The number of Puritans actually martyred by this act is not clear; but suffering and hardship were widespread in the Puritan community. According to one reliable estimate, about two thousand ministers, or about one fifth of all the beneficed clergy, were ejected from their offices in the weeks following August 24. These ejected ministers came to be called "Bartholomeans" in recognition of the day on which their stand against the terms of an intolerable act deprived them of their pulpits. Numbered among the Bartholomeans was Dr. Samuel Annesley, pastor to the Foe family.

James Foe and his family found themselves at the very center of reaction against the Act of Uniformity, for their parish of St. Giles, Cripplegate, was the city parish most densely populated by Nonconformists, and within its boundaries was situated the most revered of all Puritan burial grounds, Bunhill Fields. When Dr. Annesley was forced to leave the Church of England in 1662, many members of his congregation, including the family of James Foe, followed his example, becoming, like Annesley, Presbyterians. Daniel Foe was not even two years old then, but unknown to him he suddenly became a member of a dissenting sect and a persecuted minority. He was an outsider, and was to remain one the rest of his life.

The oppression of the Dissenters increased after 1662. Another blow was directed at them in the form of further restrictions imposed by the Conventicle Act, which forbade by penalty the assembly of five or more persons for purposes of worship. This act was in force only for three years, but a second Conventicle Act adding a £20 fine payable by the preacher came into effect in 1670. Finally, the Five Mile Act of 1665 required all dissenting clergy who failed to subscribe to the Act of Uniformity to take the "Oxford Oath," stating, "I will not at any time endeavor any alteration of government, either in church or state." Any minister refusing to take this oath was forbidden to come within five miles of where he had acted as minister; violators were subject to fines of £40 and justices were empowered to commit offenders to jail for six months. This Five Mile Act drove Dr. Annesley from St. Giles parish because he staunchly refused to take the "Oxford Oath." The family of James Foe faithfully followed their minister into exile.[2]

That the Dissenters should have felt themselves unduly persecuted is easily understandable. The Five Mile Act, for example, was enacted by a Cavalier Parliament salubriously quartered in Oxford while the nonconformist clergy were doing their best to discharge their pastoral duties in a London slowly being decimated by the Great Plague, and soon to be scorched by the Great Fire. These were indeed times of sore affliction for the Dissenters. Harassed by a government fearful of them as breeding nests of sedition and fanaticism, they saw in the Plague and the Fire that was to follow a wrathful judgment of their God on their oppressors. The higher significance of the Plague and the Fire was interpreted by Dr. Annesley for his congregation, when he preached, "The voice of the Lord hath been crying, yea, roaring in the city, of the dreadful judgment of plague and fire." Such preaching and such beliefs made the Dissenters all the more feared and persecuted.[3]

Though young, Daniel was pious and impressionable. Much of

what he saw and suffered in those days he retained in his memory all his life. "I have known the Dissenters," Defoe recalled years later, "and with reason enough, set apart many a day in the time of their apprehensions and afflictions, to deprecate the judgments of God threatening them and the whole nation." Almost fifty years after the event he could write: "I remember very well what I saw with a sad heart, *tho' I was but young,* I mean the Fire of London." [4] Even though "the whole city was laid in ashes," including scores of parish churches, St. Paul's, the Customs House and the Royal Exchange, somehow the parish of St. Giles, Cripplegate, and the house of James Foe were miraculously spared from the flames. To the devout James Foe, as to other Dissenters, the hand of God was seen operating during those terrifying times; and perhaps because the Foe family survived the holocaust so miraculously, James Foe may have decided to dedicate his only son to the service of his church and his God.

Defoe's biographers are in agreement that "the most significant factor of his childhood development lay in his home," [5] and religion was certainly at the center of the household of James Foe. James Foe met the true test of faith and upheld his religious convictions when he left the Church of England. Defoe loved his father, whose piety and godliness apparently exerted a marked influence on the boy. The character of James Foe is revealed in a letter of recommendation he wrote for a servant once employed in his household: "Sarah Pierce lived with us, about fifteen or sixteen years since, about two years; and behaved herself so well, that we recommended her to Mr. Cave, that godly minister, which we should not have done, had not her conversation been becoming the gospel." [6] In such a household young Daniel would have been imbued with above all else a strong and abiding regard for the lessons of the gospel. From his constant quoting of Scripture throughout his long career as a writer, we know how intimately he came to know the Bible.

From Defoe's later admission we learn how completely he was caught up in the frenzied and anxious atmosphere of the dissenting community during the days of the reign of Charles II, when it was widely feared that Popery would return and the Bibles be confiscated: "How many honest but over-frighted people set to work to copy the Bible into short-hand, lest when

Popery came in we should be prohibited the use of it, and so might secure it in little compass. At which work, I myself, then but a boy, work'd like a horse, till I wrote out the whole *Pentateuch,* and then was so tired, I was willing to run the risk of the rest." [7] The tone, of course, is that of a mature and worldly-wise Defoe looking back upon an early time with restrained amusement at the excessive zeal with which he and his fellow Nonconformists responded to a threat that never materialized; yet the self-conscious turn of phrase at the close of the recollection is an afterthought, designed to take the edge off the vividness of the description. As a boy Defoe had been in the very thick of the religious ferment of his times, and as an adult he still presented himself as a devout and dutiful son during those times.

The persecutions suffered by the Dissenters during the 1660's served to unite rather than disperse them. They found comfort and succor in their shared afflictions. They felt themselves being tested for their religious beliefs, if not also on trial for their souls. After easier and more prosperous times had made the Dissenters lax early in the eighteenth century, and Occasional Conformity was being hotly disputed, Defoe wrote about the early Dissenters to emphasize that the new ministers and congregations were not made of the same tough fiber: "Their ministers were men known over the whole world; their general character was own'd even by their enemies; generally speaking, they were men of liberal education; had a vast stock of learning; were exemplar in piety; studious, laborious, and unexceptionally capable of carrying on the work they were embark'd in." The members of their congregations "were conscientious, diligent hearers of the word preach'd . . . they follow'd the substance, not the sound of preaching, they understood what they heard, and knew how to choose their ministers. What they heard preach'd, they improv'd in practice; their families were little churches, where the worship of God was constantly kept up; their children and families were duly instructed, and themselves, when they came to trial, cheerfully suffer'd persecution for the integrity of their hearts." [8] Defoe, to be sure, idealizes to some extent the former times in which he was but a boy. Even so, his sincere tribute to the dissenting clergy of the 1660's and 1670's indicates how profoundly he was impressed by them, and he conveys feelingly how he and his family probably worshipped God, both in the congregation with Dr. Annesley and in the home. A child so "duly instructed" would come to value the role religion plays in life, and it is clear that Defoe many years later still cherished the memory of those days.

Defoe was so imbued with the Presbyterian faith that he was prepared to defend his beliefs physically if necessary. The muscular side of Defoe's youth comes out dramatically in his response in the *Review* to the "Mohock" disturbances of 1712. He derides the polite, exhortative efforts at reform of the rival *Spectator* because only the "Protestant Flail" will drive the "Mohock-Monsters" from the streets, and Defoe steps forward eagerly as a "volunteer" ready to serve, just as he served when a young man in his teens. He recalls with no small pleasure the times he himself wielded this weapon during the London mob agitations over the Popish Plot of 1679: "Now this *Protestant Flail* is an excellent weapon . . . for my part, I have frequently walk'd with one about me in the old Popish days, and tho' I never set up for a hero, yet when arm'd with this scourge for a Papist, I remember I fear'd nothing." [9] Defoe's courage as a man, when threatened constantly with physical violence for his forthright writing in the *Review* and elsewhere, is well known. This quality is traceable to his vigorous youth as a Dissenter with something of a reputation as a fighter. If Defoe in later life came to look back on his youth as having been lived in heroic times, as a youth he no doubt acted in accordance with the spirit of those times.

We come to appreciate what it meant to someone like Defoe to have been "set apart for" the ministry in those early days if we consider the kind of people who exerted the most profound — and therefore the most lasting — influences on his early life. In addition to his home life, which seems to have been centered on the gospel, Defoe in his youth was taught, directly or indirectly, by four extraordinary churchmen: Dr. Samuel Annesley, his childhood pastor at St. Giles, Cripplegate; the Reverend James Fisher, his boarding school teacher in Surrey; the Reverend Charles Morton, his mentor at the Newington Green academy — a man destined to become the first vice-president of Harvard College; and the Reverend John Collins, a renowned preacher at Pinners' Hall, London. All these ministers, significantly, were Bartholomeans, having been ejected by the Act of Uniformity of 1662, and with the exception of Dr. Annesley, a Presbyterian, they were all Congregationalists.

Defoe was singularly fortunate in having Dr. Annesley as his minister and first teacher. Dr. Annesley was well educated, with two degrees from Oxford, and of gentle birth. For a time he was a lecturer at Chatham in Kent, and later served as chaplain to the Lord High Admiral. During the Cromwell era he proved himself to be a man of fierce integrity, above any party, political or religious. He had "publicly detested the horrid murder" of Charles I, had refused in 1651 to send a horse to fight against Charles II, and had even called Cromwell an arrogant hypocrite who would trample on people to get his own way: all this during the Puritan Interregnum under Cromwell! For his plain dealing he was forced out of an office worth some £200 to £300 a year and assigned to the poorest parish in all London. Cromwell repeatedly blocked his preferment until finally he was granted a modest lectureship at St. Paul's, but at a fraction of the salary paid the previous incumbent.

The Restoration did not favor a man of Annesley's firm principles either. In 1662 he was ejected from his vicarship of St. Giles, Cripplegate. Despite the further restrictions imposed by the Conventicle Acts and the Five Mile Act, he carried on his ministry as circumstances permitted. It was characteristic of his convictions that he refused to take the "Oxford Oath." He was reported holding conventicles at his house in Spitalfields in 1664. Most probably the family of James Foe was in attendance at these conventicles. In 1669 he was still preaching in Spitalfields, but now "at a new house built for that purpose with pulpit & seats," supposedly the largest Presbyterian chapel in London at the time. Dr. Annesley's relentless dedication to his calling is clear from the record that in 1670 alone he was convicted four different times for preaching. With the passing of the Declaration of Indulgence in 1672, Dr. Annesley was licensed formally as a Presbyterian minister to serve at St. Helen's, Spitalfields, where he preached until his death in 1696.[10]

We know that the remarkable character of Samuel Annesley had an enduring effect on young Daniel Foe. When Annesley died, Defoe commemorated the event by composing his *Character of the Late Dr. Samuel Annesley, By way of Elegy* in 1697, with the authorship reading, "Written by one of his Hearers." From Defoe's laudatory tone we can sense the strong affection he bore his childhood pastor and teacher, as well as the lasting impact Annesley had on this particular one of his "Hearers":

> His native candor, and familiar style,
> Which did so oft his hearers hours beguile,
> Charm'd us with godliness, and while he spake
> We lov'd the doctrine for the teacher's sake.

Defoe also singled out as memorable the integrity so notable in Dr. Annesley's entire career: "Strange were the charms of his sincerity,/Which made his action and his words agree." Dr. Annesley obviously did much to inculcate in his young parishioner the fearlessness that must attend strongly held but not always popular beliefs, especially during those dark and difficult days of persecution suffered by the Dissenters. In this personal tribute by way of elegy, Defoe pays his formal respects to an important person in his early life:

> A heavenly patience did his mind possess,
> Cheerful in pain, and thankful in distress;
>
> . . . .
>
> Now he's above the praises of my pen,
> The best of ministers, and the best of men! [11]

As a member of Dr. Annesley's congregation exiled from St. Giles, and worshipping as conditions allowed in Spitalfields, Defoe was as a youth at the very heart of Presbyterianism in London during the early Restoration.

Some time in 1668 Daniel Foe's mother died, and although James Foe offered his son all the advantages of a Christian home, he could not educate him at home, especially not a son "set apart for" the ministry. He was sent off to a boarding school for children of Dissenters taught by the Reverend James Fisher at his home in Dorking, Surrey, twenty-five miles distant from London. Not much is known about James Fisher, and what little is known makes him a somewhat controversial figure. He was well educated, possessing two degrees from Cambridge, and was for many years rector of Fetcham, Surrey, until his ejection because of the Act of Uniformity in 1662. He was described by one report as "a man of a very mean character," and by another, which exonerates him from the former charge, as "an honest upright person, and very useful." He kept a school at his house after his ejection and also continued with his preaching. In 1669 a conventicle of one hundred Independents was reported held at his house in Dorking. In 1672 Fisher was licensed as a Congregationalist. Exactly when and for how long Defoe was at the school maintained by James Fisher is not known. But it is noteworthy that Defoe, after being reared in the heart of the Presbyterian faith in London, was boarded and instructed at a Congregational, or Independent, school. Among the four major kinds of Dissenters (Presbyterians, Congregationalists, Baptists, and others, for instance, Quakers), the Congregationalists were reputed to be among the more flexible and loosely structured denominations, offering the individual more interpretative freedom than the Presbyterians. Perhaps Defoe already was being offered more latitude in his religious beliefs and training by his father.[12]

If young Foe had not been intended for the ministry, his education almost certainly would have terminated with his schooling under the Reverend James Fisher. He was now about fourteen years old, and as the son of a butcher — which was now James Foe's trade — he was of age to begin his apprenticeship. But instead of being apprenticed to a butcher, he was enrolled for more education in 1674; and not just in any dissenting academy, but in the principal Congregational and the best dissenting academy in all England: the Reverend Charles Morton's academy in Newington Green near London.

Morton, under whom Defoe was to study until 1679, was another welcome choice for young Daniel Foe, who found in his mentor an agreeable person as well as a preeminent scholar and teacher. Morton had taken two degrees at Oxford and was rector of Blisland, Cornwall, at the time of the Restoration. After his his ejection in 1662, he set up first as a preacher in St. Ives and then opened his celebrated academy at Newington Green. When Defoe arrived at the school it had about fifty students, with most of them destined, like himself, for a career in the dissenting ministry. Typical of the practical instruction Morton provided his ministerial candidates was the paper, "Advice to Candidates for the Ministry, under the present discouraging Circumstances," the text of which survives. The tone of this paper shows Morton to have been a lovable man, for it opens engagingly: "Presuming you will accept of advice from one you know loves and wishes you well; and whose comforts are much bound up in your well doing . . . I thought it my duty to deal plainly and faithfully with you, in a few suitable and seasonable admonitions to you." [13] We know from the warm descriptions of people who were acquainted with Morton that his rare qualities of heart and mind endeared and distinguished him among the ministers and teachers of his age. Morton had established a solid reputation as the man "fittest to bring up young men to the ministry of any in England." [14] It may well be that James Foe came to learn of his ability at training young men for the ministry and hoped he would perform that service for his own son.

The students at Newington Green were uncommonly well prepared for their work in the ministry. At a time when, as Defoe was to recall later, "some of the greatest scholars . . . that have the whole ministry of the gospel in their hearts, and a body of divinity in their heads . . . preach[ed] away their hearers, for want of the English tongue" — which, unfortunately, was the case at many of the dissenting academies of the time — the "master or tutor" at Newington Green "read all his lectures, gave all his systems, whether of philosophy or divinity, in English; had all his declaimings, and dissertations in the English tongue." Thanks to Morton's farsighted and sensible method of instruction, the students under his tutelage, like Daniel Foe, "were by this made masters of the English tongue, and more of them excelled in that particular than of any school at that time." [15]

It is conjectured that while at Newington Green Defoe had the chance to hear John Bunyan preach, an opportunity that a fellow student later scorned. Samuel Wesley, who later defected to the Church of England, wrote: "I remember several of us, if not all our pupils, went to hear Friend Bunyan, when he preached at Newington-Green. I'm pretty confident Mr. Morton heard him, for I'm sure he commended him . . ." [16] In an age when lay preachers were held in contempt by the learned and ordained clergy, Morton characteristically had his pupils turn out to hear what inspired preaching was like. Not knowledge of Greek and Latin or other scholarly pretensions, but "plainness in style, an affectionate delivery, preach'd with a concern for souls, and with a reverence suitable to the majesty of the work" were the simple yet sure rules taught at Newington Green. This is what Defoe, some thirty years later, could still remember so distinctly from his study under Morton. And, according to Defoe, "these were the things recommended the gospel to the last age." [17]

Defoe strangely never was ordained after leaving Newington Green about 1679. He was in London in 1681 and apparently still was wrestling with the decision about becoming a minister. Our information on Defoe in that decisive year is all drawn from a 195-page manuscript notebook, now in the Huntington Library, bearing Defoe's name, initials, and dated in his hand 1681.[18] All but the final twenty-three pages contain his meticulously neat transcriptions of six sermons he heard preached by the Reverend John Collins on February 20, March 26, May 15, June 12, and September 25, 1681 (the sixth and final sermon is left undated). A notation in Defoe's writing between the texts of the sermons for June 12 and September 25, and under a heading marked "July 10th," reads:

Note   There was a sermon preached between these two on ye proper explication of ye 16: verse which I being absent in ye country could not write

Daniel Foe

This inscription seems to indicate that Defoe copied each sermon after it was preached by Collins; and if one recalls Defoe's comment about copying the Pentateuch into "short-hand" while but a boy, it seems likely that he put that skill to good use when Collins preached, recopying the sermons later from his shorthand versions. The fact that the Huntington Library manuscript bears at the beginning two lines of cryptic — and as yet undecipherable — shorthand, in Defoe's own hand, lends added weight to this interpretation. The conscious care evident in the well-formed letters, regular lines, and neat margins suggests that young Daniel Foe probably intended this personal notebook for his permanent keeping.[19]

The text of the six sermons preached by Collins apparently

held a profound and immediate significance for Defoe. All the sermons took as their text Mark, Chapter 16, verses 15 and 16, with the final two sermons devoted exclusively to an explication of the sixteenth verse: "And he said unto them, go ye into all ye world, and preach ye gospel unto every creature. He that believeth & is baptized shall be saved but he that believeth not shall be damned." For one contemplating a career in the dissenting ministry, these two verses contain the essence of the ministerial "call" and the fundamental question of faith and salvation; therefore, we need not look far to appreciate the attraction these sermons held for the twenty-one-year-old Daniel Foe, or the self-conscious care with which he copied down and kept the record of what he heard preached for further consultation and deliberation. The year 1681 was for Defoe a year of crisis. He knew he had to arrive at a final decision about the future course of his life, and he was searching within his mind and heart for indications about his fitness in "that sacred employ" he had been "set apart for."

Since Defoe so faithfully recorded the sermons of John Collins, we might inquire into the kind of minister he was for a possible insight into Defoe's state of mind in that crucial year. Collins graduated from Harvard College in 1649. According to Cotton Mather, the life of Collins "proved so very considerable among the congregational divines of Great Britain, and especially in the great city of London, where he spent his days of public service, that it well deserves a room in our account of the worthies"; and he was honored by Mather with inclusion in the *Magnalia Christi Americana*.[20] Collins returned to England in 1653 and served as chaplain to General Monk. Although a Dissenter, he was not beneficed in 1662 and hence not ejected formally; but in time he became pastor of a substantial Congregational following in Duke's Place, Aldgate, being licensed a Congregationalist in 1672. When the Merchant's Lecture was established at Pinners' Hall in 1672, Collins was chosen one of the first six lecturers, which was something of a signal honor. He and Dr. John Owen were the only two Congregationalists chosen; the rest were Presbyterians. In these offices Collins continued until his death in 1687. It was probably at the Pinners' Hall that Defoe heard Collins preach; Defoe was known to have frequented the hall.[21]

Defoe was attracted not only to the substance of the sermons preached by John Collins but also to the man himself. According to one contemporary account of Collins, "He is one of the best preachers in or about London as most agree, some say the best." Cotton Mather also singled out for praise the extraordinary qualities of Collins as a preacher, stating "such was the life and charm, which accompanied his exercises in the pulpit; that none . . . went away unmoved or unpleased from them." That Collins succeeded in moving and pleasing young Daniel Foe is clear from Defoe's later writings: "Would God in mercy to the Dissenters send among them a few such preachers, as Dr. Owen, Mr. John Collins . . . how would they restore the taste of the hearers of the town . . ." One line of the Reverend John Collins' epitaph, as quoted by Cotton Mather, reads: *"Utrobique multos Christo lucrifecit."* Defoe, however, was not one of this number, even though he had followed faithfully the advice of his recent mentor, Charles Morton, to aspirants for the ministry: "Be diligent in hearing the most pious and practical preachers, and such as you see do most prevail with the hearts of men." [22]

The great agitation of mind and spirit Defoe experienced in 1681 is revealed in the seven verse meditations which comprise the last twenty-three pages of the notebook he kept at this time. They are a kind of "confessional" in verse, perhaps intended, as John Robert Moore suggests, for his private devotions. While they show little promise for Defoe as a poet, they do show a searching and open attempt on his part to express his spiritual needs and to set down in intimate verse matters of great moment to him. The *Meditations* are conventional in their rough imitation of contemporary poetic forms, notably the Pindaric ode popularized by Cowley. Of the seven, the first — and longest — is beyond question the best, most sustained, and most emotional work. It is entitled, "Fleeing For Refuge To The Hope Set Before Us," and since it sheds some welcome light on Defoe's mental and religious state at this time, it is worth considering in some detail.[23]

The theme expressed in the title is set forth by Defoe in the first few stanzas with decided urgency:

> Let me not go, but flee,
> My God! to hide my burthened soul with thee.

> Swift be my steps, & swifter my desire,
>   To such a refuge to retire.
>   Teach me from what, and whom,
>   With eager haste it is I come.   (p. 4)

Defoe indicates his eagerness to find a refuge with Christ, yet his desire and sense of direction for that refuge are not clear, and he asks for guidance. The stanza continues conventionally enough, cataloguing from what Defoe flees: "sin," "lusts," and "a base heart." But as the enumeration is developed we notice that Defoe is not so much confessing his sins of frailty of the flesh as of the spirit: "From all my pride . . . From an alluring world, And all the gaudy vapour there appears . . . From my presumption, & from my despair" (pp. 4–5). Most of all Defoe despairs over his gnawing doubts and want of true faith:

> From half convictions, which too hardning prove;
> From false affections, and a wandring love.
>   From all my feign'd humility,
> My outward zeal, and my hypocrisy.
>
> .   .   .   .
>
>   From all my brain-begotten faith,
>   From all my doubt . . .   (p. 5)

The confessional nature of the meditation is clear from the relentless way in which Defoe peels away his outward appearances to probe beneath the surface for his real motives and feelings. His is a "brain-begotten faith," however, which to a believing and true Puritan, as he well knows, is no faith at all — let alone to a prospective Puritan divine.

Defoe makes an anguished appeal to his God for some reassuring signs of his faith, for a sure "saving light," and for new strength spiritually:

> For a new will,
> That I may serve thee only, serve thee still;
>   For new affections to lead out,
>   And faith to conquer every doubt,
>   For saving light,
> To judge of prompting baits aright . . .
>
> Have all my doubts clear'd up, my wants supplied,
>   Not as I ask, but as I need.   (p. 9)

The desperate note injected at the close of the stanza expresses the magnitude and intensity of his spiritual problem. He makes it obvious from this meditation that only God can extricate him from his doubts and vacillations. Defoe is pious but all too poignantly aware of his human failings.

The *Meditations* of 1681 offer us a cogent explanation of why Defoe came to regard himself as "set apart from" the pulpit. The theme and substance of the first verse meditation, as well as the text of the sermons preached by the Reverend John Collins and copied so carefully by Defoe, point unmistakably to his pre-occupation with one basic question: the choice of a ministerial career and his fitness spiritually for that calling. Much as young Daniel Foe appears to have wished to find a refuge in the service of Christ, and much as he asked for a living sense of faith, the *Meditations* suggest strongly that he never was to find the refuge he so eagerly sought or the faith he so ardently hoped to achieve. After the first verse meditation, the remaining six evince less personal and religious intensity. They read like the half-hearted and uninspired religious exercises of an unsettled young man in whom the "call" already was beginning to sound somewhat hollow, and he knew it.

But was a failure of faith the only reason for his abandoning the ministry? Surveying the "decay of the ministry" among Dissenters soon after the turn of the eighteenth century, Defoe cast his eye back to this time and noted how even then the dissenting ministry was in decline. The reason, according to Defoe, was that before the erection and establishment of the private academies for Dissenters, "their ministers were generally educated abroad, from whence they came much better finish'd, than they do now from our private academies." With some bitterness Defoe was later to recall his disadvantage at not attending a public university: " 'Tis evident, the great imperfection of our academies is want of conversation; this the public universities enjoy; ours cannot. If a man pores upon his book, and despises the advantages of conversation, he always comes out a pedant, a mere scholar, rough and unfit for anything out of the walls of college." Defoe was exceedingly fortunate in attending the Newington Green academy, but he still could not refrain from comparing himself with the men he was to become associated with in the ministry, and apparently the association did not particularly appeal to someone so able and so proud as Defoe. Perhaps with himself partly in mind, he wrote further of the limitations imposed on a gifted young man at a dissenting academy: "Here and there one, a youth bless'd with an extraordinary genius, strong parts, and great application, may outstrip others," but, Defoe concludes, it leaves one with the dubious distinction of emerging "like David's second-rate worthies."

Already in Defoe's youth prospective ministers were chosen for their calling very early in life and often supported by the combined charity of the congregation. A fund was collected at the meeting house door throughout the year, the proceeds of which went for the support of the young man or men in the congregation set apart for the ministry. Too often, Defoe observed, young men were chosen for the wrong reasons: misplaced and ill-advised charity which encouraged misfits for that high office. "What natural defects do we see in the pulpit, besides those of memory, of application, of morals, and of learning?" Defoe held a firm conviction all his life that each human being had a natural calling for which nature, not man, had designed him fittest, and to disregard a person's "capacities," "temper," "inclination," and "common gifts," was to do violence to that person's career and life.[24] He undoubtedly realized that he was unsuited to the ministry by temperament and inclination. Judging from Defoe's later life, notably his attraction to things worldly, his varied interests, his aversion for pedants and fools, we begin to appreciate how he could already at this time have regarded himself as set apart from the ministry as a calling, especially when his father, now grown somewhat comfortable, no longer may have been set on his son entering the ministry if he felt he lacked the faith necessary and could find a more suitable career in business.

Probably while a student at Morton's academy Defoe first began to bend his thoughts seriously to a secular career. And Morton, although primarily charged with preparing young men for the ministry, may have helped unwittingly to sway young Daniel Foe's thoughts about a career:

He had a class for eloquence, and his pupils declaim'd weekly in the English tongue, made orations, and wrote epistles twice every week upon such subjects as he prescrib'd to them or upon such as they themselves chose to write upon. Sometimes they were ambassadors and agents abroad at foreign courts, and wrote accounts of their negotiations and reception in foreign courts directed to the Secretary of State and some times to the Sovereign himself . . . In a word, his pupils came out of his hands finish'd orators, fitted to speak in the highest presence, to the greatest assemblies, and even in Parliament, Courts of Justice, or any where; and several of them came afterward to speak in all those places and capacities with great applause.[25]

To an ambitious and imaginative "youth bless'd with an extraordinary genius," as Defoe was, this secular role-playing probably held a special fascination. If the pull of faith toward a career in the church were not strong, how much more attractive and promising were the prospects of a secular career, in which one did not have to content oneself with becoming a "second-rate worthy." Young Foe could envision himself a statesman, a mighty merchant, an ambassador, a man of affairs, and play the part with gusto in his eloquence classes. The close of the passage quoted, written by Defoe at the end of a richly varied life, contains his thinly veiled sense of satisfaction; for was not Daniel Defoe himself among those very "several" who did indeed so speak "in the highest presence" and, as he could recall it, "with great applause"?

Whatever the shortcomings Defoe may have found in the private academies for their lack of polite conversation and polish, it was a fact that they offered a more balanced and practical curriculum than the public universities, notably in the areas of science and modern languages; and in these subjects Morton's school at Newington Green excelled. Charles Morton was a remarkably versatile teacher who favored a balance between ecclesiastical and secular studies, scholarly and practical subjects; consequently, his pupils were prepared for the world as well as for the service of the church.

Morton would compile "systems" of subjects in the arts and sciences on which he lectured; they were designed for use by the students as a kind of syllabus for his lectures and were copied down. So valuable were Morton's systems that many years later Defoe still treasured his notes dating back to Morton's lectures. He wrote, "The author of these sheets happens to be one that had what little education he can pretend to . . . by, viz. Mr. Charles Morton of Newington Green, and I have now by me the manuscripts of science, the exercises and actions of his school, and, among the rest, those of politics in particular." Interestingly enough, no mention is made of any religious exercises or papers. We know that in alleging to have these school manuscripts still in his possession Defoe probably was telling the truth; for he goes on to state that "the said manuscripts, system of politics and government, as read in that school, and which are now above 25 years old, are left at the publishers of this book for any one to peruse, as a satisfaction of the truth of the fact." [26] Morton's systems had the added virtue of being comprehensive yet concise. In an age of long-winded pedantry, Morton was "a declar'd enemy to large volumes; as he signified by that saying which was often in his mouth . . . A great book is a great evil." Defoe obviously shared his mentor's regard for concision. In his first real book, *An Essay upon Projects,* he concluded his preface by stating that he "endeavoured everywhere in this book to be as concise as possible." [27]

The "manuscript of science" Defoe valued so highly that he retained it long after terminating his studies with Morton undoubtedly was a copy of the *Compendium Physicae*, which Morton was busily completing during the years Defoe studied at Newington Green. The work was finished about 1680, and shows an extensive range of familiarity with the best and latest scientific knowledge of the period: Galileo, Keppler, Newton, Harvey, Boyle, Torricelli, and Leeuwenhoek are all either quoted or discussed knowledgeably in the text. So advanced for its time and so sound in scientific content was the *Compendium Physicae* of Morton that when he finally left England to come to teach at Harvard College in 1686, he brought his work with him and within a year it became the standard text for work in the natural sciences, a position it maintained at Harvard for some forty years.[28]

Under a rare teacher like Charles Morton, then, Defoe had all the advantages of choosing a career either in the ministry or in the bustling world of trade. His mind had been encouraged by Morton to reach into exciting areas not normally falling within the neatly circumscribed province of ministerial duties and studies. The new discoveries in science were taught by Morton as well as geography, history, political science, and mathematics. Here was a fresh and fascinating body of knowledge to be mastered and put to use by a projecting mind, and, coincidentally, Morton's mind was also of a projecting turn, teeming with almost as many schemes and interests as Defoe's was to do. So from Morton young Daniel Foe received a truly "liberal education," the sort of education he was himself to champion the rest of his life, and an education that in his case happily pointed with equal promise to the pulpit or to the market place.

When Defoe finally came to decide on the course of his career in 1681, or shortly thereafter, the decision seemed to have come naturally but reluctantly. He had, after all, been exposed to some of the outstanding preachers and teachers of his period, either directly in his mentors Annesley, Fisher, and Morton, or indirectly through the lectures of Collins. He had grown up in troubled times made memorable by disasters and persecutions, a time he was to cherish as a kind of heroic age for Dissenters. He was a dutiful son and devout Dissenter. In short, everything seemed to favor his entry into the ministry as planned.

Yet Defoe decided against the calling he was "set apart for" since a boy because, as his *Meditations* indicate, he came to understand that, while he was a religious person, he did not possess a viable sense of faith and purpose about a ministerial career; his genius and inclinations pointed away from the pulpit and towards the world of trade. Even as a man of fifty, Defoe recalled how he never was too successful at exhorting his fellow Dissenters "even from a youth." He came to think of himself as "set apart from" the ministry, as one "called, but not chosen." Defoe was ever too much of a practical realist not to respond to such a personal dilemma with anything but common sense. His father seemed not to have contested his son's decision; indeed, he may even have encouraged it.[29]

But a man simply does not forget entirely his formative years. Defoe never lost his interest in the ministry entirely. Tradition holds that he served on occasion as a lay preacher. His writings further show that he never abandoned the pulpit completely; many of his works bear the unmistakable qualities of a sermon. His association with the dissenting ministry was common knowledge among his contemporaries, for a hostile pamphleteer in 1703 offered the following instructions to government officers trying to ferret Defoe out of hiding: "Follow him by the scent of his scraps of scripture, and you'll find him at *Salter's,* or *Pinner's-Hall;* there needs no farther pursuit, and whether you seek for Mr. Fo the Hosier, or Mr. Fo the Preacher; 'tis all one . . ." [30]

By 1682 Defoe had reached a final decision about the course his life was to take. He had decided to embark on a secular career and become a London "marchant." He was talented, well educated, and ambitious. But this course he had charted for himself was to turn into a "disaster."

Chapter 2. London Merchant and Athenian Wit

A wit turn'd tradesman! What an incongruous part of nature is there brought together, consisting of direct contraries! No apron strings will hold him; 'tis in vain to lock him in behind the counter, he's gone in a moment . . . his journal entries are all pindarics, and his ledger is all heroics; he is truly dramatic from one end to the other, through the whole scene of his trade; and as the first part is all comedy, so the last acts are always made up with tragedy; a statute of bankrupt is his *exeunt omnes,* and he generally speaks the epilogue in the Fleet prison or the Mint. — Defoe, *The Complete English Tradesman,* II, 58

"Of all the decades in our history," observed the historian G. M. Young, "a wise man would choose the eighteen-fifties to be young in." [1] Defoe, for one, would not necessarily have agreed. He found himself a young man in the London of the 1680's, and having resolved to pursue his fortunes as a merchant, he probably found the prospects that decade made open to him almost all he could desire. As a Dissenter who felt himself set apart from his intended calling, he had only to cast his eye about to appreciate the considerable attractions a business career held for him at that time. Many of the mighty merchants in the city of London were men of nonconformist background like himself. If one chose to excel in life, then no more obvious opportunities were needed than to set up in business at this most favorable time; for, as James Sutherland notes, "somewhere about the year 1680, in fact, the modern business world was born." Defoe also shared this awareness because he wrote in his *Essay upon Projects* that "about the year 1680 began the art and mystery of projecting to creep into the world," and most strikingly in his native London.[2]

At the heart of England's economic organization at this time was London, providing the nation with the greatest port in all Europe, accounting for over half a million people (or about one tenth of the total population), and drawing materials, raw and finished, from all parts of England and many parts of the world. To a promising, impressionable, and energetic young man like Defoe, London was a marvelous and mighty metropolis offering unlimited outlets for trade and commerce. Years later, when he wrote of London in *The Complete English Tradesman*, he expressed the same fascination and excitement for the city he undoubtedly felt when a young man: "London consumes all, circulates all, exports all, and at last pays for all; and this is trade. This greatness and wealth of the city is the soul of the commerce to all the nation; and as there is the greatest number of tradesmen in this city that are to be seen in any place in the world, so they again support and supply an innumerable multitude of shopkeepers and tradesmen of every kind in the country, and every part of the country." London was the center of both economic and political power. The seat of government and the Exchange and the joint-stock companies, like the great East India Company, all were centrally located in England's capital city and port. This localized power and this growing concentration of capital in London, according to G. N. Clark, "gave opportunities for developments in finance which were turning the English into a nation of business men."[3] Throughout the 1670's and 1680's there were pronounced increases in shipping and foreign trade, and, as Macaulay was to remark about this period of activity in London, "English writers boasted of the forest of masts and yardarms which covered the river from the Bridge to the Tower, and of the stupendous sums which were collected at the Custom House in Thames Street."[4]

London not only was pulsating with activities of all kinds, London was becoming, after the Plague and Fire had demolished its medieval vestiges, a phoenix of a new city in a new and dynamic era of growth. The Plague and Fire had driven the nobles westward out of the city to new suburbs. Meanwhile the splendid dwellings of these nobles and people of quality along the Strand were taken over by the mercantile interests and converted into fashionable apartments for their use. London itself was being rebuilt under the general supervision of Sir Christopher Wren, whose architectural genius was in evidence everywhere: the magnificent St. Paul's, new parish churches, and public buildings.

London was growing in size and in population; between 1660 and 1700 the population swelled from 450,000 to 675,000. And as the gentry followed the aristocracy westward to the suburbs in this period, the city became markedly a "mercantile stronghold," with the historic livery companies growing in influence in the rule and affairs of London, and with the aldermen, sheriffs, and the Lord Mayor himself as the city's elected representatives.[5]

Understandably, Londoners like young Daniel Foe had much to feel proud about in their new city, both in its public buildings like the Exchange and Custom House and in the many new residences for its citizens. The spirit of London in the 1680's is well characterized by Macaulay, who, in spite of an overweening bias toward his own age, still could convey what it meant for someone to live in those times:

In the seventeenth century the City was the merchant's residence. Those mansions of the great old burghers . . . were originally not inferior in magnificence to the dwellings which were then inhabited by the nobility . . . London was, to the Londoner, what Athens was to the Athenian of the age of Pericles, what Florence was to the Florentine of the fifteenth century. The citizen was proud of the grandeur of his city, punctilious about her claims to respect, ambitious of her offices, and zealous for her franchises.[6]

The 1680's, then, certainly was a bright decade for a wise man to be young in, and Defoe was at that time both wise and young. If one had misgivings about abandoning a career in the ministry, there was much to distract an ambitious man in London. That Defoe responded to the spell of London's growing greatness is obvious in most of his writings, from the early *Essay upon Projects* to the late *Augusta Triumphans* (or, as the subtitle reads, "the Way to Make London the Most Flourishing City in the Universe"). London worked its spell on Defoe in much the same way as it did on so many of its illustrious citizens, like Dr. Johnson in the following century. A characteristic contemporary attitude is presented by John Evelyn, who in 1683 wrote in his *Diary* of London as "the most august city in the world." [7]

Here was a time and place for a young man of parts to make his mark. Citizens were beginning to enjoy more religious and economic freedom than they had experienced for some years — a welcome change for Dissenters. England was the richest nation in all the world. Defoe could see numerous examples of "merchant adventurers," those *novos homines* who in a relatively short period of time amassed vast fortunes from a variety of daring speculative ventures. Whereas to the preceding generation of Puritans the shop was the slow but steady way to financial security and a modest income, to the contemporary generation, inspired by the example of some singularly wealthy businessmen, many of whom came of dissenting backgrounds, the Exchange and the call of commerce and trade afforded a risky yet invitingly rapid chance for achieving a state of affluence undreamed of by the shopkeeping generation. Everywhere one heard of fortunes being made and lost on the Exchange.

Even though there was little hope of a newly rich merchant purchasing an estate of several thousand acres and setting himself and his family up as members of the landed gentry, a city merchant still could establish himself and his family as people of fashion with a fine home, carriage, liveried servants, plate, and even a second home away from the city. Such a genteel style of life enabled the people of wealth to enjoy most of the amenities of the people of leisure. And this was precisely what merchants were doing when Defoe was deciding on a career. The sight of these successful merchants probably fired his imagination and sharpened his appetite. He, too, would become a merchant.[8]

He began as a hose factor, a middleman dealing with manufacturers and retailers of haberdashery. Within a remarkably brief period of time he prospered to the point of being established as a London merchant who had his home and place of business on the north side of Cornhill, in Freeman's Yard, a spacious high-rent district situated some twenty-five yards from the busy Royal Exchange and inhabited by noted traders dealing in expensive cloths (India silks and muslins) and merchants. How Defoe financed his almost meteoric rise to eminence as a merchant — he was but twenty-three at this time — and how he acquired his uncanny business experience remains an unsolved puzzle to his biographers. He may have inherited some money from his mother, or his father may have helped his only son launch his career.[9]

On December 28, 1683, Daniel Foe of St. Michael, Cornhill, "a batchelor, marchant and Mary Tuffley, of St. Botolph, Aldgate" filed for a marriage license; and on New Year's Day, 1684, they were duly married in the large church of St. Botolph's, with the wedding performed according to the Church of England ritual by a proper Anglician minister. The wedding was an impressive affair, especially for Dissenters, and the dowry Mary Tuffley brought her merchant husband was equally impressive, the sum of £3,700. Defoe's father-in-law was a dissenting merchant and a man of means. Through this prudent alliance Defoe now had capital to speculate with as well as his shop and warehouse in Freeman's Yard, over which was located the apartment he and his bride occupied. In 1684 the future promised fair for him.[10]

The speculative fever of the 1680's raged in all areas, political as well as financial, and apparently Defoe was not immune to it. In 1685, when he should have attended to his business and cared for his young wife, an ambitious Defoe of not quite twenty-five years rode off to join the forces of the Duke of Monmouth some one hundred miles away. It was a reckless undertaking at best, and not nearly so much a patriotic venture as an attempt to exploit a politically advantageous opportunity. Defoe was impatient to achieve a brilliant success in society now that he was bent on a secular career. He was even willing to gamble for the highest stakes to achieve his end: his life as a volunteer in Monmouth's cause in hopes of royal patronage for his loyalty and services.

We know from Defoe's own writings that he was more than casually attracted to the fashionable diversions of high life. He had a lifelong weakness for horseracing, an aristocratic pastime, and attended whenever he could. It was at these races that he first saw and admired from afar the dashing figure of the Duke of Monmouth. Defoe later recalled, "I have often seen the Duke of Monmouth, natural son to King Charles II, ride his own horses at a match, and win it too, though he was a large man, and must weigh heavy." That Defoe delighted to be among all these people of quality is abundantly evident from his descriptions of these races he attended so often: "It was my hap formerly, to be at Aylesbury, when there was a mighty confluence of noblemen and gentlemen, at a famous horse race at Quainton-Meadow, not far off, where was then the late Duke of Monmouth, and a great many persons of the first rank, and a prodigious concourse of people." To cite yet another example, Defoe shows his enthusiasm for such select events as "the annual meeting of the gentry at the horseraces near Nottingham": "But the illustrious company at the Nottingham races was, in my opinion, the glory of the day; for there we saw, besides eleven or twelve noblemen, an infinite throng of gentlemen from all the countries round, nay, even out of Scotland itself; the appearance, in my opinion, greater, as it was really more numerous, than ever I saw at Newmarket, except when the king have been there in ceremony." One who spends his time recording so carefully and knowingly who is present among all the "illustrious company," which, to him, constitutes the real "glory of the day," is not primarily a lover of fine horseflesh or of racing per se.[11] From the way we come to see and understand the Defoe of the 1680's, it is clear that a man of his economic and social ambitions was not altogether fit for the austerity and dedication attending the ministry.

If Defoe could write later that the cause represented by Monmouth was one he "never doubted of, and freely ventured for," we cannot but suspect that hope of personal preferment colored much of his patriotism at this time.[12] When Monmouth's march to glory proved abortive, Defoe escaped and made his way safely back to London; but to insure his safety he conveniently spent part of his time between 1685 and 1688 traveling in Europe to promote business as a merchant. He would have to wait for another opportunity to win favor from a royal personage, whereby he might find himself a place among all that "illustrious company" of noblemen and gentlemen he came to admire so passionately and so early in his life as a London merchant.

For a time Defoe decided to attend to his business and advance himself by the normal avenues open to him. In January 1688 he was made a member of the Butchers' Company by virtue of his father's membership. It should be noted that he joined primarily, if not exclusively, for the social distinction that went with membership in a livery company. The entry in the minutes of the Butchers' Company on his admission reads, "he further desired to pay a fine to the Company and be discharged from all offices, which was also granted, he paying £10 15s. for that purpose." Now Defoe had the privilege of appearing in appropriate costume on state occasions in London; he was a *bona fide* member of a prestigious and select company numbering no more than two hundred members in all of London.[13]

Defoe was to exercise his privileges as a liveryman later in life. In the *Review* he took a strong stand of protest against the practice of "birding," wanton destruction of birds: "I protest that I have a right to make this complaint, being born a Freeman, and for having been near 30 years a *Livery-Man* of this city, and therefore claim of right to be concern'd in the preservation of the privileges of the said city, having been twice sworn to maintain and uphold the said privileges." While he enjoyed, and on occasion exercised, the rights of membership, he appears never to have participated in any way in the affairs of the Company itself. In none of the extant records is there any sign that he even voted, as did his father.[14]

But the chance he seized with the Duke of Monmouth, which could have cost him his life, was presented again, this time with much less danger, three years later when William of Orange landed at Devon and began his march on London. This time Defoe prudently waited until the time was propitious to commit himself; he did not ride to Windsor and join the army assembling under William until the Irish mercenaries under James were beginning to mutiny and causing widespread disorder in the ranks of the opposition. In William and Mary he was to find the royal patronage he sought so eagerly in hopes of furthering his ambitions.

Defoe availed himself of his privilege as a liveryman on the Lord Mayor's Day in October 1689, when the Lord Mayor, acting on behalf of the City, invited King William and Queen Mary to a gala banquet at Guildhall. The colorful proceedings of that celebrated event are recounted by John Oldmixon in his *History*, which, in spite of its biased treatment of Defoe, still succeeds in conveying Defoe's prominent part in the festivities:

Their Majesties, attended by their Royal Highnesses [Prince and Princess of Denmark], and a numerous train of nobility and gentry, went first to a balcony prepar'd for them at the Angel in Cheapside to see the show, which, for the great number of liverymen, the full appearance of the militia and artillery company, the rich adornments of the pageants, and the splendid and good order of the whole proceeding, out-did all that had been seen before upon that occasion; and what deserv'd to be particularly mention'd . . . was a Royal Regiment of volunteer horse, made up of the chief citizens, who being gallantly mounted and richly accoutred, were led by the Earl of Monmouth, now Earl of Peterborough, and attended their Majesties from Whitehall. Among these troopers, who were for the most part Dissenters, was Daniel Foe, at that time a hosier in Freeman's Yard, Cornhill.[15]

Defoe's sense of personal satisfaction on that memorable evening, when he rode "gallantly mounted and richly accoutred" in escort of their Majesties from Whitehall, can readily be imagined. He was no longer a mere spectator looking on with envious eyes at all the "illustrious company," as he so often did at the horse races; he was a participant in all the pomp and pageantry he so ardently admired; he was one of the "chief citizens" of London.

Defoe the merchant was now also to serve in an unofficial capacity as adviser to the King and Queen. The precise beginning of this close relationship he enjoyed with royalty is not known, but it is estimated to have begun in 1689, when he seems to have been in attendance on the King in Middlesex. We know from Defoe's own account that he personally assisted Queen Mary in planning the gardens for the remodeled Kensington Palace in early 1690: "The first laying out of these gardens was the design of the late Queen Mary, who finding the air agreed with, and was necessary to the health of the king, resolved to make it agreeable to her self too, and gave the first orders for enlarging the gardens: the author of this account, having had the honour to attend her majesty, when she first viewed the ground, and directed the doing it, speaks this with the more satisfaction." [16] The young merchant of Cornhill had come a long way in a short time.

By 1689–90 Defoe was at the summit of his prosperity as a merchant, and he was just under thirty years of age. He was beginning to get ready to assume his place among those mighty merchants he saw rising to prominence in London when he first cast about for a suitable career at the beginning of the decade. Defoe was living in the style of a young gentleman. All this time he maintained his residence over his warehouse in Freeman's Yard, Cornhill, where he was building a solid reputation as a wholesale merchant doing a brisk business. In the mid-1680's he probably either owned or leased a house in the country, in

Tooting, Surrey, where he could relax on weekends and during the heat of the summer when not in London. Though he lived in easy circumstances, he still sought to live like a good Dissenter, and tradition holds him responsible for organizing the noncomformist residents in the community into a congregation under the spiritual leadership of the Reverend Joshua Oldfield. By the early 1690's he and his family had the use of another country house, probably belonging to his mother-in-law, at Kingsland, about five miles from London.[17]

Another important facet of Defoe's character was his vanity. All his life he showed himself to be uncommonly fond of fine clothes. He was always "gorgeously apparelled," and himself was guilty of that very incongruity he later so passionately ridiculed, "a tradesman dressed up fine with his long wig and sword." His enemies naturally came to deride him as something of a dandy. But Defoe's vanity did not confine itself merely to clothes; we also know of his scantly concealed pleasure at informing his friend John Fransham in 1706 about the appearance of his portrait, engraved by Michael Van der Gucht, as the frontispiece to his *Jure Divino*.[18]

Around 1690, then, Defoe was a highly promising merchant who began playing the part of man of fashion as well as man of business. His business ventures were going so well that he could even see himself retiring from business and living the life of a gentleman and man of affairs. The attractions of high life had always been strong, and now he could see the day when he might pursue such a way of life. His expensive style of living at this time, however, was to give him pause for reflection years later, when he wrote knowingly that "citizens of London," like himself, lived so ostentatiously because of "their eager, resolved pursuit of that empty and meanest kind of pride, called imitation, *viz.*, to look like the gentry, and appear above themselves, drew them into it." [19] Still, this is the sort of *ex post facto* wisdom Defoe was so generous in serving up to his readers all his life; the central fact remains that in 1690 he was aping the style of life of the gentry and playing the role of the gentleman.

A fashionable gentleman living in London, if he had any lively parts to him, was likely to engage in literary activities. Defoe, too, was not to deny himself the diversions — and reputation —

of this fashionable pastime of the town. We know of his susceptibility to reading and quoting the leading poets and wits of the
day: sacred, like Milton, but more frequently profane, like
Rochester. In his *Reformation of Manners* Defoe summed up
the taste of the town: "One man reads Milton, forty Rochester."
As even a cursory glance at the pages of the *Review* will readily
reveal, Defoe was fonder of quoting Rochester than Milton — a
curiously cultivated taste for a devout Puritan, particularly one
born in the parish of John Milton. Yet Defoe apparently responded equally to the sacred and profane authors, to the ancients and the moderns; he could write: "Who can read Virgil,
Horace, Milton, Waller, and Rochester, without touching the
strings of the soul, and finding a unison of the most charming
influence there?" It is worth noting that Charles Gildon, in his
*Life and Strange Surprising Adventures of Mr. D__ De F__, of
London* in 1719, commenced his capsule summary of Defoe's
career with, "First, I set up for scribbling of verses, and dabbling
in other sorts of authorizing, both religious and profane." Although Gildon's book is a venomous attack on Defoe by an em-
bittered old man, the criticism of Defoe's characteristic mixture
of the sacred and the profane is not without foundation.[20]

To cut a lively figure as a literary wit one had to pass for an
easy rimer as well as a frequenter of rimers. Defoe during this
time seems to have earned something of a reputation among his
circle of literary friends as a talker on almost any subject and as
a facile versifier. John Dunton wrote of him: "Mr. Daniel De Foe
is a man of good parts, and very clear sense. His conversation is
ingenious and brisk enough." Dunton also commented on Defoe's method of composition, remarking that he "can say what
he please upon any subject; and, by his printing a poem every
day, one would think he rhimed in his sleep." The ex-ministerial
student and promising merchant was becoming known as something of a dilettantish man-about-town among the literati.[21]

In 1690 and 1691 Defoe was to realize the literary fame he
sought at this time. John Dunton prevailed on him to compose a
Pindaric ode to commemorate the foundation in 1690 of the
Athenian Society, a sort of esoteric literary club. The Athenian
Society was composed mostly of Dunton's friends, including De-

foe, who now sported a reputation in London as a man of parts. The Society published a journal from 1691 to 1697 entitled the *Athenian Mercury*, a weekly which attempted to provide erudite answers to "all the most nice and curious questions propos'd by the ingenious" — as the masthead read. The masthead did not belie the contents, for the readers proved themselves "ingenious" to conjure up such "nice and curious questions" as were learnedly discussed by the members of the Society: "Where had Adam and Eve their needles and thread to sew their fig-leaves together?" "Whether it is a sin for a surgeon to cure the venereal disease?" "What sex was Balaam's ass of?" "Whether Negroes shall rise so at the last Day?" [22] To such searching questions did the distinguished members of the Athenian Society address their talents. Leslie Stephen charitably described the Athenian Society as a kind of prototype *Notes and Queries*.[23]

By 1693 the reputation of the Society had sufficient currency in London for the playwright Elkanah Settle to publish his *New Athenian Comedy*, a topical satire on the pretensions and excesses of this Athenian Society to which Defoe belonged. Among other matters, Settle's play ridiculed the bizarre queries discussed by the "Athenians" in their journal. In Act I, an "Under Turnkey of Newgate" delivers to the members of the Athenian Society, depicted as convening in a coffee-house, a letter submitted for their attention by an inmate of the prison. The letter poses the question: "Which is the more noble animal, a louse or a flea?" [24]

The members of the Athenian Society took themselves very seriously, however, as did many of their devoted readers, including such notable men of learning as Sir William Temple, who, according to Dunton, "was pleased to honour me with frequent letters and questions, very curious and uncommon," and the Marquis of Halifax, who "constantly perused our 'Mercuries.' " Jonathan Swift, who was at that time secretary to Temple at Moor Park, followed his patron's lead by contributing, like Defoe, "an Ode to the Athenian Society," which was prefixed to the Fifth Supplement of the *Athenian Mercury*.[25] According to Dr. Johnson, in his *Life of Swift*, it was on perusal of these early verses that Dryden concluded, "Cousin Swift, you will never be a poet"

— which is not far different from Theophilus Cibber's equally candid estimate of Defoe's claims as a poet: "Poetry was far from being the talent of De Foe." [26]

Yet that "knot of obscure men," as Dr. Johnson dismissed the Athenian Society, in its brief existence, particularly in the years 1690–1693, commanded both attention and respect from their contemporaries. So much so, in fact, that Charles Gildon, in a less bilious mood, thought it worth his while to write a *History of the Athenian Society* in 1693. The extravagance and gravity of the Athenian undertaking is evident from Gildon's introductory comments: "England has the glory of giving rise to two of the noblest designs that the wit of man is capable of inventing, and they are, the Royal Society, for the experimental improvement of natural knowledge, and the Athenian Society for communicating not only that, but all other sciences to all men, as well as to both sexes." [27] The claims sound outlandish now, and to some extent they certainly are, but we must remember that at that time the Athenians could be impressed with a sense of their importance and their contribution to the diffusion of all knowledge. To a certain extent they saw themselves as complementing the work of the Royal Society.

The years 1690–1693, moreover, were not exactly a golden age of English poetry. Poets were busily imitating the ponderous pindarics of Abraham Cowley, and almost any rimer could call himself a poet. According to one contemporary judgment of the literary scene, "Never was there known so many versifiers, and so few poets." It is not difficult to understand, therefore, why John Dunton might later write boastfully about Charles Gildon's *History*, "to which were prefixed several poems written by the chief wits of the age (*viz.* Mr. Motteux, Mr. De Foe, Mr. Richardson, &c.); and, in particular, Mr. Tate (now Poet Laureate) was pleased to honour us with a poem directed to the Athenian Society, in these words":

. . . .

> To sing your toils let abler bards aspire,
> While I at distance silently admire,
> How much oblig'd your country is to you,
> If wit and learning here to those charms renew
> That art's admirers once to Athens drew! [28]

To be a member of this select literary circle, and to be called upon to celebrate in his "immortal verse," as his Ode put it modestly, the self-constituted counterpart in letters of the Royal Society in science was heady stuff indeed for young Defoe. After all, had not Abraham Cowley himself established this poetic precedent by commemorating the Royal Society with one of his celebrated odes? Defoe had ample cause to consider himself one of the "chief wits of the age," an "Athenian" wit, a poet in the noble tradition of Cowley, and a coequal in a way to the man who was to become Poet Laureate of England after Dryden and Shadwell, Mr. Nahum Tate. The wit had not turned tradesman; the tradesman had turned wit.

Meanwhile, England had gone to war with France in 1689. The full significance of this event was discussed by Defoe years later in the *Review:* "The power of the French influence on our trade in times of peace has not been so much, but their influence on it in time of war has been greater. And here opens a terrible scene. The sad depredation made upon us in trade, by their privateers in the beginning of the last war, has left a black mark on the estates of many ruin'd, but then flourishing families." [29] In 1689–90 Defoe was, as we saw, flourishing, both as a merchant and as a man of fashion and a wit. But the war with France was to leave its "black mark" on his fortunes.

The extended war under William (1689–1697), like the previous two wars against the Dutch under Charles II (1665–1667 and 1672–1674), gave impetus to England's development of her trade and commerce. The war with France, however, marked the beginning of an entirely new era in public finance. The war dragged on and the costs of financing it soared. Before it was over the war was to cost forty million pounds with a debt outstanding of fourteen million pounds. In the long run the war encouraged England's economic growth and led to such revolutionary changes as the foundation of the Bank of England in 1694. Certain established industries, capable of supplying goods needed to wage the war, were expanded greatly. Other new industries and manufactures also took root and flourished during this period. In short, the war, according to G. N. Clark, was transforming England increasingly into a business nation in the modern sense.

But for some merchants and traders the war proved disastrous, notably those engaged in shipping or underwriting shipping insurance. French privateers were engaged in extensive commerce-destroying operations, which reached their height in 1691. Some French sea captains, like Jean Bart, most renowned of the Dunkirk privateers, were amassing vast fortunes for themselves and those investing in their privateering escapades on English shipping. Defoe was to recall that he "had the honour, disaster, or what else you will please to call it, of losing the first ship that was taken upon the breach of the last war, and before it was declar'd." He had good cause to bemoan his bad luck because he was then at the very peak of his prosperity as a merchant-trader, and that first loss was to be but a prelude to further losses — and "disaster." [30]

Since 1688 Defoe had been involved in the shipping business as a part owner and insurer of ships. The dowry of £3,700 his wife had brought him in 1684 was invested in these and other commercial enterprises. His business activities from 1688 on show him involved in speculative, get-rich-quick schemes far in excess of his capital resources. It is clear that Defoe hoped to capitalize on the opportunities presented by the anticipation and eventual participation of England in the war with France of 1689. He was prepared to gamble heavily again — just as he had done when joining up with Monmouth — this time even risking his credit and capital against the promise of high profits from import-export and shipping insurance undertakings. But gamblers must be prepared to be losers as well as winners, and when faced with the realization that they are becoming losers, and cannot fully cover their losses, they often are driven to underhand dealings in a desperate attempt to salvage what remains of their holdings and their reputation. When faced with staggering losses, Defoe was to prove himself no exception to this pattern of behavior.

In fact, Defoe drew directly on his own experiences when he summed up in *The Complete English Tradesman* the desperate gambling psychology of men of business confronted with losses: "The richer the tradesman is, the bolder he is apt to be in his adventures . . . but as the gamester is tempted to throw again, to retrieve the past loss, so one adventure in trade draws in another, till at last comes a capital loss which weakens the stock, and which wounds the reputation; and thus by one loss coming in the neck of another the tradesman is first made desperate, [then] in his desperation ventures it all, and so is at once undone." Defoe obviously was fully aware of how this account struck close to home, for he self-consciously added that some uncharitable readers might accuse him of writing "too feelingly upon this part of the subject." [31]

Thanks to the careful research of James Sutherland we know that between 1688 and 1694 Defoe was involved in no less than eight different law suits, all of which accused him of some sort of fraud. Most of these litigations ended inconclusively, but one noteworthy fact does emerge from all these court cases in which Defoe was named a principal: when a man is brought to suit by eight different people and publicly charged with having defrauded or cheated them in his business dealings, it is a fair deduction that he was something less than a blameless businessman. If anything young Defoe was speculating not wisely but too well, hoping for quick and high profits, even if it compromised his conscience as a Puritan just a little.[32]

These litigations suggest further the extent to which Defoe was committed to assorted business schemes, if not also to some scheming. But the full magnitude of his shipping operations during this time is revealed by his citation in the "Merchants Insurers' (War with France) Bill" of 1694. This bill named him as one of nineteen merchants known to have suffered financial ruin by their shipping and maritime insurance operations during the disastrous days of English shipping early in the war. Defoe is cited as among those "who have been known merchants and traders beyond the sea for many years past, and have paid great sums of money to the Crown for customs upon goods exported and imported." [33] If Defoe was known to have paid "great sums of money" for customs on goods he imported or exported, he was not only trading in a great way but also making a great deal of money before being overtaken by bad luck in 1689–90.

When in the early 1690's the dream of prosperity and position became transmogrified for Defoe into the barest hope of averting financial ruin and personal disaster, he grew increasingly desperate in his business dealings. In the spring of 1692 he gambled on a final frantic scheme by purchasing about seventy civet-cats from a London merchant. He bought them from £852 15s., paying £200 down and promising another payment within a month, with the total price to be paid within six months. Being destitute of funds, he prevailed on an old acquaintance and former business associate, Samuel Stancliffe, for a loan of £400, which was granted him, even though he was already in debt to Stancliffe for £1,000. When Stancliffe discovered that Defoe was on the brink of bankruptcy, he asked to be repaid; but Defoe evaded him until Stancliffe was forced in the fall of 1692 to obtain a writ of seizure for the civet-cats. The sheriffs appraised the civet-cats at £439 7s. and they were placed on public sale.

In October 1692, Defoe induced his mother-in-law to buy and maintain them, which she did, until it turned out in March of 1693 that she had purchased from Defoe civet-cats that were never legally his to sell; whereupon she found herself cullied out of over £400. The light in which we must view Defoe for his hand in this transaction is described sharply by T. F. M. Newton, who, after sifting through ten thousand words of litigation filed by Mrs. Tuffley and the other principals in 1693, concludes:

[Defoe] gambled for relief; and when he lost he turned to knavery. He had little hope in the first place of financing the Newington venture properly. He paid less than a quarter of the purchase price, gave worthless notes for part of the remainder, and had the amount of the invoice increased to fool his family. He borrowed money for the express purpose of buying the cats, used none of it to that end, and lied in saying he had . . . The proceeds of his fraud went towards payment of his personal debts, and the hapless victim was his own mother-in-law.[34]

It is an ironic twist of circumstance, and a reflection on the course of Defoe's brief business career, that the scene of these reprehensible dealings by Defoe the merchant should be Newington Green, where some fifteen years before Daniel Foe the ministerial student was preparing himself for his calling at Morton's academy. The notorious civet-cat episode was to remain a stigma on his reputation the rest of his life; whenever his enemies would want to taunt him, they had only to call him the "civet-cat merchant."

Now we can appreciate why Defoe in later life came to regard it as his "disaster" to have been "set apart from" the ministry; for if he had entered the ministry as intended, all this sordid business would have been avoided. But instead, he was to refer to himself as "a *merchant*, to which I had the misfortune to be bred." [35] The "disaster" and the "misfortune" were, however, in no small measure his own doing, as his career throughout the 1680's and into the 1690's makes self-evident. Within three years after riding so resplendently accoutred in the Lord Mayor's Day parade honoring William and Mary in 1689, within two years after commencing as a member of the Athenian Society, Defoe was bankrupt to the extent of £17,000, a figure attesting to the magnitude of his daring gamble for quick success.

Defoe's bankruptcy was one of the most terrifying events of his whole life. It convinced him that life was at best uncertain and insecure, and, of far more shattering import, it made him realize that he was capable of shameful acts when pressed hard and far enough. He was to write later about the plight of a bankrupt with the insight and compassion that stem only from personal experience:

And here I must speak a word of compassion to the unhappy, when brought to the dreadful necessities of trade, ruin in prospect, a gaol in view, the creditor at the door, and all the horrid scene of a rupture presents itself to his eyes. How does this terrible prospect drive the distress'd tradesman, honest before, and in his thought abhorring to do an unjust action? How do these necessities lead him by the hand into thousands of snares, and drive him to the unhappy commission of a thousand things, which before his very soul abhorr'd?

. . . I freely rank myself with those that are ready to own that they have in the extremities and embarrassments in trade done those things which their own principles condemn'd, which they are not asham'd to blush for, which they look back on with regret, and strive to make reparation for with their utmost diligence.

BREAK, GENTLEMEN, for God's sake, for your own sake, for your creditor's sake, and for the public good; BREAK, while you have something to pay . . . something to tempt them to refrain a statute of bankrupt to the ruin both of your family and their debts.[36]

The impassioned prose of this passage reads like what it is, a *de profundis* by Defoe. He had experienced the "dreadful necessities of trade" while still a young man and had behaved knavishly. He later tried to understand more fully what had made him and other men behave like that. These inner searchings helped to make him the astute psychologist he was to become in writing of the lives of other desperate and ambitious persons.

That Defoe should have been terrified of breaking or turning bankrupt in 1692 is readily understood when we realize the fate awaiting such a business failure and his family. So foul and so hopeless were the conditions debtors met in prison in the seventeenth century generally, that an act was passed in 1670–71 attempting to keep prisoners for debt separate from convicted felons because "in Newgate and elsewhere many distressed gentlemen and tradesmen were kept awake at night by the foul language of felons and the clanking of their chains." How ineffectual this act was in ameliorating conditions in the prisons is clear from Defoe's writing on the subject as late as 1706: "To talk of humanity and mercy, and confine men to perpetual imprisonment for debt . . . to smother men in noisome dungeons, and crowd them with murtherers and thieves; to condemn them to the temporary hell of a gaol . . . for shame." Another pamphleteer in 1714 wrote in his tract exposing the insufferable conditions of debtors — entitled evocatively "Piercing Cries of the Poor and Miserable Prisoners for Debts . . ." — that so frightening was the prospect of debtor's prison, "if any man see another coming to lay violent hands upon him, to attack his person and haul his body to prison, nature teaches him to take the assailor for his capital enemy and to act the best he may in his own defence," which, considering "the violence with which arrest was resisted," probably resulted in a high mortality rate among bailiffs.[37]

Defoe understood the psychology involved in such extreme moments only too well from his own experience, and he counseled: *"Extremity makes a knave . . . [so] make nobody desperate."* His own knavery born of desperation in 1692 enabled him to confront his self-satisfied and self-assured readers with the starkest facts about human nature as he had so poignantly come to know them:

I am of the opinion that we have generally mistaken notions in the world about honesty, and those that have never had occasion to try their integrity are too apt to censure those that have; I believe there are occasions in which the necessity is too hard, even for human nature itself, tho' backed with reason, and fortified with religion . . .

You are an honest man, you say! Pray, Sir, was you ever tried? . . .
I tell you, Sir, you would not eat your neighbor's bread only, but
your neighbor himself, rather than starve, and your honesty would
all shipwrack in the storm of necessity.[38]

Defoe knew the terrible truth of what he wrote here. He had
himself experienced such "shipwrack in the storm of necessity"
in 1692, and it was an experience he was never to forget.

Defoe owes to this period of his life his first mature encounter
with fear. We know that he scorned physical cowardice of any
kind; he was ready at any time to take up his Protestant Flail or
his sword. But when faced not with a palpable enemy but with
the unknown, the unexpected, the unassailable, he was petrified
with fear. This explains why the prospect of debtor's prison — or
indeed any kind of enforced close confinement — always would
conjure up frightful images in his mind. Going bankrupt and
facing jail was like a "shipwreck" or "being taken by the Turks"
or some equally frightful prospect; not the least reason for these
fears being that to an active and dynamic person like Defoe
imprisonment deprived one of "all that helps of art, industry,
and time" to redeem and repair one's fortunes. Fear of the unknown was the worst kind of fear because it preyed incessantly
on the imagination, and Defoe was to dramatize its effects master-
fully in *Robinson Crusoe:* "Thus fear of danger is ten thousand
times more terrifying than danger itself when apparent to the
eyes; and we find the burthen of anxiety greater, by much, than
the evil which we are anxious about." The fear of debtor's prison
in Defoe at this time probably took something of this form, although the common knowledge about existence in these institutions, with their horrid health conditions and high mortality
rates, would have been terrifying enough for anyone.[39]

More than thirty years after the event, Defoe described bankruptcy with an intensity of language and immediacy of experience strongly suggesting that he relived his own financial ruin of
1692 as he described it. Very likely this is what befell Defoe and
his family:

It put all into confusion and distraction; the man, in the utmost
terror, fright, and distress, ran away with what goods he could get
off, as if his house was on fire, to get into the Friars or the Mint; the
family fled one way, the one another, like people in desperation;

the wife to her father and mother, if she had any; and the children, some to one relation, some to another; a statute (so they vulgarly call a commission of bankrupt) came and swept away all, and oftentimes consumed it too, and left little or nothing, either to pay the creditors or relieve the bankrupt. This made the bankrupt desperate, and made him fly to those places of shelter.[40]

The passage dramatically and compellingly portrays fear in operation. Defoe was to become a master at describing this emotional state in man (for example, the footprint episode in *Robinson Crusoe* or Moll's fear of poverty or Roxana's haunting fear of her daughter). Late in 1692 a terrified Defoe fled from his creditors "to those places of shelter" like the Mint or Whitefriars.

Defoe had played for the highest stakes as a merchant. He had invested his wife's considerable dowry of £3,700 in promoting his business ventures. He was involved in import-export activities of acknowledged magnitude. He speculated in land and sank funds into new inventions, such as a diving device. He was living the life of a fashionable man about town and lively wit. But the war with France left its "black mark" on his far-ranging business operations and his pretensions to gentility. He lost heavily in goods and shipping in the early years of the war. He gambled, grew desperate, gambled desperately. He even degraded himself to the point of cheating his own mother-in-law with his civet-cat fiasco. By the end of 1692 Defoe had lost all: his fortune, his good name, his position as a "chief citizen" of London, his genteel way of living, and, temporarily, even his family in his flight. Defoe, however, was always able to draw an instructive lesson from his failures for someone else's profit: "Let the wise and wary tradesman take the hint; keep within the bounds where Providence has placed him; be content to rise gradually and gently . . . and as he is sufficiently rich, if he will make it more, let it be in the old road; go softly on, lest he comes not softly down." [41]

Chapter 3. From Sunday Gentleman to the True-Born Englishman

The English tradesman is a kind of phoenix, who rises out of his own ashes, and makes the ruin of his fortunes be a firm foundation to build his recovery. — Defoe, *The Complete English Tradesman*, II, 198–199

Nil desperandum was Defoe's terse piece of advice to fallen tradesmen, and when he himself fell in 1692 he acted upon it. Defoe was becoming well schooled in the ways of "necessity"; he knew that only his own ingenuity and efforts would restore his fortunes. He was later to describe the kind of tenacity he himself probably exercised during this period of bankruptcy: "But the vigorous restless man of diligence never lies still there; he struggles, he strives with his creditors, to get free; if that will not do, he gets abroad, and turns himself round in the world . . . if one thing fails, he meets another; if not one place, he seeks out another; he never gives out." The former student destined for the nonconformist ministry had struggled with the exigencies of life long enough to learn that hope and help lay not in prayer. He came to sum up the hard lesson life had taught him simply, "A man that will lie still should never hope to rise; he that will lie in a ditch and pray may depend upon it, he shall lie in a ditch and die." [1]

From his sanctuary as a fugitive debtor, Defoe soon entered into negotiations with his various creditors to arrange some kind of settlement. Even though officially a bankrupt, he still could have retained some goods and collateral to bargain with; for he was an overseas trader, and as he wrote in the manuscript of what was to be published in 1697 as *An Essay upon Projects*, "If the bankrupt be a merchant, no statute can reach his effects beyond the seas," which was probably the very legal loophole he tried to exploit in hopes of coming to terms with his creditors.[2]

It is safe to assume that Defoe's wife and children were not with him much, if at all, during most of 1693. They very likely were staying at Kingsland, in the parish of Hackney, where the Defoes had had a residence in the country in the time of their recent prosperity. Yet as Defoe was to write in 1706, when again dunned by his creditors, he had "been 14 years in retreat, in jeopardy, in broils, and most of the time in banishment from his family," and this particular period of "retreat" would not have found him at home. He was shifting for himself as best he could and busily avoiding his creditors, while Mary Defoe was doing her best in caring for the children in Kingsland, probably with the help and at the home of her mother.[3]

We know from a petition filed by Defoe under the pending Merchants Insurers Bill that by February 1694 he had "met and proposed to his creditors a means for their satisfaction," although, the petition continues, "some few of them would not come into these proposals." Defoe was granted his petition to have his name inserted into the Merchants Insurers Bill, which was specifically designed "to enable divers Merchant Insurers, that have sustained great losses by the present war with France, the better to satisfy their several creditors." The fact that his petition was granted, and an amendment was passed in the House of Commons "inserting the name of Daniel Foe into the Bill," attests both to his stature as a merchant-trader and to the legitimacy of his claims for relief for his shipping losses. The defeat of the bill in the House of Lords in March 1694 must have come as a bitter disappointment to Defoe, who had looked to its provisions as a means of effecting a speedy and just settlement with his "several creditors."[4]

Defoe became obsessed with his condition as a bankrupt. The great uncertainty of trade, the heavy losses in shipping suffered during the first years of the war, the harshness and unreasonableness of the debtor's laws, all these matters that had touched him so deeply of late no doubt occupied his thoughts in 1692–93 while he was hiding from his creditors and separated from his family. But he was far from idle during this period. The circumstances of his unfortunate experiences and his reflections upon them he set down in a series of schemes about improving society. In 1697 he finally published this manuscript as *An Essay upon Projects*, but since the preface reads, "having kept the greatest part of it [the manuscript] by me for near five years," we know the actual date of composition falls within the time Defoe was in hiding. The fecundity of Defoe's mind, especially in times of adversity, was truly remarkable, and it is not surprising that Defoe's American counterpart as a "projector," Benjamin Franklin, should write of the *Essay*, it "gave me a turn of thinking that had an influence on some of the principal future events of my life." [5] It was also to have an immediate influence on Defoe's life.

Defoe turned "projector" not out of a spirit of unpremeditated public welfare but in direct response to the same pressures everyone came to feel from the effects of the war: "Necessity, which is allowed to be the mother of invention, has so violently agitated the wits of men at this time, that it seems not at all improper, by way of distinction, to call it the Projecting Age." The shipping losses incurred by England, already a trading power with extensive operations by that time, were felt by many people, "and I," Defoe noted, "am none of the least of the sufferers." Those hardest hit by the war were merchants like Defoe who undertook to insure the shipping and were engaged in considerable shipping activities themselves, with the result that "an incredible number of the best merchants in the kingdom sunk under the load." Since there was no prospect of relief from the government, Defoe and his fellow merchants, "prompted by necessity," began to "rack their wits for new contrivances, new inventions, new trades, stocks, projects, and anything to retrieve the desperate credit of their fortunes." [6]

Defoe's life at this time was uncomfortable and insecure; most of what he wrote in the *Essay upon Projects* was aimed at making life more comfortable and secure. Necessity was indeed the mother of invention in his case. He clearly had a twofold purpose in mind when writing the *Essay*: he hoped to command the attention and win the support of some influential patron, perhaps even King William himself; and he also hoped to correct the conditions that had landed him in his present predicament as a fugitive from his home and his creditors, whom he owed the staggering sum of £17,000.

In the chapter "Of Bankrupts," Defoe recounts vividly the people and conditions one encounters in "those nurseries of rogues, the Mint and Friars." From his intimate account it would seem that he may well have spent some time in one or more of these sanctuaries in London where debtors could flee without fear of pursuit and arrest. At this time there were eleven such sanctuaries in London, the Mint and Whitefriars being the most notorious and the most densely populated. Perhaps it was at the Mint or Friars that Defoe heard at first hand the hardened talk of the denizens of "those dens of thieves," where a newcomer, according to him, "soon learns to speak it; (for I think I may say, without wronging any man, I have known many a man go in among them honest, that is, without ill design, but I never knew one to come away so again)." If Defoe had to seek refuge temporarily among such a "black crew," he clearly found the company and surroundings intolerable; after all, he had just recently been an important merchant living like a gentleman, and they were too sordid a reminder of how far he had fallen in fortune. So appalled was Defoe by conditions in these sanctuaries that when he did have his chance to do something about them less than five years later, he was, in his own words, "the first that complained . . . *in a day when I could be heard,* of the abominable insolence of bankrupts, practis'd in the Mint and Fryars, [and] gave the first mortal blow to the prosperity of these excesses." [7] In all events, he probably took the first chance he could and fled London for the safety of Bristol.

A tradition in Bristol holds that Defoe retired to that city at this time when he was busily avoiding his creditors. He was remembered as having been seen walking on the streets of Bristol on Sundays all "accoutred in the fashion of the times, with a fine flowing wig, lace ruffles, and a sword by his side." He evidently cut something of a figure and earned himself the sobriquet of "The Sunday Gentleman" from the townspeople, who were accustomed only to see him in his flamboyant attire on Sundays, when the bailiffs were not empowered to arrest him as a debtor. The rest of the week he discreetly spent in hiding. Defoe's residence in Bristol at about this time is supported by the story that he frequented a tavern called the Red Lion, operated by a Mark Watkins and known as a favorite gathering place for the tradesmen of Bristol. Defoe is reported to have partaken of the company at the Red Lion occasionally; at least we are informed he "was well known to the landlord under the same name of 'The Sunday Gentleman.'" [8]

Defoe's reputation in Bristol as "The Sunday Gentleman," whether accurate or apocryphal, certainly is consistent with his well developed sense of vanity as revealed in other sources, notably his own writings. Defoe's snobbery about his presumed family name is unmistakable in *A Tour through England & Wales*, where he goes out of his way to mention "the pleasant seat of an ancient Norman family of the name of De Beau-foe, whose posterity remain there, and in several other parts of the county, retaining the latter part of their sirname, but without the former to this day." Though he might have hoped his readers would infer that he obviously was related to this ancient and distinguished Norman family residing at Warwick, he knew himself to be the son of a London tallow-chandler and butcher, whose own father in turn was a "yeoman" of modest means from Etton, Northamptonshire; and instead of the "Norman" ancestry Defoe implies, his family was of Flemish stock, having settled in England in the sixteenth century.[9]

We know very little about his ancestry on his mother's side. On the basis of one passing reference biographers have seen fit to endow Alice Foe's father with a country estate. In the *Review* Defoe alludes to a grandfather who "had a huntsman that us'd the same familiarity with his dogs, and he had his Roundhead, and his Cavalier, his Goring and his Waller, and all the generals of both armies were hounds in his pack; till the times turning the old gentleman was fain to scatter the pack, and make them up of more dog-like sir-names." If, as Defoe's allusion suggests, his mother was the daughter of a Royalist country gentleman, it seems unlikely that a lady from such a background would demean herself to marry a Puritan tallow-chandler.[10]

Defoe clearly was not above making such flattering claims about himself. At another time, for example, he said that he was "related to" the blood of none other than Sir Walter Raleigh. The contention is outlandish, but understandable when we consider that, as Professor Moore notes, Defoe was "a lifelong admirer of Sir Walter Raleigh," and even owned some of his charts and manuscripts. Had he known for a fact he was related to Sir Walter, surely a man like Defoe would have found countless occasions to share the knowledge with the world more often and more conclusively. Our best indication of Defoe's social pretensions is his official adoption in 1706 of the more "Norman" and aristocratic version of his name, "De Foe," in place of the more plebeian "Foe" he inherited from his father. As early as October 1695 he had used publicly the more impressive version of his name, for so his name appeared in the *Post-Boy* announcing a royal lottery he was then running for King William. He adopted a name of quality because he wanted to become and be thought of as a man of quality.[11]

Despite his financial ruin in 1692, Defoe maintained something of a reputation among his fellow merchants in the overseas trade during the war with France, which was still dragging on. "It was about the year 1694," Defoe wrote in his *Appeal to Honour and Justice* later, "when I was invited by some merchants, with whom I had corresponded abroad, and some also at home, to settle at Cadiz in Spain, and that with offers of very good commissions." He was a logical choice for such an assignment. He had had business dealings with that part of Europe; he later remarked of Spain in the *Review* that he had "liv'd in that country" and had been for a time also "concern'd in the Portugal wine-trade." It is supposed that he had traveled in Spain when on the Continent in the mid-1680's and thereby learned to speak Spanish. Among merchants at least, his stock still stood fairly high in 1694.[12]

"But Providence, which had other work for me to do," Defoe wrote in explanation of his decision, "placed a secret aversion in my mind to quitting England upon any account, and made me refuse the best offers of that kind, to be concern'd with some eminent persons at home, in proposing *ways* and *means* to the Government for raising money to supply the occasions of the war then newly begun." He conveniently invoked "Providence" for what most likely was a calculated effort on his part to ingratiate himself with "eminent persons" like Dalby Thomas, to whom he dedicated his *Essay upon Projects* when it appeared in 1697, but with whom he already was in communication about various financial schemes in the mid-1690's. Dalby Thomas was a powerful West India merchant — later to become knighted — who was to be of great service to Defoe. By 1697 Defoe could refer to him familiarly as "a friend" and as one of King William's appointed commissioners for the Glass Duty, "under whom I have the honour to serve his Majesty." Defoe owed to the intercession of Dalby Thomas the only two official posts we know for a fact he held during the reign of William III: the accountant for the commissioners of the Glass Duty, a post he held from 1695 to 1699; and the manager-trustee of the royal lotteries, a post he held in Ocober 1695, and again in March 1696.[13]

Defoe was well on his way to reestablishing himself in society. Before 1695 he "had the honour" to offer his views to both the House of Commons and the Privy Council on behalf of reopening trade with France. He also addressed himself to the "long annual inquiry of the House of Commons for ways and means" to raise revenue for financing the costly war. Part of his purpose in the *Essay upon Projects* was a conscious attempt to make himself useful to the party in power, perhaps even to the King himself. He wrote in the introduction to the *Essay*: "Projects of the nature I treat about are, doubtless, in general of public advantage, as they tend to improvement of trade, and employment of the poor, and the circulation and increase of the public stock of the kingdom; but . . . I will allow the author to aim primarily at his own advantage, yet with the circumstances of public benefit added." The central problem faced by King William at home was how to finance the war. The Bank of England had been founded in 1694, but revenue was badly needed. Defoe pointed out to the government some as yet untapped tax sources, such as "the retailers of manufacturers," those inland traders who ran no risks in shipping overseas, "have never been taxed yet," and "now lie as a reserve to carry on the burden of the war." Such suggestions were certainly timely and welcome to a government hard-pressed for funds. He was coming back into favor with his monarch, serving him in sundry capacities, as adviser and pamphleteer and for special and trusted errands that took him riding about England. He was again to be found at Court, and when King William rode home in triumph after the Treaty of Ryswick in 1697, Defoe escorted him.[14]

He could well be pleased with his progress. Just a few years after breaking so heavily and behaving so badly in 1692, Defoe, like his "phoenix" of a tradesman, could now point to himself as a shining example of a merchant able "to fall into the very dirt of scandal and reproach, and rise with reputation." Now that he was once more in the service of King William he was again accepted in the highest circles. In 1697, for example, he was entertained handsomely as a summer guest at the magnificent estate of "the famous Sir John Fagg," the M.P. for Steyning in Sussex:

I mention the ancient gentleman on this occasion, that being enter-tained at his house, in the year 1697, he show'd me in his park four bullocks of his own breeding, and of his own feeding, of so prodigious a size, and so excessively overgrown by fat, that I never saw any thing like them . . .
While I continu'd at Sir John's, some London butchers came down to see them, and in my hearing offer'd Sir John six and twenty pound a head for them, but he refused it; and when I mov'd him afterward to take the money, he said No, he was resolv'd to have them . . . But by this may be judg'd something of the largeness of the cattle in the Wild of Kent and Sussex . . . and for this reason I tell the story.

That the size of the cattle was Defoe's only reason in digressing to tell of his stay at the estate of "the famous Sir John Fagg" remains a nice point of interpretation. There can be no ques-tion, though, that he was on easy terms with men of position and power like Sir John Fagg and Dalby Thomas.[15]

As Defoe's political star had been rising since the mid-1690's, so had his commercial undertakings. Some time after 1694 he established a brick and pantile factory on land he owned in the marshlands close to Tilbury in Essex. The idea of building a brick and pantile works close to London was as ingenious as it was daring. Bricks and tiles never had been manufactured with any success in England; they had to be imported from Holland at much inconvenience and considerable cost. The demand for bricks and tiles was high. London was growing. People were coming to the city from the country. Buildings were being erected all over London to accommodate the new needs for dwellings, places of business, of worship, of entertainment. The climate for a reliable source of sturdy bricks and tiles close to London could not have been more favorable. Defoe supplied the market with a quality product in quantity; his business flourished and he prospered handily.[16]

As his business grew so did his taste for fashionable living. "All my prospects were built on a manufacture I had erected in

Essex," Defoe explained to Harley later; "all the late King's bounty to me was expended there. I employ'd a hundred poor families at work and it began to pay me very well. I generally made six hundred pound profit per annum." The "bounty" of King William must have been substantial because Defoe on another occasion remarked in a pamphlet how indebted he was to William and how he had been, in his words, "above my capacity of deserving, rewarded." Now that he had once again established a thriving source of income, he "began to live, took a good house, bought . . . coach and horses a second time." His large house stood close to the Thames and he had the use of a small boat. He maintained a staff of servants and enjoyed being rowed by them on the river. By the late 1690's Defoe's life was comfortable and fashionable once again.[17]

In 1700 Defoe seized upon another opportunity to make himself yet more valuable to his King and "Master." In that year John Tutchin, in a coarse satiric poem entitled *The Foreigners*, gave voice to a growing sentiment of dissatisfaction with King William as both foreign-born and favoring those of foreign birth. William had been widely criticized for his actions in making such foreign families as the Keppels, Bentincks, and Schombergs members of the English nobility, and awarding them large grants of forfeited lands in Ireland. Both Houses were incensed by the King's actions. It was a tense period and Tutchin's poem, though doggerel and in bad taste, had touched a raw nerve. Discontent with the foreign-born King became widespread.

Defoe gave his version of the circumstances that prompted him to write in answer to Tutchin in 1700:

During this time, there came out a vile, abhorr'd pamphlet, in very ill verse, written by one Mr. Tutchin, call'd *The Foreigners*: in which the author, *who he was I then knew not*, fell personally upon the King himself, and then upon the Dutch nation; and after having reproach'd His Majesty with crimes, that his worst enemy could not think of without horror, he sums up all in the odious name of "Foreigner."

This fill'd me with a kind of rage against the book; and gave birth to a trifle which I never could hope should have met with so general an acceptation as it did, I mean, *The True-Born Englishman*.

The most outspoken and immoderate critics of King William

naturally were those who prided themselves on their native birth and purity of English ancestry, claims that were obviously denied the Dutch-born monarch on the English throne. By January 1701 Defoe was ready to answer Tutchin's charges against King William with a doggerel poem of his own, *The True-Born Englishman*. His composition was less a poem than a kind of political pamphlet in crude but catching heroic verse; it had, as Defoe made clear in an explanatory preface to the poem, a specific satiric intent: "But the intent of the satire is pointed at the vanity of those who talk of their antiquity, and value themselves upon their pedigree, their ancient families, and being true-born; whereas it is impossible we should be true-born; and if we could, should have lost by the bargain." The best defence of the King was an attack upon the claims of those who prided themselves on being true-born. This was to be Defoe's basic strategy.[18]

The first part of the poem is a long drawn-out exposition of the fact that "Englishmen *ab origine*" are really foreigners themselves. Defoe inquires into the Englishmen's claims of pure ancestry, showing both the multifariousness of the peoples who populated England in her early days (Gauls, Greeks, Romans, Lombards, Danes, Scots, Picts, Irish, Normans, and others) and the generally low quality of these thieves and adventurers: "From this amphibious ill-born mob began/That vain ill-natured thing, an Englishman." Yet in Defoe's time the nobility and gentry looked not so much to native ancestry as to direct descent dating from the time of the Norman Conquest, thus making them a part of the pure and refined Continental nobility. But, as Defoe is quick to point out, that claim, too, is suspect:

> And here begins our ancient pedigree,
> That so exalts our poor nobility:
> 'Tis that from some French trooper they derive,
> Who with the Norman bastard did arrive.
>
> . . . .
>
> These in the herald's register remain,
> Their noble mean extraction to explain,
> Yet who the hero was, no man can tell,
> Whether a drummer or a colonel.   (pp. 190–191)

By use of the oxymoron "noble mean" Defoe underscores the

ambiguity of claims to Norman ancestry by the English gentry and nobility.

Defoe's main method of argument is that of *reductio ad absurdum*. It is foolish to be vain about so inglorious a thing as one's hybrid ancestry, he contends. Having disabused his countrymen of their empty claims to a distinguished line of ancestors, he is free to make his fundamental point about the detractors of King William:

> These are the heroes that despise the Dutch,
> And rail at new-come foreigners so much.
> Forgetting that themselves are all derived
> From the most scoundrel race that ever lived.
>
> (p. 191)

In so defending the foreign birth of William by belaboring the foreign birth of virtually all Englishmen, Defoe was also defending himself; for he knew of his own Flemish extraction dating back only to the sixteenth century on his father's side.

Admittedly, *The True-Born Englishman* is overlong, repetitious and unpolished as a poem, but as a spirited and telling defence of King William by virtue of its attack on the very claims to exclusiveness cherished by the upper classes and the ardent patriots, it was a singularly successful tour de force. It did earn for Defoe the gratitude of the King, who "receiv'd" him, "employ'd" him, and "rewarded" him handsomely; so much so, in fact, that he ever after would invoke "the immortal and glorious memory of that greatest and best of Princes, [whom] it was my honour and advantage to call Master as well as Sovereign, whose goodness to me I never forget." [19]

But *The True-Born Englishman* is more than a defence of King William and an answer to Tutchin's poem. Despite the xenophobic atmosphere in which it was conceived and composed, Defoe managed to achieve a secondary thrust to his satire. With obvious sophistication he ridicules the qualifications of the English gentry and nobility, qualifications distinctly relevant to his own social ambitions. In Europe, nobility had remained virtually absolute for centuries, but in England gentility was derivative and variable: "But England, modern to the last degree,/Borrows or makes her own nobility,/And yet she boldly boasts of pedigree (p. 196)." Since "blood and birth" are so relative in England, the only true claim one can make to gentility is not the status afforded by accident of birth but the qualities that attend gentility as outlined in the conduct books, notably personal virtue:

> 'Tis well that virtue gives nobility,
> How shall we else the want of birth and blood supply?
> Since scarce one family is left alive
> Which does not from some foreigner derive.
> Of sixty thousand English gentlemen,
> Whose name and arms in registers remain,
> We challenge all our heralds to declare
> Ten families which English-Saxons are. (p. 196)

Despite the props provided by the heralds' offices, with their coats of arms and genealogical records, English nobility and gentility are ultimately justified only by the quality of the persons themselves, not by birth and ancestry; and quality varies vastly from person to person.

Genealogists before 1700, according to Anthony R. Wagner, Garter King of Arms, "concerned almost wholly with landed families, had naturally grounded their research on the records of land tenure. Indeed in their day there were few other records which could have been used." But society was changing, and Defoe sensed the change and appreciated its implications. By 1700, Wagner observes, "there [were] the beginnings of a new clientele — the tradesmen of England, grown wealthy, whom Defoe saw coming every day to the Herald's Office." With money one could purchase the right to bear arms and so pass legally for a gentleman.[20]

What, then, is required to qualify for the rank of gentleman in England? Defoe replies disarmingly:

> Wealth, howsoever got, in England makes
> Lords of mechanics, gentlemen of rakes:
> Antiquity and birth are needless here;
> 'Tis impudence and money makes a peer.
> (p. 197)

Defoe's remarks, though ostensibly satiric, are not without their accuracy. English society at the time was in a state of flux and no longer rigidly structured. In 1691, for example, a Swiss commentator on the English social scene could write:

Gentlemen are properly such as are descended of a good family, bear-ing a coat of arms, without any particular title. And these we call Gentlemen born.

But use has so far stretched the signification of this word, both high and low, that every Nobleman . . . may be called a Gentleman. And, on the other side, anyone that, without a coat of arms, has either a liberal, or genteel education, that looks gentleman-like (whether he be so, or not) and has the wherewithall to live freely and handsomely, is by the courtesy of England usually called a Gentle-man.[21]

Defoe's reading of his society is not as far-fetched as it seems; his satiric thrust hits home. With money and breeding a man can purchase a coat of arms and set himself up as a gentleman. With unusual good fortune and the patronage of a king, like William, a man like Defoe could envision himself in time even qualifying for the nobility.

In England, according to Defoe's *True-Born Englishman,* the best way to a peership is "money"; the best claim to gentility is "virtue." It is not without design that he concludes his long poem with the final couplet: "For fame of families is all a cheat,/'Tis personal virtue only makes us great" (p. 218). By sweeping aside the nobility's insistence on the primacy of birth and blood, he effectively clears the way for tradesmen and merchants, men like himself in short, to aspire to the status that they were coming to covet as they grew wealthy and prominent in society. Since *The True-Born Englishman* was written in answer to Tutchin's *Foreigners,* everyone read it primarily in that light; but viewed in terms of Defoe's own social ambitions, the poem is also a spirited defense of the claims of the rising middle class to social status as gentlemen, not the least Defoe's own claims.

In 1701 Defoe "gave birth" not, as he said with false modesty later, "to a trifle" but to the most popular and widely sold poem in the English language up to that time. It was a notable achieve-ment, whatever its shortcomings as poetry. In the preface to the second volume of his collected *Writings* of 1705, Defoe with much less modesty referred to *The True-Born Englishman* as "a remarkable example, by which the author, tho' he eyed in it no profit, had he been to enjoy the profit of his own labour, had gained above £1000. A book that besides nine editions of the author, has been twelve times printed by other hands . . . Eighty thousand of the small ones have been sold in the streets for 2d. or at a penny." [22] Overnight Defoe had become famous. He found himself hailed as a popular poet laureate — the official incumbent was his former fellow "Athenian," Nahum Tate — and after this he was to sign himself simply as "The author of *The True-Born Englishman*." The obscure but aspiring "Athenian" wit of 1690–91 was now, ten years later, acclaimed a national poet.

Also in 1701 Defoe experienced still another personal triumph. The peace achieved by William at the Treaty of Ryswick in 1697 was temporary at best. This uneasy truce could only last until the death of the king of Spain reopened the important question of the Spanish Succession, an issue that would in all probability lead to an outbreak of war in Europe. Knowing of the territorial ambitions of his rival, Louis XIV of France, William had counted on Parliament voting him the armies and supplies he needed to thwart the designs of the French king on the Spanish empire, but Parliament failed to support him and the death of the king of Spain in 1701 precipitated a crisis.

As rumors of war preparations in France reached England, the people became alarmed, especially the residents of Kent, the county closest to the French coast and therefore the most vulnerable in the event of invasion. Defoe captured the nervous mood of the Kentish farmers in his *History of the Kentish Petition* when he wrote that "the country people began to say to one another in their language, *That they had sow'd their corn, and the French were a coming to reap it.*" In April 1701 the gentlemen, justices of the peace, grand jury, and other freeholders of Kent met and drew up a signed document petitioning Parliament to support King William's preparedness policy against France and alerting them to the palpable threat of war posed by Louis XIV. This "Kentish Petition" was hand carried to London by five Kentish gentlemen who finally presented it to the House of Commons in May. Although the petition was entirely legal and proper, the Commons were incensed by the forwardness of the action and, after a heated five-hour debate, voted it "scandalous, insolent, and seditious," and had the petitioners taken into custody as a lesson to others presuming to meddle in their affairs.

On May 14, 1701, Defoe appeared at the door of the House of

Commons escorted by "sixteen gentlemen of quality" and presented to the Speaker, Mr. Robert Harley, his paper boldly entitled *Legion's Memorial to the House of Commons*, the substance of which was both a stern reminder that the Commons were no more than the representatives of the people who elected them and a list of grievances requiring prompt attention. Defoe wisely did not wait until Harley read his paper. Whereas the "Kentish Petitioners" performed a mild gesture of protest, Defoe perpetrated an audacious act of defiance; but instead of being arrested, he carried it off with aplomb. The *Legion's Memorial* closed with a firm and defiant note: "For Englishmen are no more to be slaves to Parliaments than to a King. Our name is LEGION, and we are many." Harley read the paper to the House, as requested, and it caused a commotion — according to Defoe's account, it "struck . . . a terror into the party in the House." Defoe's daring strategy won for him a double victory: the Kentish Petitioners were released and the Commons made a conciliatory gesture to King William in encouraging him to seek military alliances abroad. Once again his King was indebted to him.[23]

Defoe was now acclaimed by the populace. A banquet was held for the freed Kentish Petitioners at the Mercer's Hall in Cheapside. The expense of the affair was borne by the citizens of London at a cost of about £200. "Several noble lords and members of parliament" dined with the more than two hundred gentlemen on hand for that memorable evening. A medal was struck to commemorate the occasion and to celebrate the Petitioners with the legend *Non auro patriam*. At the center of the festivities sat the guest of honor, Daniel Defoe, whose presence at the banquet could not be dimmed even in the description set down by a hostile Tory writer: "Next the Worthies was placed their Secretary of State, the author of the Legion-Letter; and one might have read the downfall of parliaments in his very countenance." The year 1701 marked, in William P. Trent's estimate, "perhaps the highest stand in popular estimation attained by Defoe during his own lifetime." [24] A favorite of the people, he was also a favorite of the King.

Fortune, however, was not to favor Defoe and his fondest hopes of political preferment. Just eight months after Defoe was banqueting with the Kentish Petitioners, and a little over a year after he was nationally acclaimed for his *True-Born Englishman,* his "Master as well as Sovereign" was thrown from his horse while hunting at Hampton Court and broke his collarbone. The accident was a freak, the horse having stepped into a molehole and stumbled, throwing its rider to the ground. The King's collarbone was set properly and he appeared to be on his way to recovery when complications set in and his condition worsened until a month later he finally died. While the Whigs mourned the death of their monarch, the Tories rejoiced and drank the health of the horse that threw him.[25] For Defoe it was a black day indeed; perhaps the blackest as he later came to review the course of his career. All his hopes and dreams were suddenly and unexpectedly blighted. His career was uncertain and insecure again, and precisely at a point when he was so tantalizingly close to success a second time.

The accession of Queen Anne did not augur well for the Dissenters, who under King William had enjoyed their greatest period of peace and religious freedom since the Restoration; the Act of Toleration of 1689 had ushered in an era relatively free from persecutions. Defoe, it must be remembered, remained all his life a Dissenter, and a staunch one at that. He had written in 1697, for example, his pamphlet entitled *An Enquiry into the Occasional Conformity of Dissenters, in Cases of Preferment,* wherein he admonished his fellow Dissenters not to compromise their beliefs for purposes of personal gain. For about five years now he had been actively engaged in such a pamphleteering controversy with Dissenters about compliance with the Test Act of 1673, which required allegiance to the Church of England to qualify for public office. Defoe firmly opposed the notion that Dissenters could conform only occasionally in order to hold offices; he branded such actions as *"playing Bo-peep* with God Almighty." [26] When the young Defoe decided on a career as a merchant in 1682, he obviously did not abandon his beliefs or forget his training as a Dissenter. The dissenting side of Defoe's nature was to disclose itself more forcefully now in 1702, but with unfortunate consequences; for this time he was going to aim his pen not at his fellow Dissenters but at their antagonists, the High-flying Tories.

In December 1702, the year of King William's death, Defoe

published anonymously a satire on the extreme attitudes adopted by the High Church party against the Dissenters under the newly begun reign of Queen Anne. The Queen's religious sympathies were known to reside with the Church of England, and her feelings toward the dissenting community were less than favorable. The new reign inspired High Church zealots to unleash violent sermons against the Dissenters as the Occasional Conformity issue revived in 1702. It was a time of religious hysteria, and on the first day of December, the very day that the Bill to Prevent Occasional Conformity was going to the House of Lords for consideration, Defoe's timely *Shortest Way with the Dissenters* appeared on sale in London.[27]

In this work, Defoe again adopted the approach so enormously successful in *The True-Born Englishman* of the preceding year, a *reductio ad absurdum* of the extremist position of the High Flyers, notably well-known incendiaries like Dr. Sacheverell, but with the added satiric touch that, instead of speaking *in propria persona*, as he had done in his previous effort, Defoe now assumed the persona of an anonymous High Flyer, thereby pointing up the absurdity of that immoderate position all the more dramatically.

The conception of the pamphlet was brilliant, and the sale was spirited; but the reception of the pamphlet had been miscalculated, and the results were to prove disastrous for Defoe. The High Church party had a mixed reaction to the piece: the fanatics applauded it, the moderates deplored it; and meanwhile the Dissenters were terrified by it. When the authorship of the *Shortest Way* eventually was ascertained, everyone felt victimized by Defoe. The High Flyers felt duped; the Dissenters betrayed. Defoe had committed a costly error in judgment. The Tory party now had a perfect opportunity to silence a powerful pamphleteer for the Whig cause and the dissenting interests. As Defoe later bemoaned this surprising turn of events, he fell *"the shortest way."*

Within a month, on January 3, 1703, a warrant was issued for his arrest. A week later the Earl of Nottingham, then a Secretary of State to Queen Anne and an advocate of the High Church cause, placed the following advertisement in the official paper of the Tory party, the *London Gazette* for January 11 to 14:

St. James, Jan. 10. Whereas Daniel de Foe *alias* de Fooe, is charged with writing a scandalous and seditious pamphlet, entitled The Shortest Way with the Dissenters. Whoever shall discover the said Daniel de Foe alias de Fooe to one of her Majesty's Principal Secretaries of State, or any of her Majesty's Justices of the Peace, so as he may be apprehended, shall have a reward of £50 which her Majesty has ordered immediately to be paid upon such discovery.

He is a middle-sized spare man, about 40 years old, of a brown complexion, and dark brown colored hair, but wears a wig, a hooked nose, a sharp chin, grey eyes, and a large mole near his mouth, was born in London, and for many years was a hose factor in Freeman's-yard, in Cornhill, and now is owner of the brick and pantile works near Tilbury-Fort in Essex.

A fugitive from his creditors ten years earlier, Defoe now found himself again a fugitive, but this time he was being hunted down as an enemy of the government with a price on his head.

When Defoe took flight from the fury of the Tory party in January, he lost all chance of clearing himself of his remaining debts through the success of his pantile factory at Tilbury. He was later to write about the blow he suffered at this time: "They have since seen him strip'd naked by the government, and the foundations torn up, on which he had built the prospect of paying debts, and raising his family." What he would never forget about his losses in 1703 was how close he actually came to absolving himself of all indebtedness — let alone his personal hopes of "raising his family" and becoming an affluent gentleman. "With a numerous family, and no helps but my own industry," Defoe wrote with pride of his achievements following his bankruptcy in 1692, "I have forc'd my way with undiscourag'd diligence thro' a sea of debt and misfortune, and reduced them, exclusive of composition, from £17,000 to less than 5." In 1704 he wrote to Harley, outlining what his ruined pantile works meant to his financial fortunes: "I was rising fairly to clear it all when the public disaster you kno' of began, but, Sir, that entirely blasted all my affairs, and I can easily convince you was above £2500 loss to me all at once . . . But I was ruin'd *the shortest way* . . ." [28]

In 1703 Defoe not only saw his chance for clearing himself of debts blasted — that was bad enough — but he also realized that his was "one of the worst sorts of ruin" because it affected as well his "large and promising family, a virtuous and excellent mother to seven beautiful and hopeful children, a woman whose fortunes I have ruin'd with whom I have had £3700 . . ." As his family felt the weight of his fall, so did the hundred families of his employees at the Tilbury works, because, as Defoe later commented with bitterness, those "who so eagerly persecuted him . . . were particularly serviceable to the nation, in turning that hundred of poor people, and their families, a begging for work, and forcing them to turn other poor families out of work, to make room for them, besides £3000 damage to the author of this, which he has paid for this little experience." Defoe understandably had taken the pride of a successful businessman and patriotic Englishman in his flourishing pantile and brick products, which formerly had always been "bought in Holland" and which he had manufactured "with his utmost zeal for the good of England." [29]

The crowning irony of Defoe's misery in 1703 occurred in late November, a mere matter of days after his release from Newgate prison. At that time the most violent storm in anyone's memory struck England, sweeping across the country from the river Trent to the English Channel. Estimates of damage ran high: one hundred churches lost their roofs, hundreds of homes were destroyed, and thousands of buildings were damaged. It became known as The Great Storm, and it created an immediate and untold demand for bricks and tiles. If the elements had conspired to accentuate Defoe's already acute sense of loss, they could not have chosen a more telling way; for he no longer had his Tilbury factory, having lost it just recently while languishing in prison, and he could not capitalize on this natural bonanza for brickmakers. Once again Defoe experienced the keen frustration of having come close to success only to see it snatched away.

In 1706, a Tory pamphleteer who fancied himself "a well-wisher to trade and credit" offered a derisive synopsis of Defoe's checkered business career since his crucial decision not to enter the ministry: "Of his fame and reputation in Freeman's Yard in Cornhill . . . and how he has run through the three degrees of comparison, *Pos.* as a Hosier; *Compar.* as a Civet-Cat Merchant; and *Super.* as a Pantile Merchant." [30] Derision notwithstanding, the synopsis could have given Defoe pause for reflection. He now had ample reason to consider it his "disaster" to have been set apart from the ministry, and his "misfortune" to have become a merchant. He had risen twice, once out of the ashes of his disgrace and ruin like a "phoenix," only to have fallen twice.

Chapter 4. Prison and Pillory:
Birth of Mr. Review

I have some time ago summ'd up the scenes of my life in this distich:

> No man has tasted differing fortunes more,
> And thirteen times I have been rich and poor.

In the school of affliction I have learnt more philosophy than at the academy, and more divinity than from the pulpit: in prison I have learnt to know that liberty does not consist in open doors, and the free egress and regress of locomotion. I have seen the rough side of the world as well as the smooth, and have in less than half a year tasted the difference between the closet of a King and the dungeon of Newgate. — Defoe, *Review*, VIII, preface

The prospect of debtor's prison to Defoe in 1692 had been terrifying in the extreme. Now in January 1703 he again experienced the terrors of a fugitive. While in hiding he resorted to the same strategy that had served him so well when fleeing his creditors some ten years earlier; he sought to enter into some sort of composition with the government. He wrote to his antagonist the Earl of Nottingham on January 9, 1703:

> I had long since surrendered to her Majty's clemency, had not the menaces of your Lordship's officers possessed me with such ideas of her Majty's and your Lordship's resentments as were too terrible . . .
> My Lord, a body unfit to bear the hardships of a prison, and a mind impatient of confinement, have been the only reasons of withdrawing myself . . .
> . . . that pleading guilty I may receive a sentence from her particular justice a little more tolerable to me as a gentleman, than prisons, pillories, and such like, which are worse to me than death.[1]

Defoe's letter is revealing in several important respects. Judging from his behavior in 1692, we know that he is not falsifying or exaggerating his fear of arrest here; he most certainly was "possessed . . . with such ideas of [the government's] resentments as were too terrible" for him to face. We know also that his kind of mind could be gripped with utter despair when confined. Finally, we see him present himself to a lord and one of the Queen's Secretaries of State not as a fugitive political pamphleteer but as he had come to conceive of himself during his two previous periods of affluence and social prominence: as a "gentleman."

To a gentleman, prisons and pillories are not tolerable or fitting punishments. Defoe goes on to propose to the Earl of Nottingham that he is prepared to surrender himself to the Queen as "a volunteer at the head of her armies in the Netherlands" to serve for a year or more at his own charges. He is even willing to take upon himself the charge of raising for her "a troop of horse," at whose head he pledges to serve her as long as he should live. He is bargaining, to be sure, but it is the bargain that a gentleman would strike. In fact, when Defoe again was to raise the subject of overseas service in 1706, he argued, "a broken tradesman makes a whole gentleman . . . when he's got into a commission." Although hard pressed and frightened, Defoe petitions manfully, not meanly. It is a petition also noteworthy for its eloquence in a time of obvious adversity, a feature which speaks well for the "liberal education" he received while a student at Charles Morton's academy, where he learned in the "class for eloquence" to write, among other matters, epistles "directed to the Secretary of State." [2]

This particular Secretary of State, however, scorned to answer Defoe's appeal for a kind of composition and a "justice a little more tolerable" to a gentleman. Nottingham's answer was the advertisement in the *London Gazette* offering a £50 reward for his capture. Defoe all this time, it must be remembered, had the support of his wife and seven children to worry about in addition to his own safety, hence his repeated appeals to any and all who could be of help to him.

Defoe had reason to think of himself as a gentleman; he was, after all, an acquaintance of gentlemen. In April 1703 he addressed himself to William Paterson, a London merchant like himself, and one of the men instrumental in the foundation of the Bank of England in 1694. Paterson and Defoe both had shared the confidence and patronage of King William. But of more immediate importance, Paterson was on familiar terms with Robert

Harley, then the Speaker of the House of Commons, serving Harley as news correspondent and sometime adviser. Defoe's letter to Paterson further reveals his agitated state of mind:

As to my present circumstances I can only say as of him that repents without hope, I find them desperate and that neither sense of the offence nor future amendment will atone. So I am fled, and tho' I do already find 'tis no very difficult thing for me to get my bread, yet as I expresst to my Lord N.: methinks fleeing from her Majty's justice is a sort of raising war against her, and I would fain lay down these arms . . . but jails, pillories, and such like with which I have been so much threatn'd have convinc'd me I want passive courage, and I shall never for the future think myself injur'd if I am called a coward.[3]

The terrors of prison and the pillory preyed heavily upon Defoe's mind.

Although Paterson complied with Defoe's request and dutifully forwarded his letter to Harley, ironically it did not reach Harley until May 28, precisely four days after Defoe's capture at the house of a French weaver in Spitalfields. According to Defoe's own version of these events, Nottingham's hostile gesture of posting the advertisement for his arrest in the *London Gazette* "oblig'd him to resolve to leave the kingdom . . . In order to conceal himself more effectually, he left his lodgings where he had been hid for some time, and remov'd to Barnet on the edge of Hertfordshire, intending, as soon as he had settled some family affairs, to go away north into Scotland." Before he could flee to Scotland for safety, however, he "was oblig'd to come once more to London, to sign some writings for the securing [of] some estate." Despite the warning in a dream of his impending capture, he proceeded to London and there on the morning of May 24 "was taken by the messengers, just in the very manner as he had been told in his dream."[4]

On June 5, however, after a searching examination by Nottingham and the Privy Council, Defoe was released on the notoriously high bail of £1,500. But what is even more astounding is that he was able to raise the money for his bail. Some few of his wealthy friends undoubtedly helped, but, according to a recently discovered Old Bailey document in the City of London Records, "Daniel De Foe of the City of London, Gentleman" paid £500 himself. Defoe was, in his own words, "under bail and at liberty" until July 7, when he was scheduled to appear in person in the Justice Hall of the Old Bailey. "The danger was as terrifying as possible, insomuch that when I went to see an honest and good man for advice, all he would say was in the words of the disciple to our Blessed Lord, *Master, save thy self."* Even his friends counseled flight. If ever he had good reason to flee to Scotland, here was reason enough; but he decided not to compromise his reputation a second time, nor his innocence; as he said, "these outvoted fear" and he stayed.[5]

When he presented himself on July 7, he had as his legal adviser William Colepeper, one of the five Kentish Petitioners who recalled more propitious times to the now beleaguered Defoe. Despite the fact that the government did not have much of a case against him, he accepted the well-intentioned but wrongheaded advice of Colepeper to plead guilty, with the expectation that the government would treat him generously. His actions during the trial were remarkably naive. He believed without doubt the "promises of being us'd tenderly" by the government, as he later wrote William Penn, if only he would plead guilty to their charges. Instead of mercy from the Crown for his cooperation, Defoe was repaid with the full measure of punishment by the prosecution. On July 9 he was sentenced with unprecedented harshness by the Court:

a fine of 200 marks of the lawful money of England, and to stand upon a pillory, one day in Cornhill by the Exchange, London, and another day in Cheapside near the Conduit there, the third day in Fleet Street by Temple Bar, for one hour between the hours of eleven before noon and two after noon, whichever one he likes, with a paper on his head on which his offences are written, and that said Danil De ffooe alias de ffoe should find good sureties to be of good behaviour for the space of seven years then next following.[6]

Defoe apparently had assumed that the trial would be an honorable transaction among gentlemen, his pleading guilty to spare the government possible embarrassment in trying his case in return for the government's granting him his liberty and a pardon for cooperating. But he miscalculated the Court's response, just as he had misjudged the reception of the *Shortest Way,* which had landed him in this predicament. Well could he feel himself victimized by unscrupulous men and misled by misinformed friends. Even the efforts of such influential men as William Penn to intercede on his behalf were of no avail. He was at the mercy of the Tory party and held in close confinement.

Defoe suffered much anxiety throughout July. At least four different dates were officially set for his first standing in the pillory: July 19, 23, 26, 29. Defoe sought some comfort from his ordeal by inviting three leading dissenting clergymen, with whom he had disagreed over the question of Occasional Conformity and who had taken offense at his *Shortest Way with the Dissenters*, to visit his cell and pray with him. They refused. Defoe now stood alone: his family without funds; his future without hope of relief; his only prospect the dread terrors of the pillory.

The Tory *London Gazette* for July 29 to August 2, 1703, ran the following official announcement:

London, July 31. On the 29th instant, Daniel Foe alias de Foe, stood in the pillory before the Royal Exchange in Cornhill, as he did yesterday near the Conduit in Cheapside, and this day at Temple-Bar; in pursuance of the sentence given against him at the last sessions at the Old Bailey, for writing and publishing a seditious libel, entitled *The Shortest Way with the Dissenters;* by which sentence he is also fined 200 marks, to find sureties for his good behaviour for 7 years, and to remain in prison till all be performed.

What Defoe stood in fear of for so long he was certain to remember long after it finally took place, and there was much for him to remember about his experiences in the pillory. His first exposure in the pillory on Thursday, July 29, 1703, was not without its personal irony, for it took place before the Royal Exchange in Cornhill, a scant twenty-five yards from Freeman's Yard, where Daniel Foe and his bride first lived and where the young London "marchant" scored so many early successes in business before bankruptcy overtook him in 1692. It was cruelly fitting that he should have as the scene of his first public disgrace a place so close to his first home and in the very heart of the London financial section. Nor was the second exposure any less appropriate in its choice of location, for as he stood in the pillory at the Conduit in Cheapside he could recall how almost fourteen years before he had ridden majestically with the volunteer troop of horse escorting King William and Queen Mary from the gala banquet in the Guildhall on the famous Lord Mayor's Day in 1689. He had only to look across to the Mercer's Chapel to recall that even more recently, but two short years ago, he had been fêted as guest of honor at the victory celebration for the Kentish Petitioners, one of whom, coincidentally enough, was William Colepeper, on whose advice he found himself so severely treated by the government. The last day in the pillory for Defoe was also the last day of July. He was now, as a result of the ignominy of his punishment and the terms of his sentence, no longer a menace to the Tory party.

But Defoe was not to be denied at least his personal triumph even in the time of his most trying public defeat. While he stood in the pillory, his hastily drafted but spirited defense of himself, *A Hymn to the Pillory*, was being "hawked about the pillory" with his other books and pamphlets. What his *True-Born Englishman* had done for King William two and a half years earlier, his *Hymn to the Pillory* did for him now. A hostile and unruly mob, whose favorite sport at such public pillories was to pelt the helpless victims with rotten fruit and mud and stones, was miraculously charmed by Defoe; they saw in the slight, spare, middle-aged man not an object for their derision but a victim of government injustice who could bear his trial with fortitude and courage:

> Hail! *Hi'roglyphic* State *Machine,*
> Contriv'd to punish fancy in:
> Men that are men, in thee can feel no pain,
> And all thy *insignificants* disdain.
> Contempt, that false new word for shame,
> Is without crime, an empty name.

The mob responded to the engaging forthrightness of the man in the pillory. They bought his *Hymn to the Pillory* and read it while the author stood above them. Here was the man ridiculed by the Tory pamphleteers as "Daniel" in "the Lion's Den" of Newgate prison. What the mob could appreciate about Defoe and his rough poetic rejoinder to the Tory ministry was the unmistakable tone of moral outrage at the way he had been mistreated for his honesty, and being so fortified by the rightness of his cause, he could abandon discretion for outspoken declarations:

> Tell them 'twas because he was too bold,
> And told those truths, which shou'd not ha' been told.
>   . . . .

> Tell them he stands exalted there
> For speaking what we wou'd not hear;
> And yet he might ha' been secure,
> Had he said less, or wou'd he ha' said more.
>
> . . . .
>
> And thus he's an example made,
> To make men of their honesty afraid,
> That for the time to come they may,
> More willingly their friends betray;
> Tell 'em the m[en] that plac'd him here,
> Are sc[anda]ls to the times,
> > Are at a loss to find his guilt,
> > And can't commit his crimes.

What was intended as a public ignominy for Defoe — or worse — turned into a popular triumph for him. Instead of doing him violence, of bespattering him with filth, of shouting execrations at him, the mob lionized him in the pillory, garlanding him with flowers and drinking his health. Defoe was indeed "exalted" on high, and if the Tory party pilloried him, the people transformed the punishment into a popular acclamation. Even an unfriendly observer was prompted to write how the spectators "halloo'd him down from his wooden punishment, as if he had been Cicero that had made an excellent oration in it, rather than a Cataline that was exposed and declaimed against there." [7]

For Defoe, the pillory was to be a central event in his entire career; it may well have been *the* central event in his career, marking the nadir of his personal fortune — and his most difficult time of "trial." In his *True Collection* of 1705, Defoe inserted some explanatory remarks about the *Hymn to the Pillory* because, he felt, it "seems most to require it." He is perfectly specific about the intention of this poem: it was "the author's declaration, even when in the cruel hands of a merciless as well as unjust Ministry, that the treatment he had from them, was unjust, exorbitant, and consequently illegal." Throughout his life Defoe returned to this time he had stood in the pillory. In 1708, for example, he wrote: "the author of the *Review* was set in the pillory, *which being done for speaking the truth, is* HIS HONOUR, *and reflects upon those that plac'd him there*, not upon him, *since 'tis well known, he could have deliver'd himself from that ignominy, if he would have sold his friends for his own liberty, and betray'd the memory of his master* King William, *a thing too much in fashion with this honest age.* But that by the way." Although Defoe enjoyed a momentary triumph on the pillory at the hands of a jubilant mob, his enemies were never to let him forget that he was a pilloried man of letters, a disgrace he had to bear like a stigma. Even so, he managed to see in his pillory the truest test of his innocence, which the crowd corroborated enthusiastically, and "the severest trial" of his character, which he managed to pass honorably by not turning "traitor" and by daring to "stand in the pillory rather than betray his friends." [8]

Defoe's triumph in the pillory, however, was very short-lived. He soon found himself again incarcerated within the bleak walls of Newgate prison. The carnival mood of the crowd around the pillory was replaced by the unmitigated gloom of Newgate and its inhabitants. Newgate was a sink of misery and brutality, foul and noisome, affording little cheer for a man of Defoe's active and sensitive nature. Newgate, in a word, was a living "hell" for Defoe — as it was to be for his most memorable heroine, Moll Flanders. Here were no gentlemen or fashionable throngs, but people from the lowest end of the social scale: thieves and whores and rogues of all kinds. Defoe still managed to make the best of his situation. Whereas the period he spent in hiding from his creditors in 1692–93 gave rise to *An Essay upon Projects,* this period of the pillory and Newgate prison was to give birth to Mr. Review and, eventually, the father of the English novel.

The idea of the *Review* occurred to Defoe while he was imprisoned in Newgate, for he wrote in the preface to the first volume that the "design" for the *Review* "had its birth *in tenebris.*" It marked a notable departure from Defoe's previous attempts to redeem his fortunes. The avenue of trade was now closed to him; he had no money and no credit. As he wrote with sad personal knowledge in 1706, "I cannot confess but acknowledge that to recover credit . . . is almost as difficult as to restore virginity, or to make a w—re an honest woman." He now had to depend almost slavishly on his deliverer from Newgate, Robert Harley, to whom he wrote immediately after his release from prison: "I take the freedom to repeat the assurance of a man ready to dedicate my life and all possible powers to the interest of so generous and bountiful benefactors, being equally overcome with the nature as well as the value of the favour I have receiv'd." [9]

But even before Defoe could begin to serve Harley, he had first to come to terms with his creditors. His pantile works were ruined. He had no source of funds. "Tis a melancholy prospect, Sir," Defoe wrote Harley when describing his financial dilemma, "and my fears suggest that not less than a thousand pounds will entirely free me." By the late fall of 1703 a recently imprisoned and pilloried Defoe was again at liberty, but he was no longer his own man; he was now both dependent on and indebted to the Speaker of the House of Commons; he was, in Professor Sutherland's apt phrase, "Robert Harley's man," and his *Review* was to be the mouthpiece for the moderate Tory position as represented by Robert Harley.[10]

Even though Defoe now had to live primarily by his pen, writing scores of books and pamphlets on national issues of moment, especially the union with Scotland, he never gave over his interest in trade. In fact, his trips to Scotland were to enable him to play the merchant and the projector again, and with some success. Just before the union between England and Scotland was effected officially, Defoe wrote proudly of his hand in furthering trade ties between the countries:

Nor am I an idle spectator here; I have told Scotland of improvements in trade, wealth and shipping, that shall accrue to them on the happy conclusion of this affair . . .

I have told them of the improvement of their salt, and I am now contracting for English merchants for Scots salt to the value of above £10,000 *per annum*.

I have told them of linen manufactures, and I have now above 100 poor families at work, by my procuring and direction, for the making such sorts of linen, and in such manner as never was made here before.

Much of Defoe's mercantile activity in Scotland was, to be sure, a means of concealing his real mission in that country on behalf of the Tory Ministry seeking to achieve a union. The situation, however, was perfectly suited to his genius, enabling him to engage in two-sided financial schemes with equanimity, a role he obviously relished. He could write to Harley in perfect honesty that he was going into assorted partnerships for "a glass house" or "a salt work," as "a fish merchant" or with a "woolen" and a "linen manufacturer," all with a double motive: to Harley it was to promote the union, to the Scots merchants it was to promote business and make money; but to Defoe it was both. As he himself summed up so neatly his dealings in Scotland to Harley, "I am all to every one that I may gain some." [11]

If Defoe made money through his mercantile enterprises in Scotland, he lost money through his speculations on the Exchange in London. He seems never to have lost his inclination to gamble for high stakes, despite the high risks in stock speculation. Of his investments in the stock of the African Company, he wrote in the *Review*: "I have lost money by their declining stock more than enough, indeed more than I can bear the weight of. I am not like to recover that loss." In another allusion to his unsuccessful trading in stocks, Defoe spoke of two shares of stock for which he had paid £800 but which fell so while in his possession as never to yield even £100.[12]

In spite of his projecting and trading, his investing and speculating, he was never clear of his long-standing debts and his clamorous creditors from the time of his release from Newgate until about 1715. He very likely was not indulging in hyperbole when he summed up his varying fortunes as "thirteen times I have been rich and poor." Throughout this period of his life as Mr. Review he lived with the ever-present threat of litigation and arrest. It was a precarious existence at best for Defoe and his family. He was actually arrested at least half a dozen times during this period.[13]

We get a striking picture of Defoe's life from a number of the *Review* in 1705, in which he offered his readers a detailed accounting of his difficulties as the author of a controversial political journal. Some hotheads even threatened to have his throat cut, to which he remarked coolly: "Indeed, gentlemen, the mean despicable author of this paper is not worth your attempting his correction at the price; gaols, fetters, and gibbets, are odd melancholy things; for a gentleman to *dangle out of the world in a strang,* has something so ugly, so awkward, and so disagreeable in it, that you cannot think of it without some regret." While in Newgate Defoe had had time to reflect on such matters. But these threats of violence were the least of his worries; he was also plagued by sham creditors to such an extent as confounded him completely, some of the debts dating back about seventeen years: "But now he has had a storm of a more scandalous assassination, studying to ruin and embroil him, crowds of sham-actions, arrests, sleeping debates in trade of 17 years standing reviv'd; debts put in suit after contracts and agreements under hand seal; and which is worse, writs taken out for debts, without the knowledge of the creditor, and some after the creditor has been paid; diligent solicitations of persons not enclin'd to sue, pressing them to give him trouble." We can well appreciate why he could feel himself unjustly persecuted for his writings in the *Review*. He summed up his unfortunate predicament as a hired political writer by saying he suffered "the barbarous treatment shown a man just strip't naked by the Government," which is "like suing a man just ransom'd from Algier." [14]

By the summer of 1706 Defoe's efforts to free himself from the inordinate demands of his creditors reached a climax. In May he asked Harley for two or three hundred pounds to rid himself of "the immediate fury of 5 or 6 unreasonable creditors." In August he was in desperate circumstances again, as is evident from the chaotic, almost hysterical way in which he first indulges in self-pity, then lashes out at the inhumanity of his antagonists, and finally ends by imploring compassion:

For this case gives a sad instance of the madness of this age, wherein nothing but the entire destruction of the debtor and his family can expiate the crime of his own disaster . . .

They have since seen him strip't naked by the government, and the foundations torn up, on which he had built the prospect of paying debts and raising his family; and yet now, when by common reasoning they ought to believe the man has not bread for his children, have redoubled their attacks with declarations, executions, escape-warrants, and God knows how many engines of destruction . . .

> Resolv'd to ruin me the shortest way,
> They strip me naked first; then bid me pay.

. . . Gentlemen — If you are Christians . . . if you have . . . any compassion for a man in danger, and a family with seven children, that must perish in his disaster, help him.

The desperate Defoe depicted in this number of the *Review* soon passed the crisis with his creditors, and on August 21 he could write Harley, "God almighty has heard the cries of a distressed family and has given me at last a complete victory over the most furious, subtle and malicious opposition that has been seen in all the instances of the Bankrupts Act." [15]

In 1706 Defoe surrendered himself to the Commission of Bankruptcy, was subjected to "four severe trials upon oath," and made a "full free and honest surrender" of all his estate and effects; but since some of his creditors still resisted his terms, he postponed his request for a certificate from the Commission until his return from Scotland. When he returned from his successful mission a year and a half later, after the union with Scotland was achieved, he found that Parliament had since enacted an amendment to the bankruptcy act which stipulated new conditions he could not meet, and he reluctantly ceased his efforts to obtain his certificate from the commissioners. In the summer of 1708 Defoe described his life as "a banish'd condition, a distracted, unsettled circumstance, and a general war with the world, with the constant attacks of private and public enemies and misfortunes, for a series of 16 years in a state of affliction, and yet without prospect of deliverance." As it turned out, he was never to clear himself entirely from the claims of his creditors; they were to haunt him literally to his dying day. All he could hope for now were intermittent periods of peace.[16]

Despite his financial troubles, his dependence on Harley, his insecure existence, Defoe could not resist the old itch to set himself up again as a gentleman. He had been twice frustrated in his design to become a gentleman; undaunted, he tried once again. His name was now Daniel De Foe, not Foe, a change in name, in the judgment of William P. Trent, to a "more aristocratic patronymic." The motive for the change Professor Trent attributes to the fact that "after he had been disgraced by standing in the pillory in 1703, he may have wished to emphasize so comforting a belief." Actually Defoe's claims to the status of gentleman antedate his public disgrace in the pillory. The first authorized collected edition of his works, *A True Collection of the Writings of the Author of the True Born English-man*, was published on July 22, 1703, precisely one week before Defoe's first exposure in the pillory. This edition featured a frontispiece portrait of Defoe by the portrait painter Jeremiah Taverner and engraved by Michael Van der Gucht with a coat of arms. According to Professor Moore, Defoe made his intention clear when he assumed the title of "Gentleman" and chose as his personal motto the Juvenalian tag of "Laudatur et Alget," which first appeared beneath a more formal portrait engraved by Van der Gucht and a more elaborate variation of the coat of arms as the frontispiece to the *Jure Divino* in 1706. By 1706 Defoe's coat of arms consisted of a stylish design: *Per chevron engrailed, gules and or, three griffins passant counterchanged.* How Defoe came by his armorial bearings is something of a mystery, and the fact that the arms vary markedly in the 1703 and 1706 portraits suggests that his right to bear arms was not secure; but to appear so publicly with them in two carefully prepared editions at a time when he was an easy target for his many detractors and journalistic adversaries argues for his having some right to them, even if he, like the "certain tradesman of London" referred to in *The Complete English Tradesman*, being unable to find an ancient lineage of gentlemen from which he was descended, decided to "begin a new race." With his more genteel name of De Foe and his adopted coat of arms, Mr. Review consciously sought to elevate himself in status; he was not to be dismissed as just another venal Grub Street journalist but respected as a gentleman.[17]

What Harley thought of Defoe's social pretensions we are never told, although judging from their relationship, as disclosed through their correspondence, Defoe always presented himself to his employer as a man of some social standing, a friendly and familiar confidant who knew how far he could presume with his patron. The tone he used toward Harley was not far different from his tone toward the Earl of Nottingham when attempting to come to terms with the Tory ministry in January 1703, namely, that of a gentleman addressing himself to gentlemen. Even when neglected by Harley and virtually destitute from lack of funds, Defoe still could write from Scotland in 1707: "I have always, Sir, been bred like a man, I would say a gentleman if circumstances did not of late alter that denomination, and tho' my misfortunes and enemies have reduced me, yet I always struggled with the world so as never to want, till now." It is an appeal for funds from a man who takes himself and his social position seriously, if not also somewhat self-consciously; it is, in fact, a genteel solicitation considering that Defoe at this time was living on the generosity of his Scots acquaintances, being himself "without subsistence, almost grown shabby in clothes." [18] Defoe tried to make the most of his new way of life under Harley. After all, he was not meanly employed, serving as an adviser and secret agent to a prominent Tory official and as editor of an influential periodical.

Always one to seek the friendship and support of wealthy and influential men, Defoe again applied himself to these ends. In 1705 he was in correspondence with Charles Montagu, Baron Halifax (later to become Earl). By the summer of 1705 Defoe could write Halifax in profuse thanks for "the exceeding bounty" and "munificence" he had received. Although Defoe professed ignorance at the cause for this generous treatment from Halifax and the Whig Junto, now in eclipse in government affairs, it is clear that his pamphleteering efforts against the radical Tory elements were of direct service to the Whig party, especially his *High Church Legion* of 1705, six copies of which he sent to Halifax. But there was another reason for Defoe's attempts to win the favor of a man like Halifax. A poet as well as a statesman, Halifax took an interest in literature and had established a reputation for his liberal patronage of men of letters, a patronage that had earned him the august title of the English Maecenas. Defoe seized the opportunity of his contact with Halifax in 1705 to pay him a flattering tribute in the *Jure Divino* — which he is supposed to have revised in September 1705: "So sweet his voice, and all his thoughts so strong,/So smooth his numbers, and so soft his song,/Eternal music dwells upon his tongue." This flattering reference was calculated to appeal to Halifax's sense of vanity, of which, according to the Duchess of Marlborough, he "had a vast deal," delighting in "dedications and everything of that sort." So notorious was his reputation as a vain patron among literary circles that Pope years later satirized him as "Bufo" in his *Epistle to Dr. Arbuthnot.* Defoe was paid handsomely by Halifax for his political pamphleteering, but Halifax seemingly took no interest in his poetic effusions.[19]

Defoe also was careful in dedicating other works to prominent persons. While in Scotland he became acquainted with the powerful Duke of Queensberry, who now headed the Scottish Ministry as High Commissioner and who also was a staunch supporter of the union cause Defoe had gone to Scotland to promote. In December 1706 he published a long panegyrical poem on Scotland entitled *Caledonia.* "Daniel De Foe Esq." not only dedicated the poem to John Douglas, Duke of Queensberry, he also managed to have it licensed by a special act of the Privy Council and subscribed by "His Grace" and eighty-two of the most eminent nobility and gentry of Scotland. In 1709 he followed this up with his *History of the Union,* a work dedicated again to the Duke of Queensberry, and also to Queen Anne, thus bringing himself to the attention of the two people in each country who could do most for him. These flattering dedications to the Duke apparently were not without their effect. In the *Tour* Defoe could later write, "as I had the honour to be known to his Grace, so I had the opportunity to see and read by his permission several letters written to him by the late King William, with his own hand, and several more by Queen Anne, written also by her Majesty's own hand." Defoe was also a guest at the castle of Drumlanrig, "the fine palace of the Duke of Queensberry," and, judging from the familiarity of his reception, a special guest. With his adopted coat of arms, which he supposedly had engraved on a ring he carried with him, Defoe was passing for a gentleman in Scotland at least.[20]

In London, however, Defoe's claims to gentility were ridiculed and attacked by his many enemies among the tribe of journalists. His chief journalistic rival was John Tutchin, whom he had bested in 1701 by silencing his attack on King William in *The Foreigners* with his rejoinder of *The True-Born Englishman.* Defoe now again found himself in competition with Tutchin, whose *Observator,* appearing twice weekly since 1702, championed the radical Whig point of view and therefore was in direct opposition to the views expressed in his *Review,* the chief organ for the moderate Tory position. Tutchin repeatedly lashed out at Defoe personally, the way he had attacked King William personally earlier; and despite Defoe's endeavors to remain above such mean *ad hominem* attacks, defenses, and counterattacks with journalistic rivals, he was never able to treat his antagonists as he wished, "with the contempt they deserve, I mean *by silence.*" [21]

In May 1705 he devoted a number of the *Review* to answering
Tutchin by censuring him for his bad manners and establishing
his own reputation as a well-educated man. What he resented in
Tutchin's "most scurrilous manner" of treating him was the slur
on his lack of learning, a topic that for him was always delicate,
and one that was certain to elicit a strong response. "He says, I
have read but little: I believe, I may pretend to have read more
than himself, and yet make no great pretence to books; *but this
I have read*, that raillery, and ill language, is no help to an argument, much less forgery and mistake." Although Tutchin was of
nonconformist background like Defoe, his education, which consisted of attending a school at Stepney, was decidedly inferior to
Defoe's at Newington Green. Defoe had good reason to be an-
noyed with Tutchin's aspersions on his learning.

Tutchin, however, was not alone in attacking Defoe. Dr.
Joseph Browne also made mocking remarks about him, once even
going so far as to taunt him by publishing in May 1705 a paper
called "The Review Reviewed." By the end of May Defoe could
not contain his spleen at these sneering attacks from journalists
like Tutchin and Browne, and he devoted another entire number
of the *Review* to answering "the various attacks and assaults of
the ill-wishers to this undertaking"; but as the substance of the
issue shows, it was not the "undertaking" Defoe was eager to defend but rather the author of it, and even more specifically the
character and learning of Mr. Review:

He's no scholar, says one; that may be true. He was apprenticed to
an hosier, says another; that's false; and adds to the number of the
intolerable liberties Dr. B[rowne] and Mr. *Observator* give themselves; he having never been a hosier, or an apprentice.

But he has been a trader, that's true; and therefore must know no
Latin. Excellent logic this . . .

Those gentlemen that reproach my learning to applaud their own
shall have it proved, I have more learning than either of them, because I have more manners.

As is abundantly evident from Defoe's remarks, he deeply resented these personal attacks, however unfounded or ill-mannered
they were. He singled out for reply such slights to his social
standing as his low connections in trade — a matter of known
pride to Defoe, who had been an eminently successful young

London merchant — or his limited learning, notably his deficiency in the classical education associated with polite society. Dr. Browne, unlike Defoe, was educated at Cambridge.

Defoe's extensive defense of himself in this issue of the *Review* is instructive in gaining an understanding of how he saw himself and the points on which he was inordinately sensitive:

> I have no concern to tell Dr. B[rowne] I can read English, or to tell Mr. Tutchin I understand Latin, *Non ita Latinus sum ut Latine loqui*. I easily acknowledge myself blockhead enough to have lost the fluency of expression in the Latin, and so far trade has been a prejudice of me; and yet I think I owe this justice to my ancient father, yet living, and in whose behalf I freely testify that if I am a blockhead, it was nobody's fault but my own; he having spar'd nothing in my education that might qualify me to match the accurate Dr. B[rowne] or the learned *Observator*.
>
> . . . This is the language of the enemies to this paper; he was bred a mechanic, had no education; and the *Observator*, an author of his own party, upbraids him as an illiterate fellow.

Defoe's father had afforded him the best possible education available to a Dissenter at that time. If people attacked his education, then they attacked him for not having the classical education of a gentleman. They branded him a "mechanic." Defoe could answer this kind of charge only by demonstrating that his learning was as good as that of his detractors:

> As to my little learning, and his [Tutchin's] great capacity, I fairly challeng'd him, in a letter I sent him yesterday, and which I now renew,
>
> "That I'll take any Latin author he shall name, and with it one French, and one Italian, and I'll translate them into English, and after that re-translate them *cross-wise*, the English into French, the French into Italian, and the Italian into Latin; and this I challenge him to perform wih him, who does it soonest and best for £20 each book; and by this he shall have an opportunity to show the world, how much De Foe the hosier is inferior in learning to Mr. Tutchin the gentleman."

This passage states in sharpest terms what, precisely, galled Defoe about the attacks on his learning and social standing by the likes of Tutchin and Browne, who believed their learning made them gentlemen while his lack of a classical education gave them the right to dismiss him in derisive terms as a "mechanic" and a "hosier."

Defoe's poorly concealed feelings of social uneasiness about his education at a dissenting academy had been expressed more directly the preceding year, when he wrote for a nonconformist audience with some disappointment: "'Tis evident the great imperfection of our academies is want of conversation; this the public universities enjoy, ours cannot . . . conversation polishes the gentleman in discourse; acquaints 'em with men, and with words; lets them into the polite part of language; gives them style, accent, delicacy, and taste in expression." [22]

It is noteworthy that in challenging Tutchin to test their respective claims to learning he is careful to write himself "De Foe"; he is, despite the tribute to his "ancient father," who "spar'd nothing" in his education, not content to keep his father's name of "Foe." The Defoe who responds to Tutchin's taunts is Daniel De Foe, Gentleman.

What is surprising about Defoe's defense is the curiously coarse manner in which he concludes. He had assured his readers that they would "have it proved" to them that he had "more learning" because he had "more manners." Yet he apparently became so incensed over the issue of his personal status that he failed to make good on this promise:

As to his ill language, his profess'd resolution to expose me, his abusive treatment of me with his tongue, *for he dare not do it with his hands,* I'll finish all my replies of this sort with telling him a story; and if this won't do, I'll tell him another.

Two dogs liv'd near one another, a Black and a Brown. Black, *that was more addicted to bark than to bite,* would always run baying and barking after Brown, whenever he went by; Brown took no notice of him a long time, but being once more than usually teaz'd and provok'd, he gravely turn'd about, smells at Black, and finding him of a currish cowardly breed, and not worth his notice, very soberly and unconcern'd, he holds up one leg, pisses upon him, and so goes on about his business. *And so do I.*

Though certainly a graphic if gamy rejoinder to Tutchin's attacks, Defoe's conclusion can hardly recommend him for his good taste and good manners; and instead of finishing off all replies of this sort, it stands as but one of many such stories and apologies. Well might readers of the *Review* share the feeling of the "very witty gentleman" who expostulated after reading a number of the *Review: "A p[ox] of this impertinent fellow, he's always plaguing us with his apologies."* [23]

Although Defoe presented himself in the pages of the *Review* as more sinned against than sinning, he clearly invited a good many of the attacks of his journalistic rivals by engaging in a continuous sniping war with them, not only men like Tutchin and Browne but also John Dyer, author of the *News-Letter*, organ of the extremist High Flyers, and Charles Leslie, author of the *Rehearsal*, another Tory periodical. Defoe's prickly way of getting back at his rivals is to be seen, for example, in the *Little Review* of June 1705, wherein he repaid Dr. Browne for his publication of *The Moon-Calf* (1705) — a work designed, according to Defoe, "to banter the author of the *Consolidator*" — by dwelling on two supposed errors committed by Browne in a translation of Horace. In defense of his captious criticisms Defoe remarked: "Had the Dr. [Browne] begun with the author as a gentleman, and as a man of letters ought to have done, these remarks had been civilly transmitted to him by way of letter; but he having first broke all the laws of courtesy and good breeding, left us without any obligation." Again, he expected to be accorded the respect owing a gentleman, and when denied it, chid his opponent for his want of "courtesy and good breeding." [24]

In the case of a hothead like Dyer, who contemptuously described him in an issue of the *News-Letter* as "Sammen's tenant," alluding to his arrest in the home of the French weaver in Spitalfields in 1703, Defoe could dismiss him with: it is "below the design of this paper, as well of its author, to enter into the innumerable crimes of . . . Dyer's Letter." Since everyone knew that Dyer slanted his reporting shamelessly, none but partisan readers paid him much mind. But with Leslie, Defoe admitted himself up "against a much superior antagonist, both for learning and language." Leslie, like Swift, was educated at Trinity College, Dublin, and had taken holy orders. Still, Defoe attacked Leslie, calling him, among other names, a "High Church hireling." Leslie, for his part, held no lofty opinion of Defoe, either for his political views or for his literary efforts; he once condemned an anonymous piece of wretched writing entitled *A*

Fable of the Beasts and Their King by pronouncing, "It looks like a piece of De Foe's poetry." Defoe's incessant jousting with his rivals must have taught him the truth of Pope's observation, "The life of a Wit is a warfare upon earth." [25]

Nowhere during this period as Mr. Review did Defoe make himself and his position as a gentleman more obvious than in his few revealing exchanges with Jonathan Swift. But here again Defoe, not Swift, initiated the exchange. In 1705 he made an unflattering allusion to Swift's *Tale of a Tub* of the preceding year in *The Consolidator:*

A late happy author, indeed, among his mechanic operation of the spirit, had found out an enthusiasm . . . but he formed his system wholly upon the mistaken notion of wind, which . . . flew upward in blue strakes of a livid flame called blasphemy, which burst up all the wit and fancy of the author, and left a strange stench behind it that has this unhappy quality in it, that everybody that reads the book smells the author though he be never so far off, nay, though he took shipping to Dublin to secure his friends from the least danger of a conjecture.

Defoe shows himself to have been familiar with Swift's work; in fact, he even modeled his *Consolidator* partly after Swift's successful *Tale of a Tub,* and, like Swift, addressed himself to a satiric treatment of religious excesses, particularly as practiced by the High-flying zealots. Swift never had mentioned Defoe up to this time, and if Defoe's reference to him in *The Consolidator* ever reached his attention, he did not deign to respond to it.[26]

It was not until three years later that Swift actually referred to Defoe, and then the context was the old Occasional Conformity issue, on which Defoe always had been an outspoken and powerful writer. As an Anglican Churchman Swift naturally was opposed to a repeal of the act. In *A Letter . . . Concerning the Sacramental Test* (1706) he wrote of those "weekly libellers" who were of another persuasion on this subject: "One of these authors (the fellow that was *pilloryed,* I have forgot his name) is indeed so grave, sententious, dogmatical a rogue, that there is no enduring him; the *Observator* is much the brisker of the two, and I think farther gone of late in lies and impudence, than his *Presbyterian* brother," that is, Defoe. Certainly it was no secret that Defoe had been pilloried, nor was it any less a secret that he was editor of the *Review*. Surely, Swift knew Defoe's name, or could easily enough have ascertained it, but his casual dismissal of him as just another one of those "weekly libellers" is an effective attitude for a man like Swift to adopt; it signifies that such scribblers are really beneath his and the readers' contempt ("I know it may be reckoned a weakness to say any thing of such trifles as are below a serious man's notice"). He can make a more telling point by referring, metonymically, to the pillory as Defoe's distinguishing characteristic rather than to his name. So far as we know this slur by Swift never came to Defoe's notice, for he never answered it.[27]

During this time also, we must bear in mind, both Swift and Defoe were in the service of Harley and the Tory Ministry, but with an all-important social difference. Whereas Swift served Harley as a pamphleteer, he could also meet with him as a friend. Harley became a frequent visitor to meetings of the Scriblerus Club in the apartments of John Arbuthnot at the Palace, and he was connected with the Brothers and Saturday Clubs, in which both Swift and he were major members. Swift, in short, had access to Harley's front door; he could serve Harley openly. Defoe, on the other hand, had "the bad standing of a pilloried journalist," and so, in the estimate of William P. Trent, "all intercourse between the two men had to be kept private." Defoe's dealings with Harley were therefore relegated to the back door. This relationship vis-à-vis Swift must have been uncommonly trying for Defoe. He was, as Professor Trent notes, "a proud man, who liked to emphasize his standing as a gentleman, in the more technical sense of that word." It is not surprising that he should come to resent Swift's privileged position.[28]

In the latter part of 1710 this resentment came abruptly to the surface. Swift unwittingly touched off Defoe's violent eruption with the November 16 number of the *Examiner*, which treated in a supercilious fashion the leading journalists for the two parties in England and their views: "Now to inform and direct us in our sentiments, upon these weighty points, here are on one side two stupid, illiterate scribblers, both of them fanatics by profession; I mean the *Review* and *Observator.*" Swift goes on in the passage to call attention to "the mock authoritative manner" of Defoe, who with the author of the *Observator* are sarcastically termed "worthies." Mr. Examiner clearly is concerned because Defoe's *Review* is "of a level with great numbers among the lowest part of mankind." Swift acknowledges at least Defoe's success at reaching a large audience from the ranks of the less refined readers. The references, though mean, are made in passing, and are intended only to dismiss the views of the opposition so that Mr. Examiner can make his own points more effectively. It is a standard journalistic device, one that Defoe often used himself: you sweep aside the opposition views as extremist and then present your position as the *via media*. And Swift admits, after dismissing the other journalists for assorted reasons, "It was this reason, that moved me" to write.[29]

When *Examiner* No. 15 went on sale in London, Defoe had recently arrived in Edinburgh on official business for Robert Harley. A copy evidently reached him in Scotland, and despite the demands of his important business for Harley, which, judging from his letters, was of great moment and kept him very busy, he still managed to draft two lengthy responses to Swift's brief and passing remarks about the *Review* and the *Observator*. His replies to Swift were in print in the pages of the *Review* within less than a month after *Examiner* No. 15 appeared.

In the December 14 number of the *Review* Defoe wrote:

I wonder much to hear an author who first calls the *Observator* and the *Review* stupid and illiterate should then quit his talking to men of sense, and talk to these *idiots;* for a stupid fellow is an idiot . . .

Now when a man calls another fool, stupid, idiot, illiterate, etc. and then pretends to enter debate with him — 'tis absurd; I am not upon equal terms with him; when I have call'd him idiot, and fool, and illiterate, then I am upon the square with him; and it not having been my good fortune to be bred at Billingsgate, I can never come up to this man, and so it is to no purpose for me to begin.

Very well, Defoe makes his point to Swift, and here it should properly end. But instead of stopping with a reprimand, which already has begun to magnify the offense of Swift's original "stupid, illiterate" to Defoe's expanded "fool, stupid, idiot, illiterate," he launches into a protracted censure of Swift for his behavior as unbecoming to a gentleman:

Besides, among all the authors of whom the streets abound — *with my humble service to Mr. Examiner,* I recommend it to him to answer this civil question — *If, Sir, you have so much learning, how came you to have so little manners?*

I know nothing can render a gentleman so contemptible in the world as to lose his breeding. To descend to scurrility is certainly the greatest evidence of a man's having no breeding, or having quite forgot he had any; nor does the difference of persons discharge the obligation of good manners.

Defoe indicates that he is all too aware of the "difference" between Swift and himself. Swift had a university education (Trinity College, Dublin), was an ordained Anglican clergyman, and belonged to a more exclusive stratum of society than did Defoe. But what rankles him most is Swift's failure to treat him respectfully as a gentleman in his own right, hence his dwelling on Swift's lack of "breeding" and "good manners." In censuring Swift's ungentlemanly behavior, Defoe resorts to the same strategy he had employed against Tutchin and Browne earlier, even to the story of the two dogs: "There is a known story of the *mastive* and the little *spaniel,* which I could also refer him [Swift] to, as most proper for such an author; but I leave it and him . . . And so much for *Examiners.*" [30]

Although Defoe contented himself with an allusion to the dog story this time — he might have had second thoughts on its propriety and efficacy with an Anglican divine — we know precisely what story he had in mind because a year later he quoted it in the *Review* under the caption, "Advertisement for the OB-SERVATOR"; it is the very same dog story he had directed at Tutchin earlier.[31] However hard Defoe postured at being above caring about the insulting or denigrating remarks printed by men like Tutchin or Browne or Swift, he unquestionably cared greatly, even excessively, about what they said. His responses invariably were grossly disproportionate to such slighting references, and no matter how incidental detracting remarks about him might read in context — as in the case of Swift's passing reference — he simply could not prevent himself from overreacting to them.

As if one long issue of the *Review* were not more than enough to answer Swift's brief mention of him in the *Examiner,* Defoe went ahead in the very next number of the *Review* to resume his dressing down of Mr. Examiner as behaving unlike a gentleman and his defense of Mr. Review:

And now, Gentlemen, as if this was not enough, *Mr. Examiner* is falling upon me . . .

Much powder, I say, much noise, much ill language; much call-names, no argument. After *idiot,* which is the first mark of distinction, comes *illiterate* — much wit in that truly is. How should *an idiot* but be *illiterate?* . . . I know a man at this time a minister, he is a critic in the Greek and Hebrew, a complete master of Latin, yet it would make a man blush to read a letter from him, sleep to hear him preach, and sick to read his books. He is a master of languages, and buried in letters, but cannot spell his mother tongue, knows nothing of the world, and has never look'd abroad. Such learning I confess I despise, and covet to be illiterate rather than thus a scholar.

Again, I know another that is an orator in Latin, a walking index of books, has all the libraries in Europe in his head, from the Vatican at Rome to the learned collection of Dr. Salmon at Fleet-Ditch; but, at the same time, he is a *Cynic* in behaviour, a *Fury* in temper, *unpolite* in conversation, *abusive* and *scurrilous* in language, and *ungovernable* in passion. Is this to be learned? Then *may I be still illiterate.*

I have been in my time pretty well master of five languages, and have not lost them yet, *tho' I write no bill over my door,* or set Latin quotations in front of the *Review.* But to my irreparable loss I was bred by halves, for my father forgetting *Juno's* Royal Academy left *the language of Billingsgate* quite out of my education; hence I am perfectly *illiterate* in the polite style of the street . . .

I have also, *illiterate as I am,* made a little progress in *science;* I read *Euclid's Elements,* and yet never found the *mathematical description* of A SCURRILOUS GENTLEMAN: I have read logic, but could never see a syllogism form'd upon the notion of it. I went some length in physics, or natural philosophy . . . I thought my self master of geography, and could have set up for a country *almanac maker,* as to my skill in astronomy . . . from whence I conclude very frankly . . . that according to Mr. *Examiner,* I am a stupid idiot, *and a very illiterate fellow.*[32]

This is a remarkable confession, by way of catalogue, of the real reason for Defoe's personal over-reaction to Swift. Apparently Defoe sensed in Swift a man who, by implication, had cast aspersions on his background and learning, and therefore on his recently established position of gentleman as well. In a word, he shows himself taking personally what Swift most certainly intended generally; Defoe was but one of several journalists mentioned by Swift, all of whom were leading political journalists writing and editing weekly sheets at this time.

But there is more to Defoe's astonishingly emotional overreaction to Swift in these revealing numbers of the *Review*. Though he obviously resented Swift's liberty in dismissing him as a stupid, illiterate scribbler, he lashed out at Swift less as an individual than as the representative of a social class which treated him and his dearest social aspirations with contempt. Defoe was all the more maddened because when he wanted desperately to fight back publicly, to match his skills against those of his cultivated rivals, he saw his challenges and retorts going unanswered or unacknowledged. (Swift, for instance, never responded to Defoe's *Reviews* for December 14 and 18, 1710 — indeed, he never once answered Defoe directly.) It was bad enough to be attacked constantly by Grub Street hacks, but to meet with such insolent treatment at the hands of men who profess to be gentlemen was obviously more than Defoe could bear quietly. It is not Mr. Review here who answers Mr. Examiner; it is Daniel De Foe, Gentleman, defending himself as an equal in brains and breeding, and therefore status as a gentleman, with Jonathan Swift, Trinity College, Dublin.

The rub here, of course, is that Swift never had to defend his position; he, like the men of his social class, assumed their status. Defoe, on the other hand, always had to convince his readers — and himself — of the validity of his claims to be taken as a gentleman. In actuality Swift's treatment of Defoe was the standard arrogance of a cultivated member of polite society in dealing with a member of a lower social class. Even though the eighteenth century was not an age of clearly demarcated lines of cleavage between social classes, still one could easily isolate attitudes shared by segments of society, as is illustrated in the case of Swift and Defoe: Defoe is "the fellow that was *pilloryed*" to Swift, whereas Swift is "the learned Dr. S——" to Defoe. The social distinctions implied are obvious enough.[33]

The contrast in background between Swift and Defoe clearly accounted for much of their attitudes toward each other. George Sherburn offers a succinct summary of the actual basis of their differences: "Defoe was, to be sure, a tradesman, and Swift came of somewhat more genteel stock; but the real difference in the men lies in the fact that Defoe was a dissenter and had a middle-class practical education. Swift was a churchman, and *speciali gratia* a university graduate." In literature, Swift was well versed in the classics; Defoe was not. Yet Defoe, we must also remember, was hailed an Athenian wit in 1691, when Swift was still the obscure young secretary to Sir William Temple; and both men had graced the *Athenian Mercury* with odes, Defoe's coming for the first collection, Swift's for the fifth. But that was some twenty years ago, when Defoe's star rode high in the heavens and Swift's had barely begun to rise. Their respective fortunes had altered greatly by the close of 1710, at which time the exchange between them occurred.[34]

To appreciate Defoe's frustrated sense of exclusion from the elegant literary circles of his day, we must understand the state of English letters in the early eighteenth century, because what Defoe's literary contemporaries felt towards him was in large part determined by the conditions of the age. Generally speaking, the age was dominated by the "classical school" of Pope and Swift, a literary tradition founded upon ancient models and strict rules of decorum and correctness. This classical school, according to A. S. Turberville, "made literature 'gentlemanly,' and it appealed to a small educated class composed of London society and of men of letters themselves, those Wits who frequented the Coffee Houses." The writers associated with the classical school also were grounded in classical learning, which they acquired in the grammar school, where "the greater part of the young scholar's time was given to the study of Latin and Greek," and in the university with its traditional classical curriculum. "The education of a gentleman," according to Leslie Stephen, "meant nothing then except a certain drill in Greek and Latin." Given this close relationship between the classics and a gentleman's education, we can understand Defoe's sensitivity about statements which drew attention to his "illiteracy" or "stupidity." [35]

Moreover, the reign of Queen Anne saw the literary scene dominated by the clubs and coffee-houses of London and, according to R. J. Allen, historian of *The Clubs of Augustan London,* "the writer without independent means almost necessarily allied himself with a political party." There were clubs associated with the Whigs, like the Kit-Kat Club and the Calves-Head Club; there were clubs associated with the Tories, like the Saturday Club, the Brothers Club, and the October Club; there were also informal literary clubs, like the Scriblerus Club of Pope, Swift, Arbuthnot, Gay, and Parnell. In addition to the clubs there were the many coffee-houses which served as the congregating places of Londoners of the same class or party or interests, Button's, White's, Will's, St. James's being among the more celebrated names. Almost all the major writers of this period were connected with the activities of these clubs and coffee-houses. Not Defoe.[36]

Although Defoe is known to have frequented coffee-houses on occasion, he was not an active member of a club or coffee-house literati, nor was his audience well-educated or refined, as was the audience of the classical school. Defoe wrote, as Q. D. Leavis remarks, "outside what Steele called 'the circumference of wit,' and [his] audience was outside it too." In his poetry Defoe addressed himself primarily to "the unlearned," and sought to instruct more than to please. In answer to the critics who derided his inelegant style in the *Review,* he pointed out that "this paper is writ to enlighten the stupid understandings of the meaner and more thoughtless of the freeholders and electors." When Mr. Review was born *in tenebris* in Newgate, he knew himself to be a bankrupt merchant and pilloried pamphleteer. Denied re-entry to the world of trade and commerce, he turned to political journalism out of necessity and sought to make the best of his dependent position in late 1703. Harley shrewdly assessed Defoe's talents for reaching the trading middle-class readers, and it was to this growing reading public that he addressed his *Review* and his other writings, for these were the people he knew and understood, being one of their number.[37]

We can see, therefore, the gulf that always separated Defoe from the cultivated circle of writers who ruled on Parnassus in the early eighteenth century. Despite his successes with his middle-class mercantile audiences, he showed himself as resentful of the favored position of his contemporaries, and he revealed his resentment by sniping at them in his writings. Jealous of Addison's fame resulting from the publication of his resoundingly successful poem *The Campaign,* Defoe accused him of venality in *The*

Consolidator in 1705: "Ad[*di*]son may tell his master my Lord ____
. . . why he would not take the Court's word, nor write the poem
call'd *The Campaign,* till he had £200 *per annum* secur'd to
him." Defoe was envious of Addison's success in securing what
he himself wanted, and what Harley was never to obtain for him,
despite his frequent hints: a permanent post with the government
at an assured yearly income. He went on to assert in the reference
to Addison that "they have but one author in the nation that
writes for 'em for nothing," namely Daniel De Foe. In his poem
to the Duke of Marlborough, *The Double Welcome,* Defoe also
had attacked Addison: "Mecaenas has his modern fancy strung,/
and fix'd his pension first, or he had never sung." Since "Mecaenas" was none other than Halifax, whose patronage Defoe
himself sought without success that year, we can see that his attack on Addison was motivated by something more personal than
the public interest. For his part, Addison harbored no high regard for Defoe and his political pen, referring to him indirectly
in "Count Tariff" in 1713 as "a false, shuffling, prevaricating
rascal" who published "notorious falsehoods." [38]

Defoe was equally envious of the successful climb of Richard
Steele, as well as the joint success of Addison and Steele with their
Tatler and *Spectator* papers. In February and March 1713 Defoe's
hostility toward Steele came to the surface when he urged Harley
to have Steele, then recently assigned his seat in the Commons,
charged with seditious writings and ousted. He even collected for
Harley samples of questionable writings from Steele's works. If
this action was a justifiable political move, one still cannot miss
the meticulous care with which Defoe aroused in Harley an
animus for Steele ("My Ld. it is far from me to move your Ldp.
to personal resentments") nor his scantly concealed satisfaction
in urging the government to punish a rival and eminently successful journalist ("The most insolent pamphlet writer that ever
was permitted to go unpunished"). Defoe was, we must remember, an outcast, and therefore less than charitable toward successful rivals. Prior to criticizing the "deservedly approv'd author
. . . call'd *Tatler,* now *Spectator*" in 1711, he stated frankly,
"They say there is a vice in nature that gives a secret gust of
satisfaction in seeing our superiors in any virtue commit a mistake, and perhaps I am guilty of it with the rest." Clearly he was

jealous of the success of Addison and Steele, and Professor Trent's reminder of Defoe's condition helps us to understand how he probably felt and why he behaved the way he did: "we must picture him in London or with his wife and children in a large house in Newington, seeing little or nothing of the gay society of the epoch, not even acquainted with the fellow men of letters who with himself give the age its chief lustre." [39]

Even so, Defoe's writings commanded attention and were commented on by leading writers of the period. In 1711, for example, John Gay published his pamphlet on *The Present State of Wit,* a contemporary survey of the most important and influential newspapers and journals of London: "As to our weekly papers, the poor *Review* is quite exhausted, and grown so very contemptible, that though he has provoked all his brothers of the quill round, none of them will enter into a controversy with him. This fellow, who had excellent parts, but wanted a small foundation of learning, is a lively instance of those wits who, as an ingenious author says, 'will endure but one skimming.'" Gay, of course, was here trying to make a name for himself as a wit. He adopted the sophisticated and discriminating tone of a man of the *beau monde* addressing himself to a coffee-house audience. His remarks, however, are significant because they reveal the regard the Tory wits had for Mr. Review; they pick out as his main weakness his "small foundation of learning," while admitting he has "excellent parts." Two years earlier, a short-lived journal in London called the *General Postscript,* which ran for only twenty issues, dubbed Defoe with the nickname of "Verbos Enthusiasticus." Apparently he was fair game for the sneers of any aspirant to a groat's worth of wit, as well as for the real wits of the age.[40]

The salient fact of Defoe's popularity among the masses, as Swift had acknowledged, made him a prime target for the leading satirists, notably the Scriblerus Club, which saw in his great popular successes a direct threat to the "classical school" of English letters. It is not surprising, therefore, to find Defoe included among those satirized in Martinus Scriblerus' *Peri Bathous,* a project of the Scriblerus Club. Defoe is twice satirized: first as one of the "Ostridges" whose "heaviness rarely permits them to raise themselves from the ground; their wings are of no use to lift them up, and their motion is between *flying* and *walking;*

but then they *run* very fast"; and a second time for his bogus "profundity," which he is accused of affecting by imitation of George Withers, a prolific seventeenth-century pamphleteer and a notoriously poor poet. There is nothing unusual about this un-flattering treatment of Defoe's poetical powers, for his reputation as a poet never stood very high in polite literary circles, despite his popular successes as an Athenian and as the author of *The True-Born Englishman*. In the *Advertisements from Parnassus*, for instance, Defoe's claims as a poet are raised and dismissed summarily in the thirteenth advertisement as follows: "Daniel de Foe petitions Apollo to be admitted into Parnassus, but is refused that honor." [41]

Alexander Pope, like Gay, was aware of Defoe's good qualities as a writer, and he later went on record with Joseph Spence to make his opinions known: "Defoe wrote a vast many things; and none bad, though none excellent . . . There is something good in all he has written." But there was never any direct commerce between these two great writers of the age of Queen Anne. In the copious correspondence of Pope no mention is ever made of Defoe. The only times Defoe wrote about Pope were in two successive numbers of *Applebee's Journal* in 1725, when he wrote critically of Pope's translation of the *Odyssey*, accusing him of putting his name to a work largely done by translators in his employ. Defoe's criticisms are relevant, but his tone is querulous and captious; in fact, he charged Pope with perpetrating a literary fraud on the public. Pope probably never knew of De-foe's disservice to his *Odyssey*, and it had no bearing on his in-clusion of Defoe in the *Dunciad*.[42]

The *Dunciad*, according to Professor Sutherland, "was directed against a new generation of those literary upstarts (now vastly increased in numbers owing to the rapid development of literary journalism and the growth of the reading public), and whatever private scores he may be settling, Pope is genuinely concerned to maintain the threatened standards of polite literature." Defoe by this time certainly was not a member of the "new generation," but he was without question an outstanding example of the older generation of professional writers whose success the younger gen-eration could aspire to emulate. Defoe was therefore appropriately paired in the *Dunciad* with his old journalistic rival John Tutchin, long since dead from a fatal beating he suffered in 1707: "Earless on high, stood un-abash'd Defoe,/And Tutchin flagrant from the scourge, below." Like Swift, Pope simply associated Defoe with the pillory, whose stigma he was never able to escape (the variant versions of the *Dunciad* read "pillory'd" for "un-abash'd"). The "earless" was of course inaccurate, Defoe's ears never having been cropped in the pillory or elsewhere; but it served to make him look all the more ridiculous in the satire.

Pope also injected scandal about Defoe when he included Defoe's son, Benjamin Norton Defoe, in the *Dunciad:*

> Norton, from Daniel and Ostroea sprung,
> Blest with his father's front, and mother's tongue,
> Hung silent down his never-blushing head;
> And all was hush'd, as Folly's self lay dead.

Pope reportedly relied on Richard Savage for his information on the Grub Street authors, and Savage started circulating the story that Defoe had sired a bastard son named Benjamin. In the preface to Savage's *Author to be Let* appeared the statement that Benjamin Norton Defoe was "Daniel de Foe's son of love, by a lady who vended oysters." Pope in a footnote to these lines in the *Dunciad* referred to Norton as "the natural offspring of the famous *Daniel,*" a note he retained in subsequent editions until 1735, when he probably found out that his information was inaccurate and deleted the adjective "natural." Still, he retained the lines intact, apparently not thinking it worth his time to change a slur on Defoe and his venal writer of a son, however false the statement; Defoe was by then dead and his son an obscure hack.[43]

Defoe's relationship with the polite authors of his age, then, was limited only to distant and rare exchanges between men of fundamentally different social classes and literary attitudes. Defoe was always at a decided disadvantage. His literary superiors treated him with the contempt and disdain commonly accorded an "illiterate" — by their standards — writer. The fact that Defoe scored a significant success with the unrefined reading public made him all the more distrusted and dangerous to the classical school of authors. Without a classical or university education, he could not compete with them on their own terms. His only way to get back at them, and so give vent to his resentment, was to cavil at their works or reputations on occasion or, as in the case with Swift, to censure them for their want of manners, breeding, and gentility in attacking him.

Belles lettres simply was not the natural province of Mr. Review. One would look in vain for any critical commentary on contemporary authors and their works in the *Review*, even though this period saw published noteworthy works by such poets as Pope, Gay, Parnell, Watts, Tickell, Philips, Prior, Addison, and Swift. Indeed, only five authors are named more than once (Dryden, Milton, Marvell, Temple, and, of course, Rochester), and they not only are "traditional" but the comments about them are of the order of literary clichés (for example, Milton is "sublime" or Rochester a "genius"). Defoe was not equipped by education nor inclined by temperament to match wits with the polite authors of his time in belletristic matters; his natural talents inclined him toward and made him succeed with men more like himself, Dissenters and tradesmen and merchants. But his social pretensions were patterned after the upper classes, and they would not let him rest content at succeeding only with a sober and practical middle-class audience.[44]

Defoe's *Reproof to Mr. Clark* of 1710 portrays the kind of literary figure he might well have liked to become had the "disasterous" circumstances of his life not cut him off from the leading wits of the Queen Anne era. Defoe had been a leading Athenian wit in King William's reign, and only the vicissitudes of his fortunes had forced him to relinquish that pursuit for a career as a political writer. But he seemingly always harbored a secret ambition to become something of a sophisticated wit, and his *jeu d'esprit* of self-vindication addressed to the Reverend James Clark of Glasgow reveals this side of Defoe:

Mr. De Foe, whose writings make him famous, since in them is conspicuously to be seen *eminency of gifts, humility of spirit, elegancy of style, solidity of matter, height of fancy, depth of judgment, clearness of apprehension, strength of reason, and ardent zeal for truth, &c.* . . . To rail on and reproach such a phoenix of this age, such a rare and precious gentleman, *the envy and glory of his sex,* is a sort of *indiscretion* (not to call it worse) that none would have thought Mr. *Clark* capable of.[45]

Defoe presented himself here not as a "phoenix" of a tradesman,

93

who, like himself, could redeem his credit and his fortune from the ashes of his disgrace and ruin, but as "a phoenix of this age," "a rare and precious gentleman," indeed. He at least could enjoy playing the role of the wit just as he would have enjoyed sporting the reputation — as he did in 1691.

His "differing fortunes," however, had prevented him from becoming such a wit and associating with other such fashionable authors. As he informed Lord Haversham in 1706: "But Fate, that makes footballs of men, kicks some up stairs and some down; some are advanc'd without honour, others suppressed without infamy; some are raised without merit; some are crush'd without crime; and no man knows by the beginnings of things whether his course shall issue in a PEERAGE or a PILLORY; and time was that no man could have determin'd it between his Lordship and this mean fellow." These are not only brave and eloquent words from Defoe to a noble Lord, they also sum up concisely the way in which he had come to interpret the roller-coaster course of his life, a life spent of late much "in gaols, in retreats, in all manner of extremities," and often also "without the assistance of friends or relations." Unquestionably Defoe was implying that there but for the untimely death of King William might go I, a peer like you. Lord Haversham, as Defoe was quick to remind him, owed his preferment to none other than King William, "whose judgment," Defoe wrote, "I cannot undervalue, because he gave his Lordship his honour and dignity, which was some time before as mean as M[INE]." It is perhaps no coincidence that 1706 should be the year that Defoe adopted publicly a revised version of his armorial bearings for his *Jure Divino* portrait, or that in *The Complete English Tradesman* he should cite "The late Earl of Haversham [as] originally a merchant." If Haversham could be a peer on so little merit, then De Foe could at least be a gentleman.[46]

Cut off from the fashionable world of the literati in London, Defoe as Mr. Review devoted himself to pursuing interests of more immediate importance to himself and his fellow middle-class tradesmen. Understandably the question of gentility was of special interest, and he treated it in the context of his discussions on trade and morality. In imitation of John Dunton's old *Athenian Mercury*, Defoe featured for a time an "Advice from the Scandalous Club" column in the *Review*, which discussed, among other matters, such questions of moment as "the qualifications required to entitle a man to call himself a gentleman." This vehicle enabled him to express his views in a more informal way than in, say, a poem like *The True-Born Englishman* or a tract. In matters of gentility he consistently presented the view that breeding, not blood or birth, was the distinguishing characteristic of a gentleman. And through the "Scandalous Club" he could censure the gentry and nobility for their loose manners and morals: "Some people of petulant fame, have blam'd the Club for exposing crimes which they call *little ones,* whoring, drunkenness, killing folks, duelling, and the like." [47] Defoe's remarks were always pitched to the prejudices of his readers.

We must keep in mind Defoe's audience when we consider his comments in the *Review*. He was himself acutely conscious of his audience and sought to address them in the most effective way. In one number of the *Review* he admitted: "I have hitherto preach'd to my inferiors and equals, men of the same class with myself; I hope I have slip'd into no indecencies, and have studied nothing more, than to suit my language to the case, and to the persons." Defoe's course of life had taken him far from the pulpit he had been set apart for as a boy, but his formative years left their mark on him, and he could still come to regard his writings, especially when consciously directed at an audience of "the same class" as himself, to be a form of preaching, not of religious sermons to be sure, but of secular matters like trade, social status, education, manners and morals, all of which bore so directly on the lives of the readers of the *Review*.[48]

Defoe's campaign in the *Review* against the abuses in manners and morals by so-called gentlemen of the upper classes was in keeping with the prevailing atmosphere of reform during this time, a Puritan reform movement dating back to the 1690's. Whereas Defoe addressed himself to his aspiring middle-class trading audience, Steele and Addison in their *Tatler* and *Spectator* papers addressed themselves to the upper and prominent middle classes, and they also sought to reform their readers on the matter of gentility. In *Tatler* No. 21, for example, the character of Sophronius was offered as a model of what the true gentleman should be like; and in *Tatler* No. 207 Steele wrote that "the appellation of gentleman is never fixed to a man's circumstances, but to his behaviour in them." The very same emphasis on breeding and de-emphasis of birth and ancestry found in Defoe's *Review* and other writings was promulgated in the pages of the *Tatler* and *Spectator* — as well as in other works of the age. But Addison and Steele in their writings showed none of Defoe's intensely personal and passionate concern for the ambitions of his aspiring middle class; they aimed primarily at instructing by pleasing a coffee-house and club society, an audience at once more sophisticated in taste and more prominent socially than the average tradesmen of the middle ranks for whom Defoe wrote.[49]

Defoe, for his part, championed the cause of the rising trading class of the nation in their bid for acceptance socially as well as economically and politically. England, as Defoe never tired of informing his readers, is *"a trading nation,"* and as such cannot make the nice distinctions that other European countries do which "value themselves upon abstracted nobility"; unlike these other nations, England's "numerous gentry," "illustrious nobility" and "best families, owe their wealth and rise, first and last, to the opulence and profits of trade."

Defoe introduced into the pages of the *Review* the theme he had treated in the *Essay upon Projects* — that the merchant-trader is a new kind of leader in English society — and again in *The True-Born Englishman*, in which the exclusive claims to gentility by gentry and nobility were reduced to an absurdity by Defoe's *ab origine* argument. The upper classes in England were not "abstracted" in the Continental sense but a hybrid and ever-shifting class whose fortunes were governed by trade and commerce:

Nor is it any dishonour to them [the gentry who owe their rise to trade], since the exceeding wealth of our merchants, having qualified them for gentlemen, noblemen, or statesmen, they have made it appear that those characters have suited them, and sate as well upon their posterity as upon those of the best blood in the nation; and if there has been any difference, the trading branches have had it with advantage . . .

It is not the business of this paper, to examine into the real difference between ancient and modern nobility, or gentry, a nicety very few in *England* can distinguish; but to lay down the fact, in order to draw the inference from it, that *England* is a trading nation, that the wealth and opulence of the nation is owing to trade.

Defoe's panegyrics on trade served a double purpose: they demonstrated that the past, present, and future greatness of England lay not with an idle country squirearchy and an agrarian economy but with a vigorous city trading community and a dynamic mercantile economy; they also awakened the rising trading class to its true and just historic claims to eminence in this new scheme of things. England's men of business no longer were to be dismissed and despised as mere "mechanics," they were to become regarded as men of affairs and, if they amassed a large fortune from trade, as "gentlemen." [50]

To prepare the way for tradesmen to be transformed into gentlemen Defoe stressed the great importance of a "liberal education":

Education, especially in *England,* has so much the ascendant over birth, that we see the Lady's daughter a peasant, the tradesman's daughter a Lady . . .

The wealth of the trading part of this nation is so much superior to that of the gentry, especially of mere ancient families, that it has given the tradesmen opportunity to give a more liberal education to their children than the other; and education has such strange effects on children, that it makes these mechanics gentlemen, and join'd to large fortunes, has erected such great families, and so many, that if the number of gentlemen, who had the original of their greatness from trade, was set up against the ancient gentry, they would go near to make a balance; almost all our great families, many of the nobility, owe their wealth and birth to trade.

The extract of any family, therefore, especially in *England,* where there is education, virtue, and fortune, admits of no more dispute, and that objection is frivolous.

In so stressing the virtues of a "liberal education" Defoe was also defending the kind of education he himself received at Morton's academy, where the emphasis was on practical as well as scholarly learning. The Greek and Latin of the universities, however useful for qualifying a man as a member in an elegant literary coterie, were otiose in the world of business, where fortunes were to be made from trade. As Defoe had argued earlier in *The*

True-Born Englishman, gentility in England was merely a matter of money and breeding, not antiquity and birth; a "liberal education" provided the breeding and trade offered the opportunity for acquiring the money.[51]

Defoe's concern for education also embraced the English gentry, in whom he saw an alarming tendency that had national implications. He noted how effeminate the gentry had grown as a result of their eschewing a sound education and their unbridled pursuit of pleasures:

The riches of our gentry . . . [have] effeminated the spirits of our nation, and taken off the very edge of our genius, either from arms or learning . . . 'But what business has a gentleman of quality and estate to go into the field? *No, no,* your humble servant; we pay others to fight; there's no occasion for us to go ourselves . . . soldiers fight, and scholars read, and parsons preach, 'tis all for money . . . all our business is to spend our money, hunt, race, game, drink, &c.' . . .
And let no man wonder, why the *Scots* nobility and gentry obtain so much reputation abroad, at the same time that we endeavour to put so much contempt upon them at home. The reason is plain, they have the true liberal education of a gentleman; they are bred to letters first, and then to arms; the first teaches them to behave . . . the last gives the opportunity to show it . . . they are first made men of sense, men of letters, and men of arms.

Because Defoe had spent much time in Scotland for Harley and the government and had apparently been accepted by the Scottish gentry, he had had an excellent opportunity to compare the merits of the English and Scottish gentry. The English upper classes, unlike the Scottish, were relinquishing their historic leadership by default as they scorned a "liberal education" and a manly sense of military service. Defoe did not spare his contempt for the English gentry: "they are bred *boors,* empty and swinish sots and fops, and they are not capable of having a right sense of honour in the world." If only the eldest sons were bred like the younger ones, with a sound practical education to qualify them for the world of affairs, then England would once again have a gentry to be esteemed, not the disgraceful corruption that then prevailed.[52]

Defoe knew that his remarks were not read by the gentry, but that the members of his class were only too receptive to them, and he addressed his readers accordingly. He made clear to them the kind of new role he could foresee English tradesmen playing in the nation's affairs if they were properly bred and educated:

A true-bred merchant is a universal scholar; his learning excells the mere scholar in Greek and Latin as much as that does the illiterate person that cannot write or read. He understands languages without books, geography without maps; his journals and trading voyages delineate the world; his foreign exchanges, protests and procurations speak all tongues; he sits in his counting-house and converses with all nations, and keeps up the most exquisite and extensive part of human society in a universal correspondence.

He is qualified for all sorts of employment in the state by a general knowledge of things and men; he remits and draws such vast sums that he transacts more value than a large exchequer.

There can be little doubt that Defoe is here recalling his own career as a London merchant, for everything that he describes was at one time, and not that far distant, applicable to himself, when he was such a "true-bred merchant" serving King William in various capacities while also engaging in assorted and far-reaching mercantile operations. In the introduction to his *Essay upon Projects* Defoe had written that "a true-bred merchant" is "the most intelligent man in the world." Now, more than ever before, there was a significant place for such true-bred merchants to assume in the affairs of the nation, especially in the light of the effeminate and uneducated state of the landed gentry in England. He was later to pursue this theme more fully in his *Complete English Tradesman* and other works.[53]

Defoe firmly believed that education was of the highest importance to the welfare of the nation in general and to the aspirations of the middle class in particular. "Trade and learning" indeed were to Defoe "the two chief steps by which our gentlemen have rais'd their relations, and have built their fortunes." Thus, he fretted constantly over the education of his children, as is evident from his writings and his letters. When ruined *"the shortest way"* he confided to Harley that one of the worst disasters resulting from his imprisonment and bankruptcy was the uncertain future for his children's education: "seven children, Sir, whose education calls on me to furnish their heads if I can not their purses, and which debt if not paid now can never be compounded hereafter is to me a moving article and helps very often to make me sad."

Defoe further expressed his concern for the education of his children in his *Appeal to Honour and Justice* of 1715: "I have six children. I have educated them as well as my circumstances will permit, and so as I hope shall recommend them to better usage than their father meets with in the world." It is noteworthy that he concluded his pamphlet of self-defense on the point that, contrary to spurious charges alleging he never paid for the education of his children, he alone paid for their education, and if "any man in Britain" has a shilling due him for their education, "let him come for it." As we have seen, he rarely reacted with such warmth except when accusations touched a sensitive nerve. Education, as it applied to himself, to his family, and to the middle class in general, was always a serious subject with him.[54]

In the year 1715 Defoe reached a significant turning point in his fortunes. He apparently had become increasingly concerned about his life during recent years, prompted by nothing so much as his Puritan conscience. In February 1715 he had published his *Appeal to Honour and Justice,* in which he hinted that he was close to death and therefore took the occasion to clear his name of all slanders: "By the hints of mortality, and by the infirmities of a life of sorrow and fatigue, I have reason to think that I am not a great way off from, if not very near to the great Ocean of Eternity, and the time may not be long e're I embark on the last voyage: wherefore, I think, I should *even accounts* with this world before I go." Defoe at this time was almost fifty-five years old. His publisher, in an addendum to the text, stated that while the manuscript was being seen through the press the author was indeed "seiz'd with a violent fit of an apoplexy" and had "for above six weeks" been in a critical condition. Although published in 1715, the manuscript was composed toward the end of 1714. As Defoe lay critically ill for many weeks "in a weak and languishing condition," he had little else to do than to review the events of his life. A deeply religious man and a devout Puritan, he may well have despaired of his past life. He apparently resolved to make some amends for his neglect of his religious life during these many insecure and trying years as a pamphleteer-journalist and government agent. He set to work on a religious book that was to appear in 1715 as *The Family Instructor*.

Writing of Defoe's possible motivation in composing this singularly pious book at this particular time of his life, Professor Sutherland suggests: "The book has much to say about the duties that parents owe to their children, and about the need for regular family worship and religious instruction: perhaps in those busy years from 1703 onwards Defoe had been neglecting this part of his obligations as a parent, and now was offering *The Family Instructor* as a sacrifice to an angry Jehovah." The work certainly stands as a lively example of the "old Puritan preacher" addressing an audience. Defoe had an uncanny talent for reaching an audience, as he demonstrated in the *Review,* and to make his religious and moral instruction more dramatic and comprehensible, he adopted the device of the dialogue. If he needed encouragement that his religious writings were acceptable as a "sacrifice," the surprisingly successful sales record of his *Family Instructor* should have dispelled any doubts. The work went through no less than eight editions by 1720, not to mention a second volume he added in 1718 and a third (*The New Family Instructor*) in 1727. He also resumed the theme in *Religious Courtship* in 1722 and *Conjugal Lewdness* in 1727. Puritan conscience or no, Defoe was too practical a man of the world not to capitalize on a commercial opportunity.[55]

Defoe's illness late in 1714 had not been the only cause of his anxiety at this time. The death of Queen Anne on August 12, 1714, had left him adrift as a political pamphleteer; he was without any formal journalistic connections, and now he was without a patron or a party. By July 1715 his employer of so many years, Robert Harley, was in the Tower under impeachment for treason; he was never to be Defoe's employer again. His other political employer of former days, Lord Godolphin, had been dead for three years. And on the very same day that Harley was impeached, Defoe himself was tried in the Court of the King's Bench for a libel against the Earl of Anglesley published in the previous year. He was found guilty by Chief Justice Parker but sentencing was deferred until a later date. At fifty-five, he once again found himself in desperate straits — without help, without funds, and at the mercy of a new ministry.

Yet Defoe was miraculously delivered from his uncertain predicament of awaiting sentence. As Defoe was a deeply religious man, so was he also a deeply superstitious man, who always showed an uncommon fascination for the "second sight" and the significance of all kinds of dreams, voices, impulses or other such signs of commerce with the spirit world. In the third part of *Robinson Crusoe*, "A Vision of the Angelic World," he recounted his strange experience with Chief Justice Parker:

He had a particular case befallen him, wherein he was under the displeasure of the Government, and was prosecuted for a misdemeanour, and brought to a trial in the King's Bench Court, where a verdict was brought against him . . . In this extremity he felt one morning — just as he awakened, and the thoughts of his misfortune began to return upon him — I say, he felt a strong impulse darting into his mind thus, Write a letter to them . . .

However, it repeated the words daily and hourly to him, till at length, walking about in his chamber, where he was hidden, very pensive and sad, it jogged him again, and he answered aloud to it, as if it had been a voice, Who shall I write to? It returned immediately, Write to the judge. This pursued him again for several days, till at length he took his pen, ink, and paper, and sat down to write, but knew not one word of what he should say; but, *dabitur in hac hora,* he wanted not words. It was immediately impressed on his mind, and the words flowed upon his pen in a manner that even charmed himself, and filled him with expectations of success.

Regrettably, Defoe's inspired letter to Chief Justice Parker does not survive, but it obviously proved successful, as he expected it would. He was never sentenced but found himself recommended to then Secretary of State Townshend, who, like his predecessors in that office, found Defoe's political pen useful. He was a free man once more, but he had to pay a certain price for his freedom. He served the Whig Ministry clandestinely by writing for Tory journals like *Dormer's Letter,* the *Mercurius Politicus,* and in 1717 *Mist's Weekly Journal;* his undercover assignment was to take the edge off the editorializing of these sheets so as to neutralize their impact. By this cunning stratagem, in Defoe's own account, they could still "pass as Tory papers, and yet be disabled and enervated, so as to do no mischief or give any offence to the Government." [56]

A Janus-faced journalist drawing a double salary, from the

Whigs whose agent he was and from the Tories for whom he wrote, Defoe was restored to his old and familiar profession of political writer. He was now solvent again and could live like a gentleman. Since 1708 he had settled himself and his family in a house in Stoke Newington; he now kept a coach and four. He was again beginning "to live," as he once had written Harley of former and more prosperous days.

The year 1715, then, marked a decided turning point in Defoe's career. He turned to religious writing seriously and was rewarded handsomely by the huge sales success of this venture. He was delivered from the double disaster of being without a patron or party and being found guilty of libel. This communication from the spirit world which extricated him from his difficulty with Chief Justice Parker apparently had the profoundest Providential significance to Defoe, who felt his life was attended at every crisis by such a dream or impulse from above. His capture in Spitalfields in 1703 he attributed to his failure to heed a warning in a dream, and his successful undertaking of nine long years, the *Review*, he claimed was first suggested to him in a dream in Newgate. A devout and impressionable Puritan, Defoe probably interpreted his happy and promising circumstances at the end of 1715 as the work of Providence.[57]

After 1715, even though he continued as a government pamphleteer, he never again was to depend primarily on these services for his livelihood, as he had been forced to do since his release from Newgate in 1703. The success of *The Family Instructor* had convinced him of the marketability of his didactic prose works. It was only a matter of a few years before these religious books led him to other, more imaginative, nonpolitical writing. The step from 1715 to 1719 was not a great one.

The dominant image of Defoe we have for the years 1703 to 1719 is certainly that of Mr. Review. He alone accounted for the thrice-weekly four-page journal on a bewildering array of topics for nine long and eventful years, a monumental achievement in journalism that totaled 5,610 pages when it finally ceased its publication. When Mr. Review made his farewell exit from his readers on June 11, 1713, he tried to sum up, lightly, both his writings in the *Review* and his age. He decided that his age could most appropriately be termed "a Whoring Generation":

A. makes his horse his whore. B. his fine coach. C. his weekly new clothes. D. his pack of hounds. G . . . sets four hours a day to look at his new bovet (whore) fill'd with a thousand pounds worth of gilt plate.

What a Whoring Generation is this! F. is newly made a baronet, and never tires with looking at his coat of arms; like the Indian king at Virginia, who being presented with a lock to his house-door, pleas'd himself with locking and unlocking it a thousand times a day.

Defoe, we recall, had characterized the 1690's as "The Projecting Age" in his *Essay upon Projects,* and now he labeled the 1710's as an age "strangely addicted to the modish, tho' abominable vice of MODERN WHORING." Defoe was ever a man of his age: a projector in the 1690's, he also had his "whore" in the 1710's.

Defoe confessed in the conclusion to the last number of the *Review,* "this paper has been *my whore*" — and so in many ways it had. But when Defoe went on to say, "Writing upon trade was the whore I really doated on," he was less than comprehensive in this designation. If trade was what Defoe doted on in public life, gentility was what he doted on in private life; for, as we saw, he revealed an abiding concern, almost an obsession, for the very things that he cited other men as making their "whores": namely, "fine coach," "horse," "new clothes," and especially a "new coat of arms." These various trappings of gentility were the delights of his private life, and he was quick to respond whenever they were attacked or ridiculed in any way. Defoe always had a knack of criticizing in others what he frequently practiced himself.[58]

Finally, the years of experience, both as a journalist and as a writer of religious books, had prepared Defoe for his new and major career as a writer of fiction. Not only the experiences but also the special interests and personal aspirations of Mr. Review were to find their way into his works of fiction.

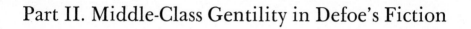

Part II. Middle-Class Gentility in Defoe's Fiction

Chapter 5. Fiction and the Age, 1714–1724

And it is in the second decade that we cannot avoid noting that literature is being influenced by the great and growing confraternity of successful merchants and their families chiefly living in London but also scattered over the country, together with all the smaller beings who lived on them and by whom they lived: from now on we begin to be aware of a great middle-class literature, a literature which was to improve with astonishing rapidity in the next few years, and was soon to constitute the main reading of the country. — Bonamy Dobrée, *English Literature in the Early Eighteenth Century, 1700–1740* (Oxford: Oxford University Press, 1959), p. 12

Leslie Stephen observed, in his discussion of *English Literature and Society in the Eighteenth Century,* that "the growth of new forms is obviously connected not only with the intellectual development but with the social and political state of the nation." In order to understand the emergence of the novel in early eighteenth-century England, we must also understand the social and political state of the nation in the decade from roughly 1714 to 1724, when Defoe stopped serving primarily as a political writer and secret agent for the Tory Ministry and Robert Harley, and wrote his major works of fiction.

The death of Queen Anne in August 1714 brought about changes that were to mark not only the end of a reign but also the end of an era. "The division between Whig and Tory," according to Leslie Stephen, "corresponded mainly to the Church and squirearchy and those who inclined towards the mercantile and dissenting sects." It is very important, therefore, that from 1714 onward the Whigs were in undisputed control of the affairs of England, a political dynasty that was to last until 1760. To insure their complete victory in March 1715, when the new Parliament met, the Whig Ministry impeached the powerful leaders of the Tory party (Oxford, Bolingbroke, Strafford, and Ormonde) for their hand in the Treaty of Utrecht. This political stratagem successfully broke any Tory opposition and secured a complete hold for the Whigs: Bolingbroke and Ormonde fled to France; Oxford was confined to the Tower for two years; and when Strafford was deemed of no consequence, the charges against him finally were dropped.[1]

The Whig government was favorably disposed to trade and to the dissenting sects which, in large part, carried on the nation's business; it was a time of encouragement to business and of toleration of minority groups. This new political climate augured well for Defoe and his middle class. When analyzing the composition of English society in terms of religious and economic interests, Defoe had recorded the following observations in his *Review* for 1710:

Those that have made calculations of the proportion of numbers, between the *Dissenters* and the *Church,* in *England,* (as to people) tell us, the *Dissenters* are not above one to eleven, or one to twelve. And I'll not dispute it with them . . . But I return upon them, calculate the trading, merchandizing, manufacturing, and shopkeeping part of *England,* and the *Dissenters* take one place with another, are at least a half, but take in the *Whig* in general, which includes those who . . . make one interest with the *Dissenter,* they will make the whole be in trade above eight parts of ten through the whole nation.[2]

Now the "trading, merchandizing, manufacturing, and shopkeeping" elements of England, predominantly dissenting in background, were at last favored with a Whig government basically in sympathy with their mercantile interests and their social ambitions.

The mighty merchants of the preceding generation, the men Defoe had tried to emulate during his career as a London merchant, were now affluent and prominent enough as a group to form an "aristocracy of wealth"; but they gravitated, significantly, not to the Court, which they saw was monopolized by the aristocracy, but to the government, by which maneuver they hoped to consolidate and enhance their position politically as well as economically. These men were now dominating the commercial world of London and living in as lavish a style as any members of the gentry. J. H. Plumb summarizes, "They owned blocks of London property; they dabbled in mortgages; they spread their money in land; whenever there was gain or security for money, they were investors and buyers." And while these merchants were adding to their fortunes and power in London, many of the landed gentry were being hard pressed to maintain their extravagant manner of living. To continue their lavish spending meant to risk mortgage and heavy debts, possibly even bankruptcy, to all but the vastly wealthy members of their class. A country estate gave only a set annual income; it was geared to an agrarian economy that was being challenged with growing vigor by the commercial classes. Faced by pressing financial problems, the old landed families increasingly were forced to have their sons marry merchants' daughters and their younger sons enter a trade.[3]

The early years of the century thus saw a continued interchange between members of the upper and middle classes. A telling illustration of this important shift in society is to be found in *Angliae Notitia; or, the Present State of England,* a perennially popular handbook by Edward Chamberlayne which went through numerous editions, with revisions, from 1669 until the middle of the eighteenth century. Chamberlayne was born a gentleman, educated at Oxford, a member of the Church of England, and a stickler for social distinctions. The edition for 1692 contains a strong denunciation of what Chamberlayne considered an alarming practice:

The English nobility and gentry till within late years judged it a stain and diminution to the honour and dignity of their families to seek their children's support by shopkeeping . . . which marks of slavery considered, herald's are of opinion that a gentleman thereby loseth his gentility forever, till he can otherwise recover it.

And yet to the shame of our nation, we have seen of late not only the sons of baronets, knights, and gentlemen sitting in the shops, and sometimes of peddling trades, far more fit for women and their daughters, but also an earl of this kingdom subjecting his son to an apprentisage and trade; but the folly of the English in swerving from their ancestors herein (and in other things) is now apparent; for those young gentlemen possessing more noble and active spirits could not brook such dull slavish lives, and being thereby unfitted for other employments have generally taken to debauched courses.

Chamberlayne was, of course, writing as a gentleman in this passage. He could not comprehend how members of the English nobility and gentry could bring such dishonor to themselves and to their station by this deplorable practice of apprenticing their sons to a trade. He even tried to intimidate his readers with the instructive lesson he found in this malpractice: the sons lead debauched lives because their fathers did violence to their "noble" spirits in setting them in trade — as if the eldest sons led less debauched lives. Chamberlayne's account, with its distortions and inaccuracies, is a passionately partisan commentary.

Curiously enough, however, both the tone and the substance of Chamberlayne's commentary were radically altered in the edition of 1700, when the paragraph quoted was deleted and only the following remark printed in its stead: "Guillum is of the opinion, that if a gentleman be bound an apprentice to a merchant, or other trader, he hath not thereby lost his degree of gentility." It is a grudging concession, as one readily infers, but certainly a significant one.

Chamberlayne died in 1703, the year Defoe was pilloried and imprisoned in Newgate; but in 1704 the work of revising the *Angliae Notitia* was carried on by the author's son John. The younger Chamberlayne, unlike his traditionalist father, was a man well attuned to his age; he was a Fellow of the Royal Society, and through his official connections with Queen Anne's Bounty Commission and the Society for the Propagation of Christian Knowledge, he became acquainted with the Whigs, Dissenters, and merchants whom his father never deigned to know. It is not surprising, therefore, that the revised edition of the handbook for 1707 adopted a more contemporary tone toward the matters of trade and gentility: "Amongst the commons of England . . . are reckoned tradesmen, among whom merchants in foreign traffic, have, for their great benefit to the public, and for their endowments and generous living, been of best repute in England; where . . . to become a merchant of foreign commerce, hath been allowed no disparagement to a gentleman born, especially to a younger brother." England was entirely unique in the high esteem with which it came to regard trade at this time. No other country in all Europe, not even Ireland, considered trade as a profession appropriate for a gentleman. In the early eighteenth century a new society was being shaped: as Defoe had long maintained, England was emerging as *"a trading nation,"* and the tone of young Chamberlayne is suited to this changing society. He even alerted his readers in the preface to his revised volume, "I have taken care to adjust it exactly to the present time." [4]

England was growing in wealth and in population. A useful index to the increase in wealth and productivity during this period following 1714 is seen in the figures for the Custom House, which show a steady rise in the value of goods imported and exported: £5,792,422 (imports) and £7,696,573 (exports) for 1714; by 1760 these figures had nearly doubled, notably the exports. The times were prosperous and the balance of trade favorable. English tonnage also was rising sharply all this time, from 421,432 tons in 1714 to 609,798 by the middle of the century. The gains in productivity and shipping were also evident in population. The population of England and Wales at the start of the century stood about 6,000,000 and by 1760 it had grown to some 7,000,000, the chief increases coming in the class of "manufacturers" and their families, whose "number, wealth, and importance," according to M. Dorothy George, "was a new development." [5]

This growth of trade and population was most distinctly felt in London, now more than ever the financial center of the British empire. London added seven new parishes to accommodate the influx of new citizens and the general growth of the city between the start of the century and the accession of George III, with most of the building coming right after the Treaty of Utrecht and the accession of George I. Even a Londoner like Defoe could not restrain his amazement at all the new buildings and squares that were erected in the decade preceding the publication of his *Tour,* wherein he wrote: "It is . . . singular to those who write in this age, and very much to our advantage in writing, that the great and more eminent increase of buildings, in and about the city of London, and the vast extent of ground taken in, and now become streets and noble squares of houses, by which the mass, or body of the whole, is become so infinitely great, has been generally made in our time, not only within our memory, but even within a few years." For the rising people of the business world, London was a booming metropolis in which to live and make money.

The effect of all this commercial reorganization in the early years of the century resulted in another important change in London. The historic city companies, like the Butchers Company to which Defoe belonged, were being superseded in power and influence by the burgeoning stock companies, like the East India Company, the African Company, and the South Sea Company, which encouraged investors, small and large, to try their capital in speculation. Stock speculation provided the readiest means to quick ascent in social and economic fortune — or even quicker descent.

The occasion of the South Sea Bubble in 1720 gave rise to countless witty expressions on this speculative fever raging in London and its repercussions on the social scene. In an anonymous farce of 1720, for example, entitled appropriately *Exchange Alley: Or, The Stock-Jobber Turned Gentleman,* a lady asks a gentleman, "How long have you been a Gentleman," to which he retorts, "About a week, Madam." [6]

Defoe, who was a frequent writer on the subject of "stock jobbing," watched these developments with keen interest:

Here are the South Sea Company, the East India Company, the Bank, the African Company, &c. whose stocks support that prodigious paper commerce, called Stock-Jobbing . . . and some have said, that there is not less than a hundred millions of stock transferred forward or backward from one hand to another every year, and this is one thing which makes such a constant daily intercourse between the Court part of the town and the city; and this is given as one of the principal causes of the prodigious conflux of the nobility and gentry from all parts of England to London, more than ever in former years, viz. That many thousands of families are so deeply concerned in those stocks, and find it so absolutely necessary to be at hand to take advantage of buying and selling, as the sudden rise or fall of the price directs, and the loss they often sustain by their ignorance of things when absent . . . they find themselves obliged to come up and live constantly here, or at least, most of the year.

Thus the growth of the joint stock companies and the growth of London supported each other: as London became more and more the financial center of all England, London grew bigger and more fashionable.[7]

In many ways the most important result of this stepped up activity and expansion was the rise into national prominence of a class variously termed "the middle class," "the middle sort," or "the middle ranks." Whatever the phrase applied to this "middle" group, they were always easily recognizable by their efforts to improve themselves in this dynamic society. The members of this great and growing middle class were the "trading, merchandizing, manufacturing, and shop-keeping" elements, who came from dissenting backgrounds in large part, for whom Defoe most consistently wrote, and with whose interests and ambitions he most closely identified. This commercial middle class was largely centered in London.

The wealth accruing to England from her overseas empire as well as the commercial reorganization evident throughout this period meant that the real wealth of England lay no longer in her lands so much as in her financial operations headquartered in London, where now even the landed nobility and gentry, as Defoe noted, came to invest their funds and watch their speculative stocks. Naturally, among those who profited most handsomely from this altered economic structure were the members of the middle class. "Without doubt the outstanding feature of this period," J. B. Botsford writes of the shifting structure of English society in the early eighteenth century, "was the rapid increase in wealth, or more exactly, the phenomenal growth of individual fortunes. Simultaneous with it was the rise of the middle class, membership of which embraced the many thousands who took advantage of opportunities offered in various fields of endeavour." The opportunities in trade and finance were open to all, and those most eager to maximize upon them were naturally the members of the middle class, who sought to improve their lot by rising to a more preferred position in the social scale.[8]

Contemporary literature reflected these shifting patterns in society. When Addison and Steele in their second *Spectator* paper first introduced to their readers the members of the Club, they included not only Sir Roger de Coverley, a gentleman of ancient descent and a baronet, but also Sir Andrew Freeport, "a merchant of great eminence in the city of London." In Sir Andrew we see portrayed a new kind of literary character worthy of respect; in fact, Steele depicts him as a contemporary hero of England's new glory: "A person of indefatigable industry, strong reason, and great experience," of whom one can say, "a general trader of good sense is pleasanter company than a general scholar." This in 1711.

By 1720, when Steele was engaged in writing *The Theatre*, a twice-weekly paper in half-sheets which was to be his last periodical enterprise, he mirrored the Whig ideal of the great merchant-trader, the kind of man Defoe had hoped to become when he began his career in the London of the 1680's. Steele was a staunch Whig who supported the mercantilist policy of the government, and he now tried to offer his readers a prototype of the merchant:

He is a true pattern of that kind of gentry, which has arose in the world this last century: I mean the great and rich families of merchants, and eminent traders, who in their furniture, their equipage, their manner of living, and especially their economy, are so far from below the gentry, that many of them are now the best representatives of the ancient ones, and deserve the imitation of the modern nobility . . . He is a man that does business with the candour of a gentleman, and performs his engagements with the exactness of a citizen.

Whatever their personal differences, Defoe and Steele certainly concurred on the honor and glory owed the merchant and trading classes, particularly those members of these classes who had been preeminently successful. Steele's comments about this "third gentry" reveal the extent to which society had changed by 1720, not the least because of the mercantilist policy of the new Whig government.

Steele wrote himself a memorandum about the play he was working on at the time he published this particular number of *The Theatre*. He wanted to be sure that his character Sir John Edgar — later to become Sir John Bevil — would be "enlivened with a secret vanity about family" and his wife would "have the same sort of pride, rejoicing in her high blood." Steele, like Defoe, was obviously sensitive to the disdain of pedigreed families among the gentry toward the "third gentry," and he made it a point to air this matter in the open and upon the English stage. In 1722 his play finally appeared on the boards as *The Conscious Lovers*, and in the words of Mr. Sealand, a powerful East India merchant, to Sir John Bevil, a member of the ancient landed gentry, we witness the dramatic confrontation of the old order of English society and the new order:

Sir John Bevil: Give me leave, however, Mr. Sealand, as we are upon a treaty for uniting our families, to mention only the business of an ancient house. Genealogy and descent are to be of some consideration in an affair of this sort.

Mr. Sealand: Genealogy and descent! . . .

. . . .

Sir John Bevil: Oh, sir, your servant! you are laughing at my laying any stress upon descent; but I must tell you, sir, I never knew anyone but he that wanted that advantage turn it into ridicule.

Mr. Sealand: And I never knew any one who had many better advantages put that into his account. — But, Sir John, value yourself as you please upon your ancient house, I am to talk freely of everything you are pleased to put into your bill of rates on this occasion; yet, sir, I have made no objections to your son's family. 'Tis his morals that I doubt.

Sir John Bevil: Sir, I can't help saying, that what might injure a citizen's credit may be no stain to a gentleman's honour.

. . . .

Mr. Sealand: Sir, as much as cit as you take me for, I know the town and the world; and give me leave to say, that we merchants are a species of gentry that have grown into the world this last century, and are as honourable, and almost as useful, as you landed folks, that have always thought yourselves so much above us; for your trading, forsooth, is extended no farther than a load of hay or a fat ox. You are pleasant people, indeed, because you are generally bred up to be lazy; therefore, I warrant you, industry is dishonourable.   (IV, ii)

As Fielding later had Parson Adams remark, this sort of passage is as good as a sermon. As a public declaration of social equality by a powerful new class of established merchants and traders, however, it is forceful and assured; and the resounding success of the play from 1722 on attests further to the favorable reception such a new attitude had with the playgoers of the time. The Whig espousal of the mercantile middle class is clear from Steele's propagandistic interpolation in this play. It is worth noting that the original title Steele chose for his play was *The Fine Gentleman*, but since it highlighted the didactic intent at the expense of the primary plot, Steele advisedly changed it to *The Conscious Lovers*.[9]

Not only the literature, but the literary life of London was changing in this period. The luster of the reign of Queen Anne was in no small part owing to the polite and fashionable literary world of coffee-houses and clubs. After the accession of George I and the installation of the Whig Ministry, the coffee-houses and clubs went into a marked decline that helped to speed the downfall of the powerful system of political patronage for men of letters. After 1714 the booksellers began to supersede the patron. A poet of rare talents like Pope could command a pre-publication subscription of £5,320 4s. for his translation of the *Iliad* and thereby be assured of an independent income. In fact, Pope's translations of Homer netted him about £9,000, and he could boast: "But (thanks to *Homer*) since I live and thrive,/ Indebted to no Prince or Peer alive." Alexandre Beljame, in his invaluable study of the relationship between men of letters and the reading public in the late seventeenth and early eighteenth centuries, interpreted Pope's dedication of his *Iliad* in 1720 as "a very important landmark in the history of English literature"; its impact was "nothing less than revolutionary," for in dedicating his work to a fellow author, Congreve, "Pope shattered at a blow the long tradition of self-seeking dedications, whether political or personal." Although Pope's grand gesture may indeed be viewed as a formal declaration of independence from the patronage system, the breakdown of that system had been in process for some time. Beljame rightly argues that men of letters prior to 1688 were slavishly dependent on the personal caprice of Court patronage; after the Revolution political patronage grew in importance, reaching a peak in the reign of Queen Anne, when most authors aligned themselves either with the Whigs or Tories. Addison and Steele, largely through the success of the *Tatler* and *Spectator* enterprises, are credited with creating a public for literature. After 1714 patronage no longer monopolized the world of letters. Under Robert Walpole's administration it became virtually extinct, both George I and George II having little interest in literature and Walpole being disinclined to encourage patronage as had his predecessors in the office of prime minister.[10]

Although the broad outlines of Beljame's study are accurate, he fails to consider adequately the significance of the emerging middle class in the creation of this new reading public. The void left by the patronage system was filled by the booksellers, men like Tonson, Dodsley, Taylor, and Lintot, who arose as the vital middle-men between author and reader. These men were attuned to the tastes and reading needs of their times, and they enabled the writers to find an audience in large enough numbers for their works to make writing profitable and attractive. Previously, an author had sought to flatter a wealthy or powerful patron, which meant he wrote for a cultivated taste common only to a small coterie of aristocrats and wits. Now, the situation was significantly reversed. The public rather than the patron determined the kind of literature it wanted. Men like Defoe now no longer had to seek a wealthy patron like Halifax; they could instead address themselves directly to an audience they knew at first hand. Defoe was himself a long-standing author and a middle-class tradesman whose contacts included both the new booksellers and the new audience of book-buyers; he was supremely suited to know what they wanted and to supply it.[11]

In displacing the patronage system of support to authors, the booksellers scored a major triumph in the literary life of England. They liberated the author from politics; so much of the patronage under Queen Anne was ultimately political. After 1714 writing became increasingly a big business, and by 1725 Defoe could write in *Applebee's Journal*: "Writing, you know, Mr. Applebee, is become a very considerable branch of the English commerce; composing, inventing, translating, versifying, &c., are the several manufactures which supply this commerce. The booksellers are the master manufacturers or employers. The several writers, authors, copyers, sub-writers, and all other operators with pen and ink, are the workmen employed by the said manufacturers, in the forming, dressing, and finishing the said manufactures." The citizen of London, whether an aspiring trader or an established merchant of Mr. Sealand's class, was making his presence felt on the literary scene. He wanted books to read, both for himself and for his family. He had, according to Bonamy Dobrée, "grown to be the main patron of literature." His impact was that great. The fears of Pope and his fellow members of the classical school were not without foundation when the *Dunciad* came to be composed; a revolution in literary taste was indeed being effected in the early decades of the century. If the aristocracy and refined readers favored poetry and classical models, the unsophisticated middle-class readers were naturally inclined toward prose, and unadorned prose at that. If the heroic couplet was the vogue around 1700, the novel was to become established as the new vogue by about 1750. The rise of the novel, more than anything else, was to be a middle-class literary triumph.[12]

With this as a general background to Defoe's new writing activities after 1715, we may now consider briefly the kind of audience Defoe had in mind when writing his religious and fictitious books. Leslie Stephen characterized the difference between Defoe and Pope simply by saying that Pope represented "the aristocratic development of literature," and Defoe "the purely plebeian." Charles Lamb also saw Defoe as addressing his works, by his "plain and homely" idiom, to "the lower conditions of readers"; he further described Defoe's novels as "capital kitchen reading." Such designations as "plebeian" or "lower conditions of readers," while suggestive, are not very precise, and we might well examine how relevant they are to Defoe's time and his works.

It undoubtedly is true that the early years of the century saw new readers coming from the lower ranks of society. We know that the Society for the Propagation of Christian Knowledge (or SPCK) did much to promote literacy among the poor folk of England who otherwise would not have received the barest education. By 1723 there were 1,329 charity schools founded in England by the SPCK, and the heaviest concentration and best-run of these schools were in London, "where the subscribers, being people of substance, not only provided adequate funds to pay for the buildings and teachers, but in some cases clothed the children and started them in life as apprentices to a trade." Although the curriculum was austere, with heavy doses of religious instruction, it did offer reading, writing, and some arithmetic. Education at the charity schools was designed to uphold class distinctions; the age was cautious in not educating a child beyond his station in life. But the important point is that these schools, particularly the better ones in London, did teach some of the poor to read, and through them others of their class could come to know what was in books that were written simply. We get a good glimpse at this situation from Charles Leslie, who wrote in his *Rehearsal* that "the greatest part of the *people* do not read *books;* most of them cannot *read* at all, but they will gather about one that can *read,* and listen to an *Observator* or *Review* (as I have seen them in the streets)." If such people could gather around one of their literate fellows in the street to hear read the words of Mr. Review, they could as well gather in the kitchen to read and hear the words of Defoe in his works of fiction. And so they apparently did, as an epigram in the *Flying Post* for 1729 indicates: "Down in the kitchen, honest Dick and Doll/Are studying Colonel Jack and Flanders Moll." Defoe's prose fiction, then, was "capital kitchen reading," as Charles Lamb suggested, and the "lower conditions of readers" found it so. Even Charles Gildon in his attack on *Robinson Crusoe* in late 1719 had to allow that "there is not an old woman that can go to the price of it, but buys thy Life and Adventures, and leaves it as a legacy, with the *Pilgrim's Progress,* the *Practice of Piety,* and *God's Revenge against Murther,* to her posterity." [13]

But what about the middle-class readers? In the *Review* of 1709 Defoe wrote of seven distinguishable classes of people in England:

1. The great, who live profusely.
2. The rich, who live plentifully.
3. The middle sort, who live well.
4. The working trades, who labour hard, but feel no want.
5. The country people, farmers, &c. who fare indifferently.
6. The poor, that fare hard.
7. The miserable, that really pinch and suffer want.

In elaborating on "the middle sort of people," Defoe estimated that they "live the best," "consume the most of any in the nation," and "are the most numerous," accounting also for "the general wealth of this nation." This middle class was composed of those "trading, merchandizing, manufacturing, and shopkeeping" families whose commercial success afforded them the means, as Defoe described, to "live well," which meant that they enjoyed some leisure in their family life and possessed the money to pursue their interests. In a word, they could now buy books and build up personal libraries. These books in the home also would be accessible to the favored servants and apprentices, who might even be encouraged by their masters to peruse some of the books in their spare time; for being largely of dissenting background, these people valued instruction in matters relating to religion and conduct. This background to the age helps us to understand the enormous popularity of a work like Defoe's *Family Instructor*, and why the single best-selling category of books in the eighteenth century remained, as in the past, books on religious subjects, of which no less than two hundred were published annually throughout the century.[14]

This middle class of readers, however, brought secular as well as religious tastes to bear on the literary market place of the early eighteenth century. They wanted to see themselves portrayed in works of literature; they wanted to identify with people of their own class, to share common problems and experiences, and to learn about matters of moment to their private lives. Leslie Stephen summed up as one of the most notable events in the history of English literature between 1714 and 1739 "the development of a new class of readers, who won't bother about canons of taste or care for skill in working upon the old conventional methods, but can be profoundly interested in a straightforward narrative adapted to the simplest understandings." What this shift heralded was no less revolutionary than the challenge of a new and assertive middle-class culture to the entrenched supremacy of the classical school of upper-class culture. And as the middle class began to buy and read books in growing numbers, it became all too clear to the writers of the classical school like Pope and Swift that their culture was being threatened by this new class of readers who read what they liked, not what they were taught to admire and to imitate; these people neither knew nor cared about Aristotle or Boileau or "the ancients."

This middle class of readers was not to be intimidated by the contempt showered upon them by the arbiters of taste of the classical school; they were anxious to develop and understand their own ideals and culture. Yet if they eschewed any imitation of the literary "rules" and tastes of their betters, they showed themselves more than eager to ape the patterns of gentility of their betters. The middle-class culture became derivative not literarily but socially, and this concern was reflected in the literature of the middle class. In her discussion of the effect of the middle-class reader on the novel, Helen S. Hughes finds, "To make a gentleman out of a prosperous Dissenting shopkeeper was, therefore, one of the serious undertakings of the period, and one variously reflected in literature." [15]

An interest in how to become a gentleman (or gentlewoman) is the natural outgrowth of wealth and leisure in any society. The members of the prominent families among the "trading, merchandizing, manufacturing, and shop-keeping" class wanted to assume their rightful positions in the structure of society; they sought instruction and entertainment from people who appreciated their needs and their backgrounds. Such a person was Daniel Defoe, whose own background was that of a Dissenter and a merchant-trader, and who in his own career, however chaotic its course, managed at three different times to establish himself and his family in the manner of gentlefolk, and between 1703 and 1706 even managed to adopt a coat of arms. Defoe believed in the mighty world of trade in which the middle class operated and prospered. He, more than any other writer of the time, was their man.

By 1719 Defoe was long since settled in his comfortable suburban house in Stoke Newington. He was busy as ever with his pen, but his life now had taken on a comfort he had not known for fifteen years, since before the ruin of his pantile works in Tilbury. His religious books were selling very well; he was securely employed by the Whig government. But, most important, he could now regard himself as a man of some social standing in his community. Living in retirement from London, he was now "Daniel De Foe, of Stoke Newington in the County of Midx. Gent.," as he designated himself in a legal document of 1719 transferring some of his stock in the South Sea Company.[16] He now had the security and leisure, relatively speaking, to reflect on his life, and the fruits of these reflections he could put to use in publishing works of interest to the new class of readers who had made of his *Family Instructor* such a success. He had lived almost three score years and had much to relate. The time and the man were right for the novel to come into being as the unique literary form of middle-class expression.

Chapter 6. Major Middle-Class Themes

The novel is that form of literary expression which belongs to the middle class, and is the only one which that class created. It did not, and doubtless could not, come into existence until the middle class had so increased in importance that it demanded a means of projecting into imaginary realms its own conception of the morals and meaning of the world. — "Moll Flanders' Way," *The Collected Essays of John Peale Bishop,* ed. Edmund Wilson (New York, 1948), p. 50

On April 23, 1719, Defoe's publisher, William Taylor, registered *The Life and Strange Surprising Adventures of Robinson Crusoe* at the Stationers' Hall, and two days later the work was published, marking the beginning of Defoe's brief career as a writer of prose fiction. On February 29, 1724, *The Fortunate Mistress* was published, a work that Defoe could not bring himself to finish. How Defoe suddenly came to write novels when almost sixty years of age, and why he abruptly stopped writing them less than five years later, no one really knows.

We do know, however, that in so turning his hand to fiction in 1719 Defoe is generally regarded as the father of the English novel. We also know that the novel proved an instantaneous and popular success with the reading public. New editions of *Robinson Crusoe* were called for in May, June, and August following publication, and by August the prolific pen of Defoe was ready to satisfy the demands of the public with a second volume. In writing about the career of Robinson Crusoe, Defoe knew he had happened upon something of importance both to himself and to his middle-class readers. How he developed and gave expression to the theme of gentility in his major works of fiction during this intensely creative period from 1719 to 1724, and how the gentility theme was integral to other major middle-class themes, indicates the central importance he attached to it.

The heroes and heroines of Defoe's fiction are not common to any one stratum of society. At one extreme of the social scale Defoe depicted a Moll Flanders born in Newgate, whose father was unknown and whose mother, a convicted felon, saved her life when she "pleaded her belly." At the other extreme was a Colonel Jacque, whose father was "a man of quality" and whose mother was "a gentlewoman." Between these extremes of low and high birth, he offered his readers characters born in the middle state of life: men like Robinson Crusoe, whose father "got a good estate by merchandise" and whose mother came of "a very good family"; or women like Roxana, whose father and mother were "people of better fashion" and "lived in very good circumstances." Even the obscure beginnings of a pirate like Captain Singleton show him to have originated from a comfortable middle-class home, for he was as a child "very well dressed" and had a nursery maid to attend him. Thus, of five protagonists in the five novels of the period, Defoe portrayed three as deriving from the middle class, one from the upper class, and one from the lower class: the range is not without its significance.

Defoe regarded birth as irrelevant to the kind of individual one became in society. The rights of primogeniture, to be sure, transferred a title and an estate, but these did not make a gentleman of the eldest sons of the nobility and gentry in Defoe's eyes. These sons he saw all too often grow up into ignorant, idle, swearing, whoring, drunken profligates. Surely their gentle birth did nothing to make them act like gentlemen. What really mattered to Defoe was the environment in which a person was raised, how his natural abilities were developed, whom he learned to emulate, and how and what he was taught. Birth could determine initial social standing and heredity could determine things like beauty or parts, but environment and breeding were what molded the true qualities and values of a person.

When judged by the conditions of their birth, Defoe's characters are representative of all the different social classes. What they all share, however, as a result of what befalls them early in life, is an ambition to better themselves and their fortunes and so move to a more preferred position in the social hierarchy, and in this common attitude they are all middle class. Defoe purposely reduced to insignificance not only the matter of birth but also the question of ancestry. Both birth and ancestry were sources of pride to the vainglorious gentry and nobility, and Defoe had all his life written about how unfounded and vain such pretensions were in England of all countries. Now in his fiction he continued to present his views on the irrelevance of both birth and ancestry to true gentility.

What use Defoe made of ancestry was consonant with the position he expounded in *The True-Born Englishman*. When Defoe defended the foreign birth of his beloved King William, he defended as well the foreign birth of his own ancestors, who on his father's side originated from Flemish stock. In *Robinson Crusoe*, for example, we notice that Crusoe's father is not English-born but a German ("a foreigner of Bremen") named Kreutznaer, whose name in time became Anglicized to Crusoe — the way Foe in time undoubtedly became Anglicized from Foo or some other Flemish original. It is instructive to keep in mind that Crusoe, whom generations of critics have hailed as the prototype of the true-born Englishman, is indeed but a first generation Englishman on his father's side, whose very name is not Anglo-Saxon but bastardized German. In the character of Roxana, Defoe created a French-born heroine whose parents were business people who fled to England in the seventeenth century to escape religious persecution. Defoe always wrote with the highest regard for the industry and value of these European immigrants to England; they contributed to the greatness and overall prosperity of the nation. To him, a Dutch-born King William or a French-born weaver in Spitalfields was as "true-born" an Englishman as those vain members of the gentry and nobility who puffed themselves up with pride over their Anglo-Saxon or Norman ancestry. In the England of Defoe's fiction, as in his other writings, birth and ancestry counted for little or nothing in determining one's right to be called a true English gentleman; more basic considerations like breeding and wealth were what really mattered. In this position he naturally mirrored the social ambitions of himself and his middle class of readers.

Since they are all middle-class individualists, "all Defoe's heroes," as Ian Watt notes, "pursue money"; in fact, they can be seen as "an embodiment of economic individualism." Their attitude toward money is that of tradesmen, an attitude as appreciated by Defoe's middle-class readers as it was by himself. In the *Review* he was forever reminding his readers that "the great medium of trade is what I call money" or "in the *language of trade,* money is the *alphabet* that forms the sound; all labour is valued in it, paid by it, rated, and bargain'd for under its title." It is easy to see how economists, political theorists, sociologists, and literary critics have fastened upon Defoe's fictional creations as the classic examples in literature of *homo economicus.* As David Riesman has observed, in *Robinson Crusoe* "the motive of economic self-sufficiency is expressed in its classical paradigm." Defoe's characters conform to the formula by their steadfast pursuit of money and by their inevitable evaluation of everything by its golden standard.[1] But such an interpretation cannot be applied too rigidly to Defoe's fiction. His characters, for all their pursuit of money, are unique in their *nouveau riche* point of view, which they owe to their creator; they do not worship wealth for its own sake but are fascinated by it because of the style of life they know it can buy in the fluid society of the late seventeenth and early eighteenth centuries, hence their keen interest in such details as fine clothes, gorgeous equipages, liveried servants, handsome houses. Defoe's characters, in short, do not pursue wealth so much as they pursue gentility, which they know wealth can buy them.

We already perceive in the pages of Defoe's novels the ambiguity of his dissenting society and of himself toward money. The Protestant Ethic and Luther's concept of the *Beruf,* or calling, which was a fundamental dogma in Protestant denominations and provided the impetus to capitalism, regarded the consuming duty of the individual to be his salvation through the dogged pursuit of his calling. "Wealth," according to Max Weber, "is thus bad ethically only in so far as it is a temptation to idleness and sinful enjoyment of life, and its acquisition is bad only when it is with the purpose of later living merrily and without care." The old-style Puritans preached and practiced a fundamentally ascetic life of work and prayer, "and the parvenu ostentation of the *nouveau riche* . . . [was] detestable to asceticism" and, therefore, to the Puritan community. The most important point about the "idea of the calling," in the finding of Max Weber, is that it "was born . . . from the spirit of Christian asceticism." [2] Whereas Defoe's strenuously didactic works, like *The Family Instructor* or *Religious Courtship,* reflect this basically ascetic approach of the old-style Puritan way of life, his novels reveal a different approach entirely. Although still bearing the marks of the Protestant Ethic in their pursuit of wealth, Defoe's characters also bear the contemporary signs of the pursuit of pleasure, even luxury. The traditional concept of the calling and the respect for one's station in life were being neglected by Defoe's time.

The gradual emergence of the modern business world toward the end of the seventeenth century, and the countless new opportunities for acquiring wealth it ushered in, undermined the foundations of the old-style Puritan way of life. If the primary pursuit was to be money, as it was in Defoe's heroes and heroines, then it was inevitably done at the expense of one's calling, both secularly and spiritually; for the Puritan was not expected to earn his salvation *in vocatione* but *per vocatione*. "The calling," according to R. H. Tawney, "is not a condition in which the individual is born, but a strenuous and exacting enterprise, to be undertaken, indeed, under the guidance of Providence, but to be chosen by each man for himself, with a deep sense of his solemn responsibilities." [3]

Defoe presents us in *Robinson Crusoe* with an excellent example of this conflict between the old order of Puritan values and the contemporary acquisitive unrest of the new generation. Crusoe's father counsels his son on the accepted wisdom of the "middle state," which would insure his being "well introduced" into business with every prospect of raising his fortunes gradually yet surely "by application and industry":

He told me it was for men of desperate fortunes on one hand, or of aspiring, superior fortunes on the other, who went abroad upon adventures, to rise by enterprise, and make themselves famous in undertakings of a nature out of the common road; that these things were all either too far above me, or too far below me; that mine was the middle state . . . not exposed to the miseries and hardships, the labour and sufferings, of the mechanic part of mankind, and not embarrassed with the pride, luxury, ambition, and envy of the upper part of mankind.[4]

This sermon on the middle state delivered by Crusoe's father is the discharge of an important parental duty in the Puritan home; Crusoe's father is here trying to caution his son on the choice of his calling and to reconcile him to "the station of life

[he] was born in" (I, 4).[5] Yet Crusoe is young (his father even presses him "not to play the young man" — I, 4) while his father is old ("My father, who was very ancient" and "confined by the gout" — I, 2). This opposition between the old and new generations, if we follow the chronology of the novel, takes place in the mid-seventeenth century (Crusoe was born in 1632), but actually Defoe dramatizes a phenomenon drawn more from his own generation and his own experience. For what Defoe suggests in the opposition between the orthodox Puritan attitude of Crusoe *père* and the radical adventuring spirit of Crusoe *fils* is the sharp shift in values he witnessed among his fellow Dissenters — and, indeed, himself practiced — in the heady mercantile society stemming from the 1680's.

Defoe gambled for high stakes when he gave up a ministerial career and turned merchant in the London of the 1680's. He was not content to learn a skilled trade or tend a shop, as was usual in the preceding generation, and as his father had done before him; he chose the more risky and adventurous path of a merchant-trader, an ambitious beginning that took him traveling, introduced him to fine company, and in a short time saw him prospering handily. When he did fail, his losses amounted to £17,000. Defoe underscores the basic difference between Crusoe *père* and *fils* in their approach to their callings by having young Crusoe set sail on his first voyage from Hull, the very town where his father had made his fortune by "merchandise" a generation before as a middle way trader. The world of young Crusoe, like the world of young Defoe, is a new and challenging world; the old and sure steps to success no longer are as attractive in the face of new and bold opportunities for making quick fortunes. Defoe apparently appreciated the parallel between his early business career and that of his protagonist because he has young Crusoe reflect shortly before the disastrous voyage that was to "shipwreck" him and his fortunes: "And now, increasing in business and in wealth, my head began to be full of projects and undertakings beyond my reach, such as are, indeed, often the ruin of the best heads in business" (I, 40). The cause of Defoe's own "shipwreck" of his fortunes in 1692 was precisely this kind of overreaching.

The central significance of money in Defoe's novels is to be seen as a reflection of the values of his society, especially the readers for whom he writes. On his last trip to the wreck of the ship to salvage what he can use for his existence on the island, Crusoe comes upon a locker containing "about thirty-six pounds value in money": "I smiled to myself at the sight of this money. 'O drug!' said I aloud, 'what art thou good for? Thou art not worth to me, no, not the taking off of the ground; one of those knives is worth all this heap. I have no manner of use for thee; even remain where thou art, and go to the bottom as a creature whose life is not worth saving.' However, upon second thoughts, I took it away; and wrapping it in a piece of canvas, I began to think of making another raft" (I, 62). Coleridge esteemed this passage worthy of Shakespeare, yet the touch is supremely worthy of Defoe — and natural of Crusoe — because, as Bonamy Dobrée notes, "the 'second thoughts' suggest the whole structure of the society Crusoe has been formed by." What Defoe intended simply as an expostulation by Crusoe at the sight of the money, and a brief reflection on the irony of his find, becomes transformed into an apostrophe to Money ("O drug! . . . Thou"), as if Defoe suddenly became conscious of his audience observing Crusoe, hence the "second thoughts" and the renewed idea of "making another raft" in hopes of getting to spend this money.[6]

The very idea of ever leaving any money, even on a deserted island, was incomprehensible to Defoe and his middle- and lower-class readers. He makes it a point never to leave his readers in doubt about the presence of the money. He finds at least three more occasions in the story to allude to it, and so reassure his readers about it. On the island Crusoe reflects sagely how "the most covetous, griping miser in the world would have been cured of the vice of covetousness, if he had been in my case" (I, 143). But the very next thing we learn is that he still keeps his "parcel of money." What bothers him is that "the nasty, sorry, useless stuff" cannot be spent, and he lets it "lay in a drawer." Even after he has been on the island more than twenty-three long and lonely years, he cannot resist the temptation of removing yet more money from a Spanish wreck, despite his contrary reflections: "I had no manner of occasion for it; 'twas to me as the dirt under my feet" (I, 215). As if twenty-three years of solitude and contemplation were not enough to cure him of covetousness, Crusoe comments: "Well, however, I lugged this money home to my cave, and laid it up, as I had done that before which I brought from our own ship; but it was a great pity, as I said, that the other part of this ship had not come to my share, for I am satisfied I might have loaded my canoe several times over with money" (I, 215). Again, the "however" for Crusoe's contrary actions. Crusoe's attraction to money of any kind in any circumstance is as instinctive as the moth's attraction to any source of light. And Crusoe's fascination for wealth is inseparable from Defoe's. In passages like this Defoe had his eye on his readers, for whom money always had an immediacy since it could be converted in their imaginations into material things or social status, hence its significance in the novels, no matter how awkward the context in which it appears nor how inconsistent the behavior of the character dealing with it. In the end Defoe makes it all come right. When Crusoe finally leaves his island, he makes a special point of reassuring his readers: "I forgot not to take the money I formerly mentioned, which had lain by me for so long useless that it was grown rusty or tarnished . . . as also the money I found in the wreck of the Spanish ship" (I, 310). After twenty-eight years, two months, and nineteen days, Crusoe departs from his island home with his hoarded wealth intact: his foresight has paid off; the money no longer is "useless," and his readers can be relieved.

In Defoe's England wealth brought the possibility of purchasing an estate and even a title. The middle-class readers of Defoe's novels were eager to know about anything that mirrored their interests and ambitions, and it is natural that the matter of acquiring land should find its way into his fiction. A number of estates were sold to wealthy merchants and tradesmen at this time. But the number of middle-class families fortunate enough to secure such an estate and title, let alone amass the fortune necessary to make the purchase, was very limited. For most of them the prospect of an estate was only a fond dream; even so, the fact that some of their number had indeed purchased estates was enough to fire their imaginations.[7] Defoe was sensitive to these middle-class dreams; he shared them himself. *Robinson Crusoe*, accordingly, can be read not so much as an imaginary adventure story as an accurate reflection of a society's attitudes and values. Consider, for instance, how Defoe depicts Crusoe's existence on the island in terms relevant to his readers' social ambitions: "I descended a little on the side of that delicious vale, surveying it with a secret kind of pleasure, though mixed with my other afflicting thoughts, to think that this was all mine; that I was king and lord of all this country indefeasibly, and had a right of possession; and, if I could convey it, I might have it in inheritance as completely as any lord of a manor in England" (I, 110). Crusoe's baronial pleasure at the prospect of all this land as his to keep and pass on by right of inheritance was a thought equally appreciated by Defoe's readers, for whom there was certainly the same "secret kind of pleasure" at contemplating how grand it would be to possess such lands in England and live like any "lord of a manor"; and if not in England, where such thoughts only rarely could become realized, then in some far-off and exotic part of the world.

Defoe cannot forgo the natural temptation of speaking of Crusoe's island in the terminology of the landed gentry of his native England. Crusoe's place of habitation, appropriately, becomes his "estate." He even comes to fancy himself as absolute monarch of all he surveys. But more to the mark is Crusoe's description of his second plantation, on the other side of the island, as his "country seat" (I, 168). The metaphor of the "estate" obviously interested Defoe, for he never failed to refer to Crusoe's enterprises abroad in terms of this figure, whether on the island or in Brazil: "I was now master, all on a sudden, of above £5,000 sterling in money, and had an estate, as I might call it, in the Brazils of about a thousand pounds a year, as sure as an estate of lands in England" (I, 318). Defoe's prose betrays his self-consciousness about terming Crusoe's plantation an "estate," but the idea of having a plantation worth thousands of pounds was a delicious concept to contemplate, particulary when the overseas plantation was the equivalent of an English estate worth £1000 a year, a sum that elevated it to the upper level of landed estates in England (the lower level of country squires in the Age of Anne, for example, had estates worth about £300 a year).⁸ Crusoe's Brazilian "estate," furthermore, was a thriving enterprise, whereas a good number of the English estates of the gentry and nobility were mortgaged, debt-ridden, and run-down. Defoe knew the difference only too well, hence his delight in converting Crusoe's wealth and property into English terms and, undoubtedly, the equal delight of Defoe's readers in hearing about such singular successes possible overseas.

Defoe's interest in places overseas involved something much more relevant than the adventure and exoticism it introduced into his fiction. England was undergoing a period of colonial expansion in the seventeenth and eighteenth centuries, and Defoe was a vigorous exponent of colonization whose works of fiction advocated both the establishment of new colonies around the world and the increasing settlement of established colonies.[9] In such episodic adventure stories as *Captain Singleton* and *A New Voyage Round the World,* he hoped to excite the imagination of his readers to undertake voyages to distant and uncharted parts of the world in quest of land and riches, two commodities dearly sought after by any true-blooded Englishman but with a special appeal to the more adventurous members of the rising middle or lower classes who aspired to become affluent gentlemen. Whereas in times past the work of colonizing fell, as Crusoe's father reminds his son, to "men of desperate fortunes on one hand or of aspiring, superior fortunes on the other," the time now was ripe, in Defoe's judgment, for the men and women of "the middle state" to take a responsible part in this great national enterprise — as Crusoe himself does, eventually even setting up a "colony" on his island before returning home to England.

One of Defoe's personal heroes was Sir Walter Raleigh, a man whose life and exploits fascinated him. It is probably no coincidence that Defoe in 1719, the year *Robinson Crusoe* appeared, wrote *An Historical Account of the Voyages and Adventures of Sir Walter Raleigh*, a tract specifically designed to set forth the glories of Sir Walter's "discoveries and conquests" and to suggest to the South Sea Company in particular and to Englishmen in general how Guiana, which Raleigh had tried abortively to settle, "might now be with ease possess'd, planted and secur'd to the British nation, and what immense wealth and increase of commerce might be rais'd from thence." The colonial theme was very much on Defoe's mind throughout the fertile period of his fiction writing, and his pamphlet on Sir Walter Raleigh shows that it received expression from the very outset of this period.

The search for gold underlies most of the adventures of *Captain Singleton;* Defoe at one point even speaks of gold as "the make-bait of the world." [10] In *A New Voyage Round the World,* written in 1724, he carried forward and made even more explicit the colonizing ideas of *Robinson Crusoe* and *Captain Singleton;* in fact, the themes of adventure and travel aside, the book is a sustained piece of propaganda on colonization and the wealth accruing to England from her overseas settlements. Defoe, like Raleigh, seemed especially drawn to the possibilities of establishing colonies in South America. In the *New Voyage* he interpolated, for example, a special observation calculated to excite interest in colonizing parts of South America; it is entitled appropriately, *"An Observation concerning the Soil and Climate of the Continent of America, south of the River de la Plata, and how suitable to the genius, the constitution, and the manner of living of Englishmen, and consequently of an English colony."* [11] Whatever the technique employed by Defoe, whether a break in the narrative in which he addressed his readers directly or an oblique reference in context, he clearly was anxious to awaken in his audience an interest in the limitless opportunities for personal and national wealth through the adventures of colonization.

More specifically, however, Defoe employed the colonial theme as a means of showing his middle- and lower-class readers how they could better their fortunes, regardless of their ancestry or birth, through industry in the already established colonies in America, specifically Virginia and Maryland. In 1722 he made a conscious effort to encourage his readers to emigrate to the New World and make for themselves a new life there. Both the novels Defoe wrote that year, *Moll Flanders* and *Colonel Jacque,* use the colonial theme to dramatize that even convicted felons like Moll and her mother could get a second chance in the colonies and become affluent and socially prominent. Moll's mother tells her that the colonists can be divided roughly into two main sorts: those brought over by ship's masters to be sold as servants, like Colonel Jacque, and those felons transported to work the plantations, like Moll's mother — and later Moll herself. But the colonies are drawn by Defoe as a land of equal opportunity for all: "When they come here," according to Moll's mother, "we make no difference; the planters buy them, and they work together in the fields, till their time is out" [12] Under such an attractive scheme any person can make something of himself; as Moll's mother sums it up aptly, "many a Newgate-bird becomes a great man." In England it is a permanent stain to have been burnt in the hand; in Maryland or Virginia "some of the best men in the country are burnt in the hand, and they are not ashamed to own it" (I, 86). Given the picture of life in the colonies popularized by Defoe's fiction, it is little wonder that the Tory Dr. Johnson held so contemptuous an opinion of the American colonies: "Sir, they are a race of convicts, and ought to be thankful for anything we allow them short of hanging." [13]

Actually, Defoe's impression of the equal opportunities afforded even convicts in the American colonies had its grounding in historical fact; for at its third session the 1717 Parliament passed "an act . . . for the more effectual transportation of felons," which was to serve as the basis whereby convicted criminals were sent to the colonies in the eighteenth century. Since the last quarter of the seventeenth century the colonies of Virginia and Maryland had enacted statutes prohibiting the importation of convicts. Now in 1718 the flow of convict labor to these colonies began again, and convicted felons were spared their lives on condition that they be transported, depending on their crimes, for a term of seven to fourteen years. The impact of this act was pronounced. Although no complete records are available showing the precise number of persons transported, we know that the three major contractors of convict labor for the colonies from 1719 to 1772 accounted for 17,740 felons drawn from Newgate and the Home Counties shipped to America, with nearly all going to Maryland and Virginia. One estimate puts the number of malefactors transported from Old Bailey alone as 10,000 by 1775. Some 30,000 felons were so transported to the colonies in the eighteenth century.[14] This renewed traffic in convict labor was moving into full swing when Defoe began writing novels, and being a man close to his times, a long-standing journalist, Defoe turned this renewed traffic to propagandistic uses. He could extend even to the lower class the promise that in America they could with hard work and good luck hope to become wealthy.

Middle-Class Gentility in Defoe's Fiction

The heroes and heroines of Defoe's fiction are all in a way tradesmen, and since Defoe always had such an abiding faith in and respect for the dignity of trade, it is worth observing that in his fiction he is at pains to show his readers the exemplary behavior of his heroes and heroines whenever they transact any business. The virtual absence of dishonest or imprudent business transactions in his novels is remarkable. Indeed, the business decorum and skill of the characters, major and minor, is idealized to a fault, as if Defoe were unable to bring himself to portray any improper actions when it came to the transaction of business. The English sea captain, his widow, and the Brazilian planter in *Robinson Crusoe*; the governess in *Moll Flanders*; the Major and the Custom House clerk in *Colonel Jacque*; the pirates and Quaker William in *Captain Singleton*; the Dutch merchant and Sir Robert Clayton in the *Fortunate Mistress*: all of these assorted people, planters and pirates, sea captains and merchants, even whores and highwaymen, when entrusted with money, often ill-gotten, wisely invest it or generously share it and, when the hero or heroine returns from an adventure or escapade, the money is waiting to be claimed — and in the absence of the owner it has been invested shrewdly and has increased substantially. Clearly Defoe held trade of any kind in the highest regard, as well as the people who dealt in it, and he felt compelled to paint it in its purest colors for his middle-class trading audience. His characters almost invariably transact their business like gentlemen.

Later in *The Complete English Tradesman* he was to write that a "gentleman-tradesman is not so much nonsense as some people would persuade us to reckon it." [15] The ideal of the "gentleman-tradesman" was in Defoe's mind when he wrote his novels as well. Even in *Captain Singleton* he made a special point of introducing to his readers the character of a gentleman whose trade was that of a "factor" — as was Defoe's early trade in London. This English gentleman appears in the most unlikely of places, the heart of black Africa, where he is found by Captain Singleton and his band of pirates. His description is worth considering: "He appeared to be a gentleman, not an ordinary-bred fellow, seaman, or labouring man; this showed itself in his behaviour in the first moment of our conversing with him, and in

spite of all the disadvantages of his miserable circumstances"
(p. 138). The "disadvantages" of the gentleman's condition are
indeed formidable, for although he immediately conveyed the
unmistakable impression that he was an English gentleman, he
did so in spite of the natural handicap that he was unshaved,
unkempt, unwashed and "stark naked."

Defoe stressed the importance of the gentleman in the story by
highlighting him in the subtitle (". . . Of his meeting with an
Englishman, A Citizen of London, among the Indians . . ."),
Though the gentleman helps to break up the monotony of the
transcontinental odyssey of Singleton and his band, his appearance in the story clearly is intended by Defoe as something more
than a variation, however arresting, in the episodic and rambling
plot: "We found his behaviour the most courteous and endearing
I ever saw in any man whatever, and most evident tokens of a
mannerly, well-bred person appeared in all things he did or said,
and our people were exceedingly taken with him. He was a
scholar and a mathematician; he could not speak Portuguese indeed, but he spoke Latin to our surgeon, French to another of
our men, and Italian to a third" (p. 139). Defoe is here not so
much portraying a person as an ideal. (We are never, for instance,
told the name of the gentleman; he is always referred to simply
as "this gentleman" or "our new gentleman.") He had his eye
on his audience in making the gentleman a trader, for the man
is an illustration of the "gentleman-trader" ideal, an ideal with
which Defoe's middle-class audience could easily identify. No
mention is made of birth or ancestry and the like, when "the
sum of his history" is related; Defoe was not concerned with
such matters. What was important to him was that this man's
conduct and manner were such that, despite his rude and "stark
naked" state, he could charm a ruthless band of pirates in the
steaming jungles of Africa; and his knowledge and learning were
such that, despite the disadvantages of being without books or
supplies, he could subsist more than adequately by his practical
knowledge. He knows modern languages from his trading career,
as well as Latin, mathematics, and geography. His knowledge is
more of the world than of the study: he knows where to find gold
or water, how to travel through the jungle; in short, he proves
himself as adept at survival among the aborigine tribesmen as at

leadership among the pirates. In *The Complete English Tradesman* Defoe was to comment on how "knowledge of the world . . . is the best education." [16] This anonymous English gentleman is an embodiment of the "liberal education" Defoe received at Newington Green Academy.

Education and the profound effect it had on the careers of his characters was of particular interest to Defoe. In the novels he sought to show how the aspirations and success of the middle class in large part rested on the kind of education they received. In this regard he was consistent with the care he exercised in the education of his own children. Without the proper kind of education, a "liberal education," one could not hope to succeed in business and eventually become a person of wealth and position. From *Robinson Crusoe* to *The Fortunate Mistress* he detailed how education helps to shape the careers of his heroes and heroines. We know how Defoe valued the practical education he received at Morton's academy. In the novels he exhibited the same respect for a practical education. Captain Singleton's life as a pirate, for example, is in no small part the result of a faulty early education. As a child Singleton was shifted from parish school to parish school, where he was taught nothing of practical value; he received only the admonishments of a minister who told him that though he was a poor boy, if he minded his Bible and served God, he might be a good man — small comfort to an indigent lad without a means of livelihood. Thus, when Singleton falls in with a "thieving, lying, swearing, forswearing" crew, he is quick to remind the reader, "Education, as you have heard, I had none" (p. 13). Singleton must remain just another member of that devilish crew until he can develop his innate talents through education.

In *Captain Singleton* Defoe is careful to stress the importance of education in general and its effect on Singleton's career in particular. Singleton is eager to learn; he simply has never had the opportunity presented him. The parish schools were remiss in preparing him for a decent place in society. Without a trade, he had little control over his destiny, hence his consorting with a band of pirates. Fortunately, he meets a gunner in the band who undertakes to educate him:

This gunner was an excellent mathematician, a good scholar, and a complete sailor; and it was in conversing intimately with him that I learned afterwards the grounds of what knowledge I have since had in all the sciences useful for navigation, and particularly in the geographical part of knowledge . . .

In an especial manner, *he filled my head with aspiring thoughts,* and with an earnest desire after learning everything that could be taught me; convincing me, that nothing could qualify me for great undertakings, but a degree superior to what was usual in the race of seamen; *he told me, that to be ignorant was to be certain of a mean station in the world, but that knowledge was the first step to preferment.*   (p. 64, italics mine)

The passage has an unmistakably didactic intent; Defoe is addressing himself to his audience, urging them to prize education as the readiest means of realizing their "aspiring thoughts" and rising in society. Once Singleton is exposed to the right kind of education he takes to it heartily. It is significant that on the very next page we learn Singleton is chosen leader of the group; armed with useful knowledge, he is now no longer just another seaman but "Captain Bob." This general pattern applies to the careers of all Defoe's characters: education determines the course their lives take and the successes they attain.[17]

The road along which Defoe's heroes and heroines pursue their ambitions for wealth and social position may be paved with good intentions, but it is also laid with all kinds of snares. Every rise in society is attended by serious moral compromises, hence the central importance of the repentance theme in all of his novels. Defoe's own life as a businessman exemplified this scheme of moral compromise and general human failings, notably in 1692 when he acted so dishonorably toward his creditors and even sunk so low as to cully his own mother-in-law in the notorious civet-cat scandal. As a devout Puritan and former ministerial student, he was never able to erase from his mind how churlishly he had behaved when frightened by his failing credit and pressed by his creditors. Since he could not forget his past conduct, he could at least attempt to understand and justify it on the grounds of being gripped by a "necessity" over which he had no human control. In their pursuit of money and position Defoe's characters find they cannot be overnice in their consciences as to the means by which they succeed. But Defoe is too much aware of his readers, and the strong dissenting background he shares with many of them, not to attempt some reconciliation of the compulsive acquisitive activities of his characters with the Puritan concept of repentance and salvation.

In the personal essays comprising the *Serious Reflections of Robinson Crusoe* we find a clear presentation of Defoe's views on human nature. Every reader of the essay "Of Solitude" is familiar with Defoe's memorable passage on man's fundamental egocentricity: "The world, I say, is nothing to us but as it is more or less to our relish. All reflection is carried home, and our dear self is . . . the end of living." [18] Defoe held the traditional Calvinist position on the innate depravity of man; only God raises men above their sinful natures: "I readily allow all men are born knaves, villains, thieves, and murderers, and nothing but the restraining power of Providence withholds us all from showing ourselves such on all occasions" (III, 23). Given this view of man's basic condition, Defoe could hold that man was unable to withstand the power of necessity, regardless of the individual or the circumstances. There was no such thing as absolute honesty or goodness; it was all relative in man. Men simply have different "necessities." Some succumb easily, some succumb only after great struggle, but all succumb eventually. Defoe could envision a world without an honest man in it, given the right circumstances. He therefore concluded: "Necessity is above the power of human nature, and for Providence to suffer a man to fall into that necessity is to suffer him to sin, because nature is not furnished with power to defend itself, nor grace itself able to fortify the mind against it" (III, 35).

Robinson Crusoe's "original sin," as he terms it, is his failure to follow "the excellent advice of [his] father," just as "the general plague of mankind," according to Defoe, is the direct result of their "not being satisfied with the station wherein God and Nature has placed them" (I, 216). But, significantly, Crusoe does not accept full moral responsibility for his "original sin"; rather he attributes his shipwrecked condition on the island ultimately to "Providence," which, if it had "blessed [him] with confined desires," might have made him "by this time . . . one of the most considerable planters in the Brazils" (I, 216). The conditional tense used by Crusoe in describing his predicament on the island may read like a clever piece of moral casuistry, but it is strangely consistent with Defoe's view of human nature and necessity. Crusoe's failure to heed his father's "excellent advice" was the means of his coming to his "miserable condition" but not the cause. Providence had simply not seen fit to favor him with "confined desires" and he therefore could not be content to remain in his "station."

Defoe's position on Crusoe's "original sin" underscores again the essential conflict between the Puritan attitude toward the pursuit of a calling for the greater glory of God and the mercantilist attitude toward the pursuit of business for the greater glory of Mammon. The care exercised by Puritans in choosing a suitable calling in the seventeenth century was the result of their conceiving, as we saw, a calling as a profoundly serious religious duty. The eminent Puritan divine Richard Baxter, accordingly, admonished parents to "choose such trades and callings for them [their children] as have least dangerous temptations, and as tend most to the saving of their souls, and make them most useful in the world, and not those that tend most to the ease of the flesh, or worldly ends." [19] Seen in this light, the advice of Crusoe's father is well taken both secularly and religiously. But Crusoe is determined to pursue "worldly ends" in his trading adventures to Guinea. He is a kind of representative of the mercantilist society, and as such is set in opposition to the Puritan society. Defoe seemingly accepted without question the right, indeed even the necessity, of men to raise themselves and their fortunes, despite the risks they so obviously ran in neglecting or even doing violence to the religious side of their lives and callings. This conflict between the solemn and austere work of achieving salvation and the attractive and dangerous course of amassing a fortune Defoe sought to harmonize through the theme of repentance; as he stated: "They who repent, and their ill lives amend,/Stand next to those who never did offend" (III, 24). The repentance formula probably served Defoe well in his life, for it served him well in his novels, which were often little more than imaginative self-dramatizations drawn from his own life.[20]

All of Defoe's heroes and heroines pursue their careers beyond the pale of the Puritan religious life in their relentless quest for money and status, and only by repenting can they re-enter the orthodox fold after they have made their money and achieved their social status. All of Defoe's stories are, then, as Bonamy Dobrée observes, "success stories," but with a serious qualification: "his heroes and heroines all make good, indeed reach affluence, in the end, after tottering at the edge of the abyss." [21] The "abyss" is a fitting Puritan figure, connoting the damnation with which Defoe's characters flirt during their careers; they all at some time fall on evil days and into evil ways for which they must atone and repent sincerely.

Once their quest for money and position is consummated, and they find themselves in easy and secure circumstances, safe from the irresistible temptations of necessity, they are free to address themselves to higher matters and repent. Defoe's position on repentance for his characters comes through clearly at the conclusion of *Colonel Jacque,* where he has Jacque finally come to terms with the course of his life: "Here, I say, I had the leisure to repent. How far it pleases God to give the grace of repentance where He gives the opportunity of it is not for me to say of myself. It is sufficient that I recommend it to all that read this story, that, when they find their lives come up in any degree to any similitude of cases, they will inquire of me, and ask themselves, Is not this the time to repent?" [22] Defoe implies that repentance, if it be lasting, must be done in "leisure," that is, the ease of financial and social security. Without these conditions one is still subject to the duress and temptation attending necessity, and therefore one cannot foreswear one's past life and transgressions; with these conditions met, however, a character would be culpable of the inexcusable sins of avarice or unfounded wickedness if he did not repent sincerely. Roxana alone of Defoe's major characters does not conform to this pattern of atonement and repentance, although even she is made to see, at times in her wicked career, the "necessity" of preparing for "the great work . . . of repentance." [23] Defoe had to leave her story unfinished.

"Popular literature revived in Defoe," in the estimate of Ernest A. Baker; "the lower middle classes, and orders still humbler, saw their lives and circumstances, their interests and ideals, represented with a sympathy and a seriousness that had hitherto been accorded only to their betters in the social scale." [24]

Defoe faithfully presented his readers with pictures of life with which they could identify, as well as into which he himself could project his own middle-class ambitions and values. By purposely playing down such matters of interest to the upper classes as birth and ancestry, he made it easy for his readers to participate more directly in the lives of his heroes and heroines; the importance of money, land, clothes, servants, manners, and education is evident in all the novels. But being a Puritan, Defoe hoped to square the checkered careers of his characters with the scheme of repentance in the end. In this way he tried to offer a satisfactory means of reconciling the social and economic dynamics of his middle-class protagonists with the spiritual side of their lives. The ambiguity of Defoe's position, and that of his characters, is a revealing reflection of the ambiguity of his mercantile society.

Chapter 7. Moll Flanders

"It isn't difficult to be a country gentleman's wife," Rebecca thought. "I think I could be a good woman if I had five thousand a year." . . . And who knows but Rebecca was right in her speculations — and that it was only a question of money and fortune which made the difference between her and an honest woman? — William Makepeace Thackeray, *Vanity Fair* (Modern Library ed.), p. 436

On January 27, 1722, Defoe saw published *The Fortunes and Misfortunes of the Famous Moll Flanders.* It was a great success with the public and underwent three editions in 1722 alone. It was also an important event in the history of English prose fiction, marking the first major novel which had for its story the career of a common girl.

Since early in life Defoe had demonstrated an interest in the role and education of women. In his *Essay upon Projects,* written some thirty years before, he had shown himself well in advance of his age in his enlightened attitude toward women as equal to men in their capacity to learn. He wrote, "the great distinguishing difference which is seen in the world between men and women is in their education." In Moll Flanders he created a character who not only embodied some of his ideas on the education of women but also owed her abiding ambition in life to her early education, both formal and informal.[1]

Critics have variously interpreted the career of Moll Flanders, finding it "our classic revelation of the mercantile mind," as does Mark Schorer; or a "novel in which a character is everything and is given freest play," as does E. M. Forster. Dorothy Van Ghent calls it "a complex system of ironies and counterstresses," and several other scholars have examined the question of irony in *Moll Flanders.*[2] Most modern critics from Virginia Woolf to John Peale Bishop have had the highest regard for the novel. Strangely enough though, despite the different approaches taken to the novel and the generally high esteem accorded it, no one has attempted to interpret *Moll* closely and consistently in terms of the important theme introduced at length in the opening pages of the novel, the theme of gentility and its significance in Moll's career.

There is little doubt that Defoe's experiences in the "school of affliction" had a direct effect on his novel writing, particularly the writing of *Moll Flanders*. "It is no accident," Mark Schorer writes, "that Moll's paralyzing fear of Newgate is her most forcibly urged emotion." Defoe was, as we saw, terrified at the prospect of arrest, both in 1692 and again in 1703, when he was actually imprisoned for months in Newgate. But fear in his life became transmuted into a quest for security, as is evident from the tenor of the *Essay upon Projects* and other works. Professor Schorer rightly discerns in *Moll Flanders* signs of "the middle-class striving for security." In this regard Defoe reflects his age. In the estimate of the social historian M. Dorothy George, "The dominating impression of life in eighteenth-century London, from the standpoint of the individual, is one of uncertainty and insecurity." Defoe perhaps as much as any man of his times experienced the uncertainty and insecurity of life, and he more than any man of his age addressed himself to finding ways for making life more secure. In Moll he created a character who embodied his own fundamental desire for security. It is no coincidence that Moll admits all she really wants from life is "to be placed in a settled way of living" (I, 131). This is Moll's *modus operandi*. But in order to understand Moll and her career, we must come to understand what she means by "a settled way of living" and the kind of security she craves.[3]

Defoe portrays in Moll's early life the plight of an unfortunate girl ("the offspring of debauchery and vice") who, because of her beauty and brains, comes to aspire to a life much higher than the drudgery of going out to service. Moll's aspirations are the result of her education. In Colchester she is put to school by the parish with a woman who had previously lived in "good fashion," and Moll is "brought up as mannerly as if [she] had been at the dancing school" (I, 4). Moll instinctively takes to this fashionable education, and she first experiences fear when at the age of eight she is "terrified" at the news that the magistrates had ordered her to "go to service." Her fear is prompted by the realization that wherever she might be sent, she could do little except "run of errands" or "be a drudge to some cookmaid."

Even after her tears move her teacher to ask the mayor not to send her out to service yet, Moll cannot control her "apprehension" because, as she explains it, "to think of going to service at all was such a frightful thing to me" (I, 5). At the age of eight, Moll is already endeavoring to avoid at all costs her expected fate of being sent out to service, and no small part of her eagerness to avoid her calling clearly is the taste of fashion she has received from her teacher.

When Moll's frustration over the prospects of her future cause her to weep, her teacher asks in exasperation, "What! would you be a gentlewoman?" She innocently snatches at the hyperbole and says, "Yes." The absurdity of her grandiose choice of a station in life naturally sets her teacher "a-laughing," "as you may be sure it would," Moll adds as an afterthought; for Defoe's readers knew only too well what Moll's teacher knows, and what Moll writing her memoirs in retrospect now knows:

"Well, madam, forsooth," says she, gibing at me, "you would be a gentlewoman; and how will you come to be a gentlewoman? What! will you do it by your fingers' ends?"
"Yes," says I again, very innocently.
"Why, what can you earn," says she; "what can you get a day at your work?"
"Threepence," said I, "when I spin, and fourpence when I work plain work."
"Alas! poor gentlewoman," said she again, laughing, "what will that do for thee?" (I, 6)

Moll the child does not even know what a gentlewoman is or does; she is indeed "innocent" of such worldly and grown-up notions of life in her society. But she recognizes intuitively that to be a gentlewoman is better than going out to service. From this chance remark passed by her teacher, and the ensuing discussion, Moll charts the course of her life. She will learn in time what it means to become and be a gentlewoman.

Moll's aspiration to become a gentlewoman reaches the ears of the mayor and his family, who derive much amusement from its absurdity; but their mirth gives way to curiosity and Mrs. Mayoress soon comes to meet "the little lass that is to be a gentlewoman"

(I, 7). Even though Moll has no clear conception of what she means by becoming a gentlewoman, all the fuss people make over her when she says she wishes to become a gentlewoman encourages the eight-year-old Moll to hold fast to her ambition. For one thing, it pays for her to do so. She is flattered and rewarded. Mrs. Mayoress assures her she has "a lady's hand" and gives her a shilling, saying she "might be a gentlewoman for aught she knew" (I, 7). The pattern of flattery and reward is repeated when the mayor's daughters visit little Moll. They ask her if she is resolved to be a gentlewoman and she answers, yes. They like Moll's "little prattle" and give her money, too. All this attention turns her head and soon she is known all over town as "the little gentlewoman" (I, 9). Even to her teacher she is now "the gentlewoman" (I, 9).

By the age of ten Moll knows herself to be "very mannerly" and "pretty," as she "often heard the ladies say." And because their flattery is accompanied by money ("they often gave me money" — I, 9), she can afford "headdresses, and linen, and gloves." Moll, however, is still unclear on what it means to be a gentlewoman. When she would speak to her teacher or Mrs. Mayoress or the townspeople about wanting to be a gentlewoman, it seemed to Moll "they meant one sort of thing by the word gentlewoman, and I meant quite another"; all she wants is to support herself and not go out to service, but her interlocutors think she "meant to live great and high" (I, 7-8). Only gradually does Moll's tutoress realize what she means by becoming a gentlewoman:

My old tutoress began to understand what I meant by being a gentlewoman, and it was no more than to be able to get my bread by my own work; and at last she asked me whether it was not so.

I told her, yes, and insisted on it, that to do so was to be a gentlewoman; "for," says I, "there is such a one," naming a woman that mended lace and washed the ladies' laced heads; "she," says I, "is a gentlewoman, and they call her madam."

"Poor child," says my good old nurse, "you may soon be such a gentlewoman as that, for she is a person of ill fame, and has had two bastards."

I did not understand anything of that; but I answered, "I am sure they call her madam, and she does not go to service nor do housework"; and therefore I insisted that she was a gentlewoman, and I would be such a gentlewoman as that. (I, 8)

This scene is ironic, of course, highlighting as it does young Moll's innocence about gentility and foreshadowing her later career.

Moll's social education is significantly furthered by her association with gentlefolk. By the time she is twelve, she already has achieved the status of a gentlewoman ("as I understood that word" — I, 10); she earns her bread by making linen and mending lace — a genteel commodity — for the ladies of the town. But soon Moll's appetite for another kind of gentility is awakened. She receives fine cast-off clothes from the ladies of the town and so, with the help of her tutoress, goes about dressed like a little gentlewoman. One of the ladies, taking a fancy to her, invites her to spend a week with her daughters at her home. As her tutoress wisely predicts, however, this exposure to fashionable living will do "the little gentlewoman more harm than good" (I, 10). Moll's old nurse has good reason to be concerned about the adverse effects exposure to a fashionable household as a guest would have on an impressionable girl like Moll, who already has shown a more than passing interest in gentility. Now that she will live on familiar terms with ladies she will want to emulate her social betters, the consequences of which must be bitter frustration and difficulty in reconciling herself to her proper station in life.

Defoe was keenly aware of the imitative social behavior of his age; all classes tried to dress and behave as did their immediate superiors in society. The most outrageous class in Defoe's eyes, however, were the domestic servants. In 1724 he was prompted to write a book of more than three hundred pages entitled *The Great Law of Subordination Consider'd,* in which he deplored "the unsufferable behaviour of servants" in England and "how hard it is sometimes to know the chamber-maid from her mistress." This matter had become a national grievance to Defoe's mind, and in 1725 he was back with a prickly pamphlet entitled *Everybody's Business is Nobody's Business,* wherein he again complained of seeing everywhere "the maid striving to out-do the mistress." There is little question about Defoe's position on the matter of the servant class and its proper place in the scheme of society; he believed firmly in "the great foundation, the Rule of Subordination," which he saw as "essential to all family-economy." [4]

In *Moll Flanders,* however, Defoe seems to have adopted a different attitude entirely about the "little gentlewoman" and her ambition in life, outrageous as it was socially and unlikely as it was economically. Somehow he could not prevent himself from championing the cause of his plucky little heroine. She is not depicted as saucy or pert but innocent and engaging; everyone who meets little Moll is drawn to her. Defoe sees his heroine as a natural lady who, owing to the misfortune of her birth in Newgate, is deprived of the eminence nature had fitted her for within society. As she becomes educated like a gentlewoman, Defoe regards her less as a servant, although that remains her station, and more as a "little gentlewoman." His ambiguous attitude toward Moll is easily explainable if we see her not so much as a servant girl with genteel aspirations but as an extension of her creator. Moll is unmistakenly "obsessed with gentility and keeping up appearances," as was Defoe throughout his life. "Defoe's identification with Moll Flanders," Ian Watt concludes, "was so complete that, despite a few feminine traits, he created a personality that was in essence his own." [5]

After direct exposure to gentility in the home of the lady, Moll at fourteen has a more sophisticated idea of what it means to be a gentlewoman: "I had such a taste of genteel living at the lady's house that I was not so easy in my old quarters as I used to be, and I thought it was fine to be a gentlewoman indeed, for I had quite other notions of a gentlewoman now than I had before; and as I thought that it was fine to be a gentlewoman, so I loved to be among gentlewomen, and therefore I longed to be there again" (I, 11). It is precisely at this point, when Moll has become thoroughly acquainted with a life she feels the strongest attraction for and a life she has been imitating for years in her modest way by her clothes and manner, that her old tutoress and protectress dies suddenly. Once again Moll is distracted with fear. "I was frightened out of my wits almost, and knew not what to do" (I, 11) is Moll's apt summary of her predicament.

Happily, Moll is taken into the home of a "new generous mistress" where she is allowed to nurture her aspirations for gentility. Defoe makes an obvious point of stressing the genteel education Moll is privileged to acquire in the next three years or so in her new household: "Here I had all the advantages for my education that could be imagined; the lady had masters home to teach her daughters to dance, and to speak French, and to write, and others to teach them music; and as I was always with them, I learned as fast as they . . . I learned by imitation and inquiry all that they learned by instruction and direction; so that, in short, I learned to dance and speak French as well as any of them, and to sing much better, for I had a better voice than any of them" (I, 12–13). Defoe had a special interest in the education of women, and in this passage he outlines in essence the kind of education he had recommended in his *Essay upon Projects*. Women, he wrote, "should be taught all sorts of breeding suitable both to their genius and quality"; they should be taught "music and dancing" as well as "languages, particularly French and Italian," and "all the graces of speech." Moll learns music and dancing and French by "imitation and inquiry." She even becomes proficient at the fashionable instruments of the harpsichord and the spinet, being taught by the daughters of the family. "By this means," Moll concludes with satisfaction, *"I had all the advantages of education that I could have had if I had been as much a gentlewoman as they were with whom I lived"* (I, 12–13; italics mine). At the age of about eighteen, then, Moll has been educated like a gentlewoman, is living in a household of gentlefolk, and wants desperately to be a gentlewoman in her own right.[6]

By placing Moll in a household with born ladies of approximately the same age, Defoe contrasts sharply the difference between the natural attributes of beauty and parts evident in Moll and the artificial advantages of birth and position enjoyed by the daughters. As Moll herself realizes, "in some things I had the advantage of my ladies, though they were my superiors, viz., that mine were all the gifts of nature, and which all their fortunes could not furnish" (I, 13). She is decidedly "handsomer," "better shaped," and endowed with "a better voice." The town regards her as "the handsomest young woman in Colchester." But despite her natural advantages, Moll lacks the one factor that would make her sought after for marriage by gentlemen — money. As the daughters of the household know only too well, "if a young woman has beauty, birth, breeding, wit, sense, manners, modesty, and all to an extreme, yet if she has not money she's nobody" (I, 15). Since "nothing but money recommends a woman" in the world, Moll is faced with a peculiar problem. She is a gentle-woman by breeding and a woman of beauty by nature, but none the less a woman without money.

Having brought Moll's genteel education to completion, Defoe introduces the marriage theme. Through marriage Moll will at-tempt to realize her ambition of becoming a gentlewoman de-spite her impecuniousness. Defoe foreshadows the action by having the younger brother comment to his sister, in the presence of Moll, "beauty will steal a husband sometimes in spite of money, and when the maid chances to be handsomer than the mistress, she oftentimes makes a good market, and rides in a coach before her" (I, 16). The theme is revolutionary in its social implications but appropriate to the audience for whom Defoe writes because it panders to the dreams and aspirations of the middle- and lower-class readers. The theme clearly anticipates the fiction of Samuel Richardson a generation later, especially the central ac-tion of *Pamela,* wherein precisely this kind of an idea will be ex-ploited to the delight of a middle- and lower-class reading public.

Moll, unlike Pamela, does not hold out for marriage; her vanity and attraction to wealth and gentility result in her fall from virtue. Moll is taken up with the pride "of being loved by such a gentleman" as the eldest brother, who is always putting "a handful of gold" in her hand while playing to her vanity by flattering her beauty. The pattern of flattery and reward was, as we saw, instrumental in Moll's holding fast to her ambition of being a gentlewoman when a small girl; now Defoe again resorts to this design in staging her capitulation to the advances of the eldest son. She is not a little taken with the prospect of becoming a lady by marriage to the eldest son, who is destined to inherit the family estate. She also appreciates the necessity of money in furthering her social ambitions: "As for the gold, I spent whole hours in looking upon it; I told the guineas over a thousand times a day" (I, 21).

Although money certainly helps to bring about Moll's fall, it is by no means the only factor. When the eldest brother shows her "a silk purse with a hundred guineas in it," and promises her such a one each year until he marries her, Moll cannot resist the temptation. We notice, however, that the temptation is founded not only on money but also on fashion — and the promise of marriage. The purse used as the bait is made of "silk," and it is "at the sight of the purse," not the money inside, that Moll's "colour came and went" (I, 24). If Moll became a whore for money, she unquestionably was influenced not a little by the symbols of gentility she hoped to enjoy with her wealth and the expectation that she would become a lady through marriage to the eldest son of the family.

It is worth observing also how the scene of Moll's seduction is laid by Defoe in the most fashionable way so as to play to Moll's weakness. The assignation is planned carefully and executed with great skill and excitement. The eldest brother sets off in a coach on the pretense of seeing Sir W——, a neighbor, but Moll is quick to notice he is dressed up in his best gentlemanly attire; he even "calls for his best wig, hat, and sword." Moll, as prearranged, leaves a quarter of an hour later, and although she cannot change dresses without arousing suspicion, she still manages to dress herself like a lady: "I had a hood, a mask, a fan, and a pair of gloves in my pocket" (I, 23). Moll's actions are symbolic; she believes the eldest brother's promises of marriage, and even though she sneaks off to have an assignation with him, she already shows herself to be dressing for the role she hopes soon to act in reality, that of a fine gentlewoman married to an eldest son destined to inherit his father's estate. What she overheard at the discussion of money and marriage among the children of the family seems to be coming true for her; the eldest brother compliments her beauty, gives her money, and even promises marriage. Moll is in love with him; she is of a passionate nature and his declarations of love fire her blood; but she is equally in love with the idea of becoming the wife of such a gentleman. Paradoxically, it is her desire to become a gentlewoman that results in her becoming a whore.

When the eldest brother refuses to marry her, after having enjoyed her favors, she has no choice but to marry Robin, the younger brother who loves her, even though she, by her own admission, still loves the other brother. As the eldest brother counsels her, knowing Moll's weakness, it is to her advantage to accept Robin's offer, even though she does not love him, because in this way she can "marry a gentleman of a good family, in good circumstances" after all (I, 52). He helps to assuage Moll's disappointment by giving her £500 for the liberties he has taken with her person. Moll accepts the advice, and the money, because she is "terrified" at the idea of "being turned out to the wide world a mere cast-off whore" (I, 54). She is also influenced in her decision by "the easy, prosperous life" she will lead as Robin's wife. Thus Moll finds herself a gentlewoman by marriage.

Robin's death leaves Moll a widow with about £1,200. She is now a changed and worldly-wise woman: "Being still young and handsome . . . and with a tolerable fortune in my pocket," she remarks, "I put no small value upon myself" (I, 57). She has even become something of a social snob. Courted by several tradesmen, Moll declares herself "not adverse to a tradesman," but she insists on having a tradesman "that was something of a gentleman too." Defoe reflects the values of his audience in the description Moll offers of what she seeks in a "gentleman-tradesman": "When my husband had a mind to carry me to the court, or to the play, he might become a sword, and look as like a gentleman as another man; and not like one that had the mark of his apron-strings upon his coat, or the mark of his hat upon his periwig; that should look as if he was set on to his sword, when his sword was put on him, and carried his trade in his countenance" (I, 58). Such a "gentleman-tradesman," in Defoe's mind, and the mind of his audience, was a contradiction in terms, hence his derogatory description of this meretricious ideal as an "amphibious creature," a "land-water thing," to distinguish it from the true ideal of the "gentleman-tradesman" in *Singleton*. Defoe made this important distinction concerning the "gentleman-tradesman" explicit a few years later when, in his *Complete English Tradesman*, he devoted an entire chapter to showing how all this extravagance and vanity by some tradesmen was the shortest way to their ruin, and was nothing more than "their eager, resolved pursuit of that empty and meanest kind of pride, called imitation, viz., to look like the gentry." [7]

Moll finally marries such a showy "gentleman-tradesman" whose trade is that of a draper but whose pretensions are "to look like quality." The expensive way of living pursued by Moll and her husband presages their financial ruin. They ride around in "a rich coach," with an entourage of ostentatiously attired attendants: "a coachman, postillion, and two footmen in very good liveries; a gentleman on horseback, and a page with a feather in his hat upon another horse" (I, 59). They go to Oxford where they instruct the servants to address them "my lord" and "Countess" as a finishing touch to their masquerade as people of quality. In so portraying the genteel antics of Moll and her draper husband, Defoe was drawing an instructive and relevant lesson for his audience. In *The Complete English Tradesman* he was to outline the four surest ways to ruin for a tradesman:

1. Expensive housekeeping, or family extravagance.
2. Expensive dressing, or the extravagance of fine clothes.
3. Expensive company, or keeping company above himself.
4. Expensive equipage, making a show and ostentation of figure in the world.   (I, 112)

Moll and her "gentleman-tradesman" husband are guilty of all four extravagant expenses to a fault. Such expensive living, Defoe warned, was especially insidious to a tradesman because "it eats into the two most essential branches of his trade, namely, his credit and his cash." Predictably, the draper, despite his "coming to a lump of money at once," breaks in little over two years of such profuse living and retires to the Mint.

In offering his readers an account of this "gentleman-tradesman" Defoe may well have had in mind his own career in London prior to his bankruptcy of 1692. In those days, as we saw, he was himself something of a "land-water thing," being both a London merchant and an Athenian wit. Young Defoe also emulated the patterns of people of quality by establishing something of a reputation as a dandy in dress and frequenting fashionable throngs, like the horse races, whenever possible. Defoe from costly personal experience knew how such extravagant and pretentious living could speed the ruin of a tradesman. In the dramatic account of the ruin of the draper, Defoe was probably to some extent indulging in a self-dramatization of the London merchant he was before ruin overtook him in 1692.

Moll must flee to the Mint herself and she is "filled with horror at the place" (I, 64). Casting about for ways to extricate herself from her surroundings, she finds her thoughts returning to the idea of marriage. The subject of marriage was of great interest to the age, especially to the middle class, which looked upon marriage almost exclusively as a means of social betterment or business aggrandizement. In the middle class, according to G. M. Trevelyan, "husbands were found for girls on the principle of frank barter." Swift spoke for the age when advising his young lady that a match her parents made for her was preferable, since it was "without any mixture of that ridiculous passion." [8] Moll's first mistake had been to allow herself to be "tricked once by that cheat called love"; she was not going to be victimized by the "ridiculous passion" a second time. Yet she realizes only too well what her predicament entails; for while "it was requisite for a whore to be handsome, well-shaped, have a good mien, and a graceful behaviour," in a wife only "money was the thing" (I, 65). Moll decides to barter for herself. She pretends to possess a fortune. The stratagem succeeds. "With the reputation of this fortune," Moll reports, "I presently found myself with admirers enough" (I, 76). The centrality of money in matters of marriage was readily understood by Defoe's readers, and it was for their benefit that he spent so much time detailing how one can catch a husband even without a fortune to bargain with. This kind of material understandably made capital reading for the class of readers who soon would thrill to such stories as *Pamela*.

Moreover, Defoe experiments when treating the subject of love. He shows himself to be introducing any material that may be of interest to his readers. The attempts at witty love poetry by Moll and the man who is to become her third husband are a good illustration of this. Defoe appears to be imitating the genteel romances of the upper-class reading audiences:

One morning he pulls off his diamond ring, and writes upon the glass of the sash in my chamber this line: —
    "You I love, and you alone."
I read it, and asked him to lend me the ring, with which I wrote under it, thus: —
    "And so in love says every one."
He takes his ring again, and writes another line thus: —
    "Virtue alone is an estate."
I borrowed it again, and I wrote under it: —
    "But money's virtue, gold is fate."
He coloured as red as fire to see me turn so quick upon him, and in a kind rage told me he would conquer me, and wrote again thus: —
    "I scorn your gold, and yet I love."

I ventured all upon the last cast of poetry, as you'll see, for I wrote boldly under his last: —

"I'm poor; let's see how kind you'll prove."   (I, 77)

And so it goes on. Finally, Moll's suitor acquiesces in this war of wit, laying down "the cudgels, that is to say, the pen" (I, 78). Defoe's self-conscious attempt at witty repartee between lovers in the style of the genteel romances or Restoration comedy is awkward in the extreme. The efforts of Moll and her suitor hardly threaten the Congrevian tradition of Millamant and Mira-bell, but they are noteworthy as the clumsy first attempts of middle-class prose fiction to take over some of the fashion and sparkle of the polished literature of the upper classes. Defoe is not sure of himself in this passage, as he is when dealing with what he knows first-hand, and it is no surprise that we find little more of this kind of writing in his novels.

Defoe depicts Moll's third husband as the prosperous owner of three plantations in Virginia. He and Moll go to the colonies for eight years, and Defoe introduces the colonial theme by having Moll notice in astonishment that a new class of gentry has grown up there, a gentry that owes its beginnings largely to Newgate prison. Moll's mother points out to her officers in the army who were once pickpockets, justices who were shoplifters. Whereas England with her Newgate spawns "thieves and rogues," the colonies offer all a fair chance at making something of their life, with the result that men no longer desperate can with time and industry succeed and prosper. Although Moll must leave the colonies after discovering her incestuous marriage to her brother, she first is instructed by the *exemplum* of her mother's life. In her younger days Moll's mother was a "whore and thief" — as Moll herself is to become — but she was able to "repent sincerely of both" and in the colonies find a new and prosperous life (I, 89). Defoe thus foreshadows Moll's repentance of her own life and her return to the colonies as a transported felon.

Moll's formative education in gentility has a lasting effect on her and when she returns to England, she is drawn almost in-stinctively to the favorite resort of people of quality, Bath — "a place of gallantry enough," where she "kept good company, that is to say, gay, fine company" (I, 106–107). Here she manages to meet "a complete gentleman," whose mistress she eventually becomes. Moll makes no pretense about her compelling desire to live like a woman of quality. She admits to a passion for fine things ("I loved nothing in the world better than fine clothes" — I, 114). She takes a maid, hires a coach, and is given enough money "to subsist on very handsomely" (I, 117). To live "handsomely" is immensely important to Moll, and she uses that term advisedly. She is, after all, the product of her early shaping environment.

When Moll loses her paramour she again experiences fear and anxiety. She is forty-two years old and is terrified by her uncertain future ("the terror of approaching poverty lay hard upon my spirits" — I, 131). Moll's intermittent periods of gripping fear after the loss of the security of a husband or lover (that is, a provider) are to be understood only in terms of her true goal in life: "I knew what I aimed at, and what I wanted . . . I wanted to be placed in a settled state of living" (I, 131). This frank admission by Moll is our key to understanding both her and her career. Moll's particular problem, however, is that a settled state for her means to be able to live like a gentlewoman. When she absolves herself of all moral responsibility for her actions, saying "vice came in always at the door of necessity, not at the door of inclination" (I, 131), her understanding of "necessity" must be read carefully; for she, like Defoe, has a unique understanding of that important word. Moll must live "handsomely" or she feels she is not really living at all. Defoe appreciated Moll's motivation when he wrote earlier in the *Review*: "Men rob for bread, women whore for bread; necessity is the parent of crime. Ask the worst highwayman in the nation, ask the lewdest strumpet in the town, if they would not willingly leave off the trade if they could live handsomely without it, and I dare say not one but will acknowledge it" (VIII, 303). Defoe writes about "necessity," but we notice that the key word in the passage is "handsomely"; obviously men would not steal and women whore if they had the means to live "handsomely" without recourse to such desperate "trades." A century later, another celebrated female character of English fiction, Rebecca Sharp, would preach and practice this same kind of moral relativism. Becky, like Moll, schemes only to obtain the kind of secure and genteel living that "five thousand a year" could provide.

The only consistent way to understand the workings of Moll's mind is to see her as she came early in life to see herself, and as her creator came to regard her: a gentlewoman. Her necessity is the relative necessity of an assured income and the fine things and easy life that accompany such a status in society. Defoe knew that in an absolute sense Moll's actions could not be justified ethically or morally; he wrote in 1714, when examining the actions of others, and therefore not confusing them with his own: "Necessity is pleaded by both Parties for doing things, which neither side can justify. I wish both sides would for ever avoid the necessity of doing evil; for certainly it is the worst plea in the world, and generally made use of for the worst things." [9] Moll could avoid the "necessity" of dissembling and whoring if she would live frugally and honestly on her remaining stock, which even when she was fifty amounted to the tidy sum of £450 — certainly enough to last Moll a long time if she does not insist on living "handsomely." But this she clearly cannot do. Her necessity is to live like a gentlewoman, hence she can no more live from her remaining funds than she could from her "needle" as a child; she can be satisfied only with a place of fashion like London or Bath and with equally fashionable company, all of which are expensive. In short, Moll simply is unable to resist the temptation of gentility or to dispel the haunting fear of losing her privileged place in society.

Moll's next marriage to James, her Lancashire husband, is a direct result of her inability to resist the trappings of gentility. She is deceived by the meretricious show of wealth he puts on for her benefit ("my eyes were dazzled" — I, 147) because she, like James, is attracted to external appearances; thus they succeed in deceiving each other about their respective want of wealth. She uses her clothes to pass herself off as "a widow of great fortune" I, 145) and James has, in Moll's eyes, "the appearance of an extraordinary fine gentleman" (I, 147). Moll's susceptibility to the symbols of genteel living is abundantly evident in her description of how she was courted: "he . . . talked as naturally of his park and his stables, of his horses, his gamekeepers, his woods, his tenants, and his servants, as if he had been in a mansion-house, and I had seen them all about me" (I, 147). In accounting for what had resulted in her deception, she admits the cause as "the glittering show of a great estate and of fine things" (I, 148). Even so, Moll loves her husband and takes genuine pleasure in knowing that, although reduced to a low fortune by bad luck, "he was bred a gentleman" (I, 154). Virginia Woolf perceives in Moll a woman "haunted . . . for the quality which to her perception makes a gentleman." It is entirely in keeping with this quality that Moll can derive a curious kind of comfort in viewing her deception by James: " 'Tis something of relief even to be undone by a man of honour, rather than by a scoundrel" (I, 155). James, after all, is no common deceiver but a "gentleman" with a "true, gallant spirit," and she cannot help responding to these qualities.[10]

When Moll begins her career of crime, Defoe makes it clear that she is driven to it by necessity. At the age of fifty she finds herself friendless and low in funds, a condition that induces her to become obsessed with fears of poverty and even starvation. Her state of mind is paranoid: "I saw nothing before me but the utmost distress; and this represented itself so lively to my thoughts . . . my very apprehensions doubled the misery, for I fancied every sixpence that I paid for a loaf of bread was the last I had in the world, and that to-morrow I was to fast, and be starved to death" (I, 199). When Moll comes to steal a bundle of goods, we have been prepared for the action by her distraught state of mind; she has lived for two years "like a distracted woman," growing "desperate" as she grew "poor apace" (I, 199). Her career as a thief is brought on by circumstances, both physical and psychological, beyond her control; she is "driven by the dreadful necessity of [her] circumstances" (I, 202).[11]

Defoe justifies Moll's entry into crime by the Biblical injunction, "Give me not poverty lest I steal," an injunction he had recourse to often in his writings and his career. But he is explicit in his condemnation of her continued thieving when she has the opportunity to abandon her life of crime and refuses: "the temptation of necessity, which is the general introduction of all such wickedness, was now removed; that I had near £500 by me in ready money, on which I might have lived very well, if I had thought fit to have retired; but, I say, I had not so much as the least inclination to leave off" (II, 29–30). Since Moll now is culpable by her own frank admission, she must atone for her crimes. Defoe adds a touch of poetic justice to Moll's career by having her taken by a constable for stealing and locked up in Newgate prison, the very place where she began her life some sixty years before: thus her life has come full circle. Moll's mother had been convicted for stealing "three pieces of fine holland" (I, 2); now Moll herself is convicted for stealing "two pieces of flowered silks" (II, 87). Like mother, like daughter.

Newgate marks the nadir of Moll's fortunes. She cannot describe the "terror" of her mind at surveying "all the horrors of that dismal place"; indeed, Newgate prison to Moll seems "an emblem of hell itself" (II, 89). Only after many days of living "under the utmost horror," and after her conviction and sentence to death, does she become ready for repentance. With the assistance of a minister she becomes "a true penitent" (II, 105). Moll's mother had repented of her life of crime and then begun her rise in fortune, culminating with her plantation in Virginia. Now that Moll has repented of her past life as a whore and thief, she, too, is ready to begin her rise in fortune.

The colonial theme is Defoe's means of restoring Moll to her status as a gentlewoman. He has prepared the reader for her deliverance by the remark passed by Moll's mother at the time of her first trip to the colonies: "many a Newgate-bird becomes a great man" in America (I, 85); now Moll sums up her lot: "in a word, I was become a mere Newgate-bird" (II, 95). The nexus is intentional. Moll becomes reunited with her Lancashire husband, James, whom she had once tried to persuade to go with her to the colonies to make their fortunes. Now they find themselves both convicted felons sentenced to death. They avail themselves of the transportation option and, with a stock of £354 between them, sail for the colonies.

Defoe does not over-idealize conditions in the American colonies, especially for gentlemen. As Moll soon discovers about James: "The case was plain; he was bred a gentleman, and was not only unacquainted, but indolent, and when we did settle, would much rather go into the woods with his gun, which they call there hunting, and which is the ordinary work of Indians; I say, he would much rather do that than attend to the natural business of the plantation" (II, 147). Success in the colonies requires hard work and some good luck; once a plantation is thriving, then one can play the gentleman and hunt. Fortunately, however, they have some money with them and Moll has prosperous relatives in the colonies. With their money they can buy servants and a plantation in Maryland, and Moll's relatives help them to stock the plantation. In time their enterprise flourishes and they grow rich.

Affluence affords Moll the chance to make of James and herself the moneyed people of quality they both pretended to be when deceiving each other into marriage many years earlier. Virginia Woolf oberves that it is in keeping with Moll's fascination with the idea of a gentleman that she shows such pleasure in catering to her husband's gentlemanly needs: "I took especial care to buy for him all those things that I knew he delighted to have; as two good long wigs, two silver-hilted swords, three or four fine fowling-pieces, a fine saddle with holsters and pistols very handsome, with a scarlet cloak; and, in a word, everything I could think of to oblige him, and to make him appear, as he really was, a very fine gentleman" (II, 161). Moll is prouder of outfitting James like a "very fine gentleman" than she is of outfitting herself; her pleasure in gentility is now in large part the vicarious pleasure of knowing she is securely married to a true gentleman at last.[12]

Defoe consummates the career of Moll and her quest for gentility by providing her with a plantation worth £300 sterling a year. With this "estate" and the other trappings of gentility, Moll and her husband return to England resolved to spend what remains of their lives "in sincere penitence" (II, 164). Moll must be seen, then, as Dorothy Van Ghent has remarked, as "a woman of the bourgeois world; her aspirations are thoroughly middle-class — she wants, above all, economic security and middle-class respectability."[13] All Moll says she ever really wanted was "to be placed in a settled way of living," which she now certainly has at the close of her life. But her "settled way of living" and her representativeness of "the bourgeois world" must be seen in terms of Defoe's characterization of her as an extension of his own middle-class values. Interpreted in this way, we must see her as seeking and in the end fully realizing the bourgeois dream of gentility, a dream that Defoe shared intensely with his heroine. Throughout her life Moll, like Defoe, pursues the status of a gentlewoman, and what she aspires for as a child she achieves in the end. Thus Defoe neatly rounds off his novel through the theme of middle-class gentility.

Chapter 8. Colonel Jacque

My father . . . charged her [the nurse], that if I lived to come to any big-ness, capable to understand the meaning of it, she should always take care to bid me remember that I was a gentleman . . . and that I would cer-tainly act like a gentleman, if I believed myself to be so. — Defoe, *Colonel Jacque,* ed. George A. Aitken, I, 1–2

Moll Flanders and Colonel Jacque, in the estimate of George Sherburn, "form two of the best contrasting genre pictures of the century." Moll begins her life in Newgate, the bastard child of an unknown father and a convict mother. Colonel Jacque, on the other hand, although also a bastard, is raised in the knowledge that he is the child of "a gentlewoman" and a "man of quality." Thus Moll is born with bad blood, Jacque with genteel blood; but despite the enormous differences between them owing to the accident of birth, they both aspire to achieve the same end by their careers: Moll to become a gentlewoman and Jacque to be-come a gentleman.[1]

The careers of Moll and Jacque are indeed contrasting. Moll only chances upon the idea of becoming a gentlewoman, at first innocently seizing upon it as a child and then holding fast to her ambition as it takes shape in her imagination and assumes a di-rect bearing on the course of her career. Jacque, however, has the idea firmly planted in his mind from the outset by his fa-ther's charge to his nurse. The knowledge that he is a gentleman does, as his father predicted, "inspire" him with "thoughts suit-able to [his] birth" when even a small boy; it makes him ambi-tious of social distinction.

Jacque's nurse has a son of her own and another "son of shame" to care for, and in order to keep the three boys straight she assigns them titles of military rank, designating her own son, the eldest of the three, "captain." Jacque, though a child, senses the distinction and is "provoked" at not being himself the cap-tain; he is a "gentleman," by the good nurse's admission, and even though he is not at all clear about what that means, he feels he should have the distinguishing rank. To keep the peace the nurse promotes Jacque to the rank of "colonel," which pleases him mightily. As Defoe comments on Jacque's behavior, "so universally is ambition seated in the minds of men that not a beggar-boy but has his share of it" (I, 3). The nurse also encourages Jacque's social ambitions by assuring him that "none but gentlemen are ever made colonels" and that "colonels come to be lords and generals, though they were bastards at first" (I, 3).

The significance of what Defoe sets forth in these early pages of *Colonel Jacque* becomes clear when we bear in mind his audience. They were middle- and lower-class readers who were eager to identify with what they read, and Defoe enables them to identify with Colonel Jacque from the outset. The accident of birth does Jacque no material good; he is still an abandoned bastard, a "child of shame" who, though the offspring of "quality," is fobbed off on a nurse with the expectation that he "should not be seen or heard of" (I, 1). Defoe even goes so far as to suggest that Jacque is a kind of Everyman: "I was left to call myself Mr Anything, what I pleased, as fortune and better circumstances should give occasion" (I, 2). The name "Mr Anything" can be read as Defoe's invitation to his readers to see themselves and their ambitions embodied in Jacque and his career. If the bastard of unknown parents can set out to become a gentleman because he believes himself to be one, surely Defoe's readers can do the same.

Defoe always had an almost reverential regard for the ideal of the gentleman as a social force in support of the best institutions of society. Education was central to the making of a true gentleman in Defoe's scheme of things. His preface to the novel stresses the crucial importance of "a sober and well-governed education," without which so many thousands of youths in England are ruined and for lack of which Jacque is compelled "by necessity to be a thief" (xv). Defoe introduces the gentleman theme at the very beginning of the novel to demonstrate that the ambition to become a gentleman imbues Jacque with "a strange rectitude of principles" that remain with him and inspire him to realize his ambition. But Defoe derives still another moral from Jacque's career: "If he had come into the world with the advantage of education, and been well instructed how to improve the generous principles he had in him, what a man might he not have been!" (xvi). Defoe's audience was invited to take notice.

Education and gentility were, for Defoe, inseparable. "I need not give instances, or examine the character of a gentleman with a good estate and of a good family and with tolerable parts," Defoe wrote in the *Essay upon Projects*, "and examine what figure he makes for want of education." [2] In *Colonel Jacque* he intended to dramatize the importance of education to Jacque's career in general and to his attempts at becoming a gentleman in particular.

From the outset, Jacque's primary problem is his want of education. He is, like Singleton, "willing enough, and capable too, to learn anything" (I, 5), but he is not enrolled in a school. When he is only ten years old his nurse dies, and the uneducated "three Jacques" find themselves "turned loose to the world." Colonel Jacque instinctively is drawn to learn, if only indirectly; he "was always upon the inquiry, asking questions" (I, 10). But Jacque's life is that of a street arab who exists by begging or running an occasional errand.

Significantly, Jacque never gives serious thought to the idea of being a gentleman so long as his primary needs of food, clothing, and shelter remain unfulfilled. He falls in easily with a "gang of naked, ragged rogues" like himself, and his "schoolmaster" is the "devil" (I, 5). Jacque's thoughts appropriately turn first to his being a gentleman when the Major shares some stolen booty with him: "This was very welcome to me, who, as much as I was of a gentleman . . . never had a shilling of money together before in all my life, not that I could call my own" (I, 15). With the money Jacque buys himself some much-needed stockings and shoes: "I found myself so refreshed with having a pair of warm stockings on, and a pair of dry shoes — things, I say, which I had not been acquainted with a great while — that I began to call to my mind my being a gentleman" (I, 15).

Jacque next accompanies the Major to a boiling cook's in Rosemary Lane, where they put away a hearty meal. Now that the primary needs of clothing and food are satisfied, and they are seated in the warmth of the boiling cook's establishment, Jacque is in a position to appreciate the advantages of being a gentleman. The maid and serving boy at the boiling cook's look in periodically while the Major and Colonel Jacque eat their boiled beef, pudding, and beef broth, and they cry out, "Gentleman, do you call?" and, "Do ye call gentlemen?" This is not without its effect on Jacque, who comments, "I say, this was as good to me as all my dinner" (I, 16). Jacque's pleasure at being called "gentleman," however matter-of-factly, is drawn with disarming naturalness by Defoe, who himself probably appreciated the kind of secret pleasure he ascribes to Jacque — "so universally is ambition seated in the minds of men," as he wrote.

Jacque's entry into a life of crime is the direct result of his lack of education and his not being bred to any trade. "I looked on picking pockets as a kind of trade," he comments innocently, "and thought I was to go apprentice to it" (I, 19). Like all of Defoe's heroes and heroines, Colonel Jacque is not to be held responsible for his initial criminal actions: "I was made a thief involuntarily" (I, 20). Although apprenticed to a gang of pickpockets, Jacque is so uneducated that for a long time he cannot even "tell money" (I, 50), a deficiency he corrects by becoming the "scholar" of an "eminent pickpocket."

Eventually he falls in with a roguish crew of footpads. He notices, however, that he does not share "the general wickedness of [his] companions"; unlike his fellows, he does not swear or get drunk. He learns indirectly — as he has learned almost everything he knows — that in not conforming to the swearing and drinking of his colleagues he is behaving like a gentleman. One day in Rosemary Lane, he witnesses the glassmaker reprove a gentleman for his swearing because " 'tis not like a gentleman to swear" (I, 69). The episode serves a double purpose: it instructs Jacque in the manners becoming a true gentleman ("it made as great an impression upon me as it did upon the gentleman"), and it affords Defoe an occasion to condemn in passing, for the benefit of his readers, the fashionable vice of swearing by so-called gentlemen among the ranks of the gentry and nobility, whose manners and morals he had censured all his life (gentlemen "know better, and are taught better").

All this time as a pickpocket and a footpad, Jacque has been totally unaware that he was doing wrong; now he must develop a sense of right and wrong. The notion that he is a gentleman furnishes him at least with an inchoate principle of moral rectitude: "Then as to principle, 'tis true I had not foundation laid in me by education; and being early led by my fate into evil, I had the less sense of its being evil left upon my mind. But when I began to grow to an age of understanding, and to know that I was a thief . . . I would stop short, and ask myself if this was the life of a gentleman" (I, 70). Defoe effectively climaxes this second phase of Jacque's moral development with the robbery of Dame Smith, an aged woman from whom the gang steals "all she had left in the world" (I, 73). The act awakens Jacque's compassion ("it made my very heart bleed to see what agony the poor woman was in at parting with it") and he resolves to repay the woman and leave off such a life, which he now is convinced "was not the life of a gentleman" (I, 76). He breaks off with the gang and leaves for Edinburgh with Captain Jacque; but first he seeks out Dame Smith and makes restitution.

Although Jacque is now endowed with a proper conscience, he is still without a practical education or a trade. He realizes how ill prepared he is for life. Defoe uses Jacque's predicament to stress the value of a proper training to his readers: "Here indeed I felt the loss of what just parents do, and ought to do, by all their children — I mean, being bred to some trade or employment; and I wept many times that I knew not what to do or what to turn my hand to, though I resolved to leave off the wicked course I was in" (I, 96). The fault of Jacque's criminal career, as Defoe argued in his preface to the novel, lies not with Jacque but with his parents and his society. Even when he gets to Edinburgh and seeks honest employment, he finds he can get no job ("two or three things which I had offered me I lost, because I could not write or read" — I, 119).

Jacque fortunately is "delivered" from the "anxiety" of his dilemma by the generous intercession of a stabler who, in about half a year, teaches him to read and write. By becoming literate Jacque staves off the "necessity" of returning to crime for his livelihood; he is now "fit for business" and soon locates a job working for an officer of the customs. His ambition to become a gentleman cannot, however, be realized as a clerk, and he enters the army in Scotland. He no longer is under the "necessity of stealing" (I, 121) and, in the army, he can even aspire to becoming a "gentleman officer."

But commissions in the army must be bought, and Jacque is without money. Only after he has prospered, in the second part of the novel, does Jacque succeed in the army, because with "some money" he obtains "a company" in the regiment of a lieutenant colonel he knows. As an officer he takes pleasure in thinking that he is living "the life of a gentleman" (II, 41), as an officer was then regarded; in fact, he even fulfills the prediction of his nurse (I, 3) and becomes a lieutenant colonel. But first Jacque must be brought to a level of affluence that, in Defoe's mind, can best be attained in the American colonies. He deserts the army, is kidnapped by an unscrupulous sea captain, and is sold as an indentured servant in the colonies.

The third phase of Jacque's career takes place in Virginia and it affords Defoe the occasion to highlight the colonial theme. Jacque's own capsule summary of his career underscores his rapid rise to a position of prosperity in the colonies despite the lowness of his beginnings: "from a pickpocket to a kidnapped, miserable slave in Virginia . . . then from a slave to a head-officer or overseer of slaves, and from thence to a master-planter" (I, 176). In short, Jacque acquires in the colonies the wealth he needs to realize his ambition of becoming a true gentleman ("I was grown really rich" — I, 184).

Defoe also exploits the colonial theme for its propagandistic value. Colonel Jacque digresses from the narration of his career in the colonies in order to address himself to his audience on the subject of opportunities awaiting them in Virginia or Maryland. After a man completes his term of service, he is allotted fifty acres of land for planting. Thus everyone becomes a planter with credit from the very outset, and Jacque assures his audience, "no diligent man ever miscarried, if he had health to work and was a good husband; for he every year increases a little, and every year adding more land and planting more tobacco, which is real money, he must gradually increase in substance, till at length he gets enough to buy negroes and other servants, and then never works himself any more" (I, 177–178). This ostensibly foolproof rags-to-riches formula expounded by Defoe through Colonel Jacque, as it was earlier by Moll Flanders' mother, was aimed at encouraging the bolder and more enterprising members of the English middle and lower classes to seek and make their fortunes

166

in the New World, where men may begin "without a hat or a shoe" and in time rise to the eminence of owning "estates of £40,000 or £50,000" (I, 177). Surely such a formula must have had its appeal for Defoe's readers, and designedly so; for he wanted the members of his class to take part in the great work of colonization, the rewards of which were, as Defoe made clear, the prospect of an "estate" and the life of an affluent gentleman-planter.

Now that Defoe has brought Colonel Jacque to the point of being a thriving plantation owner, and he is "arrived to an independent state," Jacque finds "different sentiments of things taking place in [his] mind" (I, 180). He now has the leisure to reflect upon what it means "to be a gentleman," and he recalls the exchange between the glassmaker and the gentleman about the behavior proper to a true gentleman, "that to be a gentleman was to be an honest man" (I, 181). Being a prosperous planter, Jacque has no need to concern himself about being "an honest man"; he is not put to the test by any necessity. All he really lacks now to qualify as a complete gentleman is an appropriate education. His "prosperity" is but the "foundation" of his new life, which still requires "the superstructure," and this only a "liberal education" can provide.

The fourth and final stage of Colonel Jacque's development as a true gentleman is reached when he embarks on his program of self-education. If his daily demands of attending the plantation had not precluded it, Jacque "would have been content to have gone to school" (I, 183). Still, he comes "to love books" and to read widely in histories and other books he either buys or borrows. Just as he had found in the stabler in Edinburgh a tutor to instruct him to read and write, he now finds in a transported felon from Bristol a man who is "an excellent scholar" and from whom he gladly learns Latin. Jacque becomes both a "planter" and a "student," and from his "pedagogue" he acquires a "liberal education" (I, 183, 186).

The process of education is consummated when Colonel Jacque learns from his tutor the importance of repentance. The felon from Bristol is an example of what, to Defoe, was "the case of most of the wicked part of the world, viz., that to be reduced to necessity is to be wicked; for necessity is not only the temptation, but is such a temptation as human nature is not empowered to resist" (I, 187). He, like Defoe's other characters, first succumbed to the "necessity" of crime. But once begun, a life of crime is not easily abandoned, and the tutor remarks that sincere repentance requires "leisure." Now, in the colonies, the tutor informs Jacque, "God has found me leisure to repent" (I, 188). Jacque's tutor finally introduces him to the Bible, and his education is completed when he asks his teacher, after some thought about God and the Bible, to "leave off teaching me Latin, and teach me religion" (I, 198).

In this way Defoe rounds off the education of Colonel Jacque as a complete gentleman. Jacque has a true liberal education, has discovered God and the Bible, has two thriving estates worth thousands of pounds, and has the manners and morals of a proper gentleman (he does not drink or swear or wench). At the conclusion of Volume I Colonel Jacque is a model of the self-made gentleman, a model with which Defoe's readers could identify completely — and probably did.

Defoe had in mind yet another aspect of the gentleman theme when he described Colonel Jacque's youthful career in crime. The era of George I witnessed an alarming rise in the crime rate, especially crimes of theft and highway robbery. This trend, in turn, gave rise to a proliferation of books and pamphlets by hack writers on the lives and exploits of this swelling class of criminals. "An examination of the lowest class of thieves' literature of the time," according to William Lee, "shows that successful highwaymen and burglars were exalted into heroes, whose deeds were more held up as examples for imitation, than as warnings to be avoided." And, George A. Aitken notes, "it was between 1720 and 1730 that the greatest number of lives of criminals — told in the wrong spirit — appeared." In the year 1722, for example, in December of which Defoe's *Colonel Jacque* was published, such works as *Tyburn's Worthies, Compleat Account of Robberies committed by James Carrick and others, Account of Robberies committed by Wilson, History of the Robberies of all the celebrated Highwaymen to the year 1722,* and many similar accounts glutted the market — the works cited all being published within one month.

Defoe was certainly aware of this trend in the literature of thieves at the time he was writing his novels. He was closely in touch with booksellers and the tastes of readers. Moreover, during the years 1720 to 1726 he was in the employ of Applebee, who was a printer widely known for his interest in publishing criminal lives. While connected with *Applebee's Journal* in the early 1720's, Defoe was authorized by Applebee to represent the magazine as a criminal reporter, an assignment that gained him entrance into Newgate and enabled him to obtain first-hand accounts from convicted criminals of their exploits and confessions. His interviews with criminals and his readings in criminal biographies made him see the disparity between the actual careers of criminals and the falsified biographies by "hackney Grub Street writers [operating] upon the old pickpocket principle of publishing anything to get a penny."

Admittedly, he himself wrote books and pamphlets about famous pirates, like the *General History of the Robberies and Murders of the Most Notorious Pyrates* (1724), as well as lives of celebrated criminals, like *A Narrative of all the Robberies, Escapes, etc. of John Sheppard* (1724) and *The True and Genuine Account of the Life and Actions of the Late Jonathan Wild* (1725), which were printed and sold by John Applebee. Defoe obviously had no compunctions about the sensational side of these criminal accounts so long as they included a useful moral for the reader. Defoe, for example, could write *Unparallel'd Cruelty: Or, The Tryal of Captain Jeane of Bristol* (1726), a lurid work that dwells on the gory details of the slow torture and death of an innocent cabin boy at the hands of a sadistic sea captain; but his prevailing tone in the narrative is that of an outraged moralist and the story is designed to serve as an *exemplum* for the readers. What concerned Defoe during this period was the vulgarization of the ideal of the gentleman in these cheap and eulogistic criminal biographies. It was one thing to offer vivid, even lurid, accounts of desperate or depraved men for purposes of moral instruction, but it was something else entirely to idolize these villains as heroes. Such "romantic reports," as Defoe called them, not only were spurious, they also invited approbation, even emulation, from the readers.

Defoe's fundamental position on crime and criminals in general is unmistakably set forth in such works as *Some Considerations*

Upon Street-Walkers (1726), *Second Thoughts Are Best, Street-Robberies Consider'd* (1728), and his last published work, *An Effectual Scheme for the Immediate Preventing of Street Robberies* (1730). In all these works he addressed himself to the problems attending the sharp rise in the crime rate during this time and the very practices glorified by the criminal biographies of the 1720's. Defoe, in short, wrote as a social reformer anxious to discover ways of curtailing the crime rate and alerting the citizens of London on how to protect themselves and their property.[3]

In *Colonel Jacque* he tried to check this trend in the criminal biographies of treating the rogues as if they were gentlemen. The main purpose of the section dealing with Jacque's brief membership in the gang of the footpad Will is to underscore the essential distinction, to Defoe, between the vulgarized notion of the "gentleman thief," as exemplified in the character of Will, and the true gentleman in the making, as exemplified by Jacque himself.

In Will we have Defoe's representation of the typical hero of rogue biographies; he is "a lusty, strong fellow, and withal very bold and daring" who "would fight anybody and venture upon anything"; he is, in a word, "above the mean rank of a poor pickpocket" (I, 67). Jacque naturally is drawn to so dashing a person as Will, and he is invited to fall in with Will's band of thieves: "'I'll bring you into a brave gang, Jacque,' says he, 'where you shall see we shall be all gentlemen'" (I, 68). Defoe tellingly punctures this inflated promise of gentility by having Jacque remark innocently, "that is to say, in the evening they were footpads, and in the night they were housebreakers." Defoe takes special care to show that Colonel Jacque, although a member of the gang, is different from his comrades in crime. Whereas Will and the others are guilty of "raking and vice," not to mention swearing and intemperance, Jacque is free of "the general wickedness" of his companions.

Jacque gradually is led to intuit — he is still at this time without any proper education — that his personal understanding of a gentleman differs radically from Will's; for when Will assures him he will be "a gentleman," he comments: "Will, it seems, understood that word in a quite different manner from me; for his gentleman was nothing more or less than a gentleman thief, a villain of a higher degree than a pickpocket, and one that might do something more wicked, and better entitling him to the gallows, than could be done in our way. But my gentleman that I had my eye upon was another thing quite, though I could not really tell how to describe it either" (I, 71). Defoe clearly is attacking the notion of the "gentleman thief" as popularized in the low life literature of the time. But not until the gang robs Dame Smith are the pretensions to gentility by thieves the likes of Will and his companions shattered completely and finally. The robbery of Dame Smith is described in the most affecting manner; she is a poor honest woman from whom the gang takes "all she had left in the world." The wickedness of the act causes Colonel Jacque such moral anguish that "it came into [his] head with a double force that this was the high-road to the devil, and that this was not the life of a gentleman" (I, 76). Only Jacque can respond to the viciousness of stealing from a pathetic old woman like Dame Smith; his mind is full of "abhorrence" over the act, but his cohorts are totally inured to it.

Defoe further elaborates the point. Will informs Jacque that the gang will "take the highway like gentlemen," get a lot of money, and "live like gentlemen" (I, 76–77). Will's persistent use of the term "gentleman" in describing actions that are obviously anything but gentlemanly enables Defoe to make his point with his readers about the debased ideal of the gentleman promulgated by the cheap and trashy pamphlets so popular in the period. In a dramatic confrontation between Will and Jacque the distinction between a real gentleman and the so-called "gentleman thief" is forcibly drawn:

"Why, Will, do you call this way of living the life of a gentleman?"
"Why," says Will, "why not?"
"Why," says I, "was it like a gentleman for me to take the 22s. from a poor ancient woman, when she begged of me upon her knees not to take it, and told me it was all she had in the world to buy her bread for herself and a sick child which she had at home?"   (1, 77)

The contrived emotional appeal of Jacque's question is irresistible to anyone but the hardened Will, whose retort, "Did you ever see any of them cry when they see gentlemen go to the gallows,"effectively reinforces the reader's impression of Will's basic wickedness as well as his misconception and misuse of the word gentleman.

Defoe leaves absolutely no doubt in the reader's mind about his purpose in the passage dealing with Will and the gang of footpads who like to think of themselves as gentlemen. Will is soon captured by the authorities and put in Newgate, where Jacque visits his former "master and tutor in wickedness." Will's final words to Jacque are, significantly: "I was far out, Jacque. . . . when I told you, to be a notorious thief was to live like a gentleman" (I, 94). In so having Will recant his mistaken notion of the "gentleman thief," Defoe drives home his lesson for his readers by noting that Will was condemned in the "very next sessions" and executed three weeks later. Will is not even offered the option of being transported, so strongly did Defoe obviously feel about the lesson he wanted to leave with his readers that he would not risk softening its impact. He also managed to compress his treatment of the "gentleman thief" theme into some twenty-five pages, thereby insuring that his point would not be missed or misinterpreted by his readers.

Defoe, however, did not restrict his treatment of the gentleman theme in *Colonel Jacque* to a condemnation of the misuse of the ideal by the lower classes; he also addressed himself to censuring the fashionable excesses of the upper classes. The second part of the novel has always presented problems for critics because it marks a dropping off from the first part, which traces in ascending action the rise of Colonel Jacque to the full stature of a true gentleman. Even so partisan a critic as John Masefield, for example, who valued *Colonel Jacque* as Defoe's "best work of fiction," remarked that "no one cares for *Colonel Jacque* after he begins his disgusting series of marriages." But the very fact that the marriages are "disgusting" is Defoe's way of condemning most compellingly the failings of the gentry to act like true gentlemen. The gentleman theme, in a different color, continues to thread its way through the second part of the novel.[4]

Although Colonel Jacque is basically a gentleman at the end of part one of the novel, he is still without the polish and sophistication generally associated with gentlemen. To acquire these finishing touches, Defoe has his hero go to France, the country where, to the English mind, such finishing touches as are appropriate to a gentleman may best be acquired. (Lord Chesterfield, to take a prominent example, went to France for his polish in gentlemanly matters early in the eighteenth century, as did many other fashion-conscious English gentlemen.) Up to now Defoe has omitted entirely the theme of marriage — so central in *Moll Flanders* — because Jacque was busy becoming educated and prosperous; now, however, he is "at the height of [his] good fortune" (II, 15) and can turn to other pursuits.

Jacque's reputation as "a great merchant" (II, 16) makes him a target for the machinations of women of quality, and being "a mere boy in the affair of love" (II, 17), he soon falls victim in marriage to a lady who sets her cap for him. It is worth remembering, though, that Jacque's series of marriages begins with the motivation, on his part at least, that in so frequenting the company of ladies in France he will learn to become a polished and refined gentleman. He went to France with "a perfect indifferency for the whole sex," having no more regard for women than for "a picture hanging upon the wall" (II, 19). Gradually, however, he is attracted to such genteel diversions as playing cards with ladies and dancing with them. His motivation is made perfectly clear by Defoe: "for in France I accomplished myself with everything that was needful to make me what I believed myself to be even from a boy — I mean a gentleman" (II, 22).

The "disgusting series of marriages" which offended John Masefield's critical sensibilities is to be read as Defoe's commentary on how the conjugal state was being subverted by the very vices made fashionable by the upper classes. Typical of Defoe's position on the low state of morality in England is the following statement drawn from his *Review*: "As in the common vices of the nation, 'tis not so much the common-people, as the gentry, clergy, and magistrates, that are the authors of our general debaucheries, by their encouraging the crimes of the meaner sort in their example" (VI, 255). In Jacque's first marriage Defoe exposes the evils of gambling and adultery and their ruinous effects on marriage. Even though Jacque's wife brings him the handsome dowry of £1,500 a year, she is an incorrigible gamester, and as Jacque remarks ruefully, "no estate is big enough for a box and dice" (II, 26). Jacque must secure a divorce from his wife in the ecclesiastical court when he discovers her guilty of marital whoredom, and he is "sick of wedlock" (II, 31).

The first marriage proves disastrous for Jacque even after he has rid himself of his unfaithful wife because he must satisfy debts from her "extravagance of three years." His difficulty with creditors makes him realize that he cannot defend himself and his honor with a sword, as was expected of a gentleman in so chivalrous a country as France: "though I had learned a great many things in France to make me look like a gentleman, I had forgot the main article of learning how to use a sword, a thing so universally practised there" (II, 33). Jacque soon finds himself challenged to a duel because of his unfamiliarity with the customs of the gentry. He tries to settle his disagreement with the French gentleman peacefully and lawfully, but the Frenchman, true to his code of honor, misinterprets "law" to mean "Gentleman's law," namely dueling. He addresses Colonel Jacques accordingly: "They say you are a gentleman, and they call you colonel. Now, if you are a gentleman, I accept your challenge, sir; and if you will walk out with me, I will take it for full payment of the bill, and will decide it as gentlemen ought to do" (II, 34). But since Jacque is totally unfamiliar with a sword, he cannot defend himself even if he were inclined to duel with the Frenchman, which he is not. The actions of the heated Frenchman are the stereotyped behavior of any unmannerly gentleman, for he resorts to hurling oaths with "about six or seven 'damme's' " thrown into the bargain. Jacque is taunted with being a coward and is treated impertinently by the so-called French gentleman, who later exacts a terrible vengeance by having Jacque waylaid by a hired assailant who slits his nose and almost cuts off one of his ears.

The association of gentility and dueling was particularly strong with the public in 1722. In that year Richard Steele's *The Conscious Lovers* appeared on the boards and had a prodigious success with theatergoers. Even Steele was moved to wonder why his play was "received with universal acceptance." The high point of the play was the barely averted duel between Bevil Jr. and his friend Myrtle; in fact, Steele made his intention perfectly clear in the preface later added to the printed version of the play: "Nor do I make any difficulty to acknowledge that the whole was writ for the sake of the scene of the fourth act, wherein Mr. Bevil evades the quarrel with his friend, and hope it may have some effect upon the Goths and Vandals that frequent the theatres." The Goths and Vandals, of course, were the gentry

who regarded dueling as the gentlemanly way of settling differences and so preserving their honor, a practice of which Steele
hoped to disabuse them. *The Conscious Lovers* immediately became the talk of the town. The fashionable upper-class practice
of dueling was very much in the air while Defoe was composing
Colonel Jacque.[5]

The first performance of Steele's *Conscious Lovers* took place
on November 7, 1722; the success of the play was instantaneous.
Defoe was writing at a furious pace throughout 1722 — "the
greatest *annus mirabilis* in the career of any English writer," in
the estimate of William P. Trent. On November 22 Defoe saw
published his *Impartial History of the Life and Actions of Peter
Alexowitz,* a work based partly on his previously published *History of . . . Charles XII* but none the less a production of well
over four hundred pages. Since *Colonel Jacque* was not published until December 20, it is very likely that Defoe was still
at work on the manuscript of *Colonel Jacque,* probably the
second part of the novel, when Steele's play with its attack on
dueling was sweeping the town. Defoe was a man ever in touch
with the times, and since his story dealt with the theme of the
gentleman, he probably decided to appropriate a relevant and
topical issue for his work in progress.

Besides, Defoe had long been an outspoken critic of dueling.
As Mr. Review he consistently attacked the practice, and in 1705
even printed a special fourteen-page appendix to Volume I of
the *Review* which offered an English translation, presumably by
Defoe, of King Louis XIV's edict on dueling, "containing a general regulation concerning duels made at St. Germains en Lay in
the month of Aug. 1679." Defoe's intention in printing the appendix is stated explicitly: "I cannot but wish something like
this practis'd by a legal authority in England, where we see but
this very week two gentlemen murthered in duels." In 1713 he
had assembled for the press *An Account of the Abolishing of
Duels in France*, a work, as the advertisement in the *Guardian*
for June 1, 1713, read, "humbly offered to the consideration of
the House of Commons." Clearly by the time he came to compose
Colonel Jacque late in 1722, Defoe needed little more than the
stimulus of Steele's play to prompt him to set down his opposition
to dueling in the pages of his novel in progress.[6]

Because Colonel Jacque was humiliated and almost killed in his first encounter with the "Gentleman's law" of dueling, he learns to handle a sword while serving as an officer in the army. His second marriage, designed to expose the vice of intemperance, forces him into another dueling situation, again very much against his will. Jacque, fearful of being a cuckold, confronts his wife in the presence of a marquis; but rather than seek a quarrel with the marquis, who could not have found his way into bed with his wife were she herself not "willing to be a whore" (II, 65), he rightly sees his wife as the chief offender. The marquis, however, true to his code and the "Gentleman's law," cannot let the incident pass so easily; he demands "satisfaction" from Jacque, who has no choice but to oblige him. They duel and Jacque fells his opponent. The outcome of the "Gentleman's law" this time is no more favorable than before. The marquis in time recovers from his wounds but loses his "commission in the Guards, which was worth to him twenty thousand livres" and Colonel Jacque is forced to flee France for his life.[7]

In condemning the practice of dueling among gentlemen to preserve their honor, Defoe does not adopt the heavy moralizing tone of Richard Steele. Defoe's method of censure in the novel is indirect. The behavior of the Frenchman toward Jacque is hardly calculated to recommend itself to Defoe's readers, who would see in his cursing and vicious actions only the represensible performance they commonly associated with such so-called gentlemen. Similarly the actions and fate of the marquis are aimed at underscoring the code of dueling as wrong, both by its unreasonableness and by its evil consequences for those who live by it. There is nothing fashionable or dashing in Defoe's depiction of dueling in *Colonel Jacque.*

Jacque, significantly, is represented by Defoe as seeking the same kind of goal in life as Moll Flanders; for he remarks, "A settled life was the thing I loved" (II, 72). Despite two previous marriages which ended disastrously for him, he still pursues his goal of a settled life as a gentleman. After more misadventures in matrimony, which are useful in highlighting further abuses of the conjugal state (for instance, "Oh, the power of intemperance!" — II, 80), and after a generally unfortunate career as a gentleman in the beau monde of the Continent, Colonel Jacque returns to the scene where he first realized his basic ambition of becoming a gentleman: Virginia. The reintroduction of the colonial theme enables Defoe to show, by contrast, how wholesome and prosperous life in the colonies is in comparison with the genteel and artificial life on the Continent. Returning to Virginia, Jacque finds his "plantations prodigiously increased" and is "exceedingly pleased" (II, 92) by all he sees.

To complete the picture and to secure for his hero the "settled family life" he seeks, Defoe rounds off the marriage theme by reintroducing Jacque's divorced first wife, who now turns up a reformed woman, pious and sober, on Jacque's plantation. In time they remarry and live happily together. His wife already has repented of her past life, and before the novel concludes, Jacque, too, repents sincerely. Thus Jacque and his wife, like Moll and her husband, finally return to England as sincere penitents and affluent plantation owners. They will henceforth, we may assume, live like exemplary gentlefolk.

Chapter 9. The Fortunate Mistress

Sir Robert and I agreed exactly in our notions of a merchant. Sir Robert said, and I found it to be true, that a true-bred merchant is the best gentleman in the nation. — Defoe, *The Fortunate Mistress,* ed. George A. Aitken, I, 193

The publication of *The Fortunate Mistress* on February 29, 1724, marked a further development in Defoe's treatment of the theme of gentility. In the careers of Moll Flanders and Colonel Jacque two years earlier he had detailed the rise of two bastard children from opposite ends of the social scale to the status of gentlefolk. Now he was to undertake the presentation of a middle-class girl's rise to the higher station of a full-fledged "lady." As the bill of fare offered in the full title reads: "a History of the Life and Vast Variety of Fortunes of Mademoiselle de Beleau, afterwards called the Countess of Wintselheim, in Germany. Being the person known by the name of the Lady Roxana, in the time of King Charles II." If Moll and Jacque were designed to encourage readers to look up in society with some hope of succeeding in their aspirations to become gentlemen and gentlewomen, Roxana was to serve as the embodiment of Defoe's thoughts on the advisability of looking up higher still, to the top level of society, a level traditionally restricted only to the most privileged members of any society. *The Fortunate Mistress* is Defoe's essay into the province of high society, as *Moll Flanders* and *Colonel Jacque* were his essays into the familiar province of middle-class gentility.

Roxana's early life, prior to her marriage, is set forth as consisting of the best features of a secure and prosperous bourgeois home. In this comfortable environment she acquires the graces necessary "for the sociable part of the world"; she also grows into a strikingly handsome young woman, tall and "very well made." In sum, we learn that she "wanted neither wit, beauty, or money."

She grows up "having all the advantages that any young woman could desire" (I, 3).

At the outset Roxana's career looks bright indeed, unlike the dark beginnings of Moll or Jacque. Roxana has every right to regard herself as destined for a "happy living." She is married well to "an eminent brewer in the city" at the age of fifteen. But first marriages in Defoe's fiction never turn out well. "After I have told you that he was a handsome man and a good sportsman," Roxana remarks, "I have indeed said all" (I, 4). To be a merchant-tradesman and a sportsman was, to Defoe, simply a contradiction in terms, and having told her middle-class readers that her husband liked to hunt, Roxana could assume that they would know immediately what the disastrous consequences of such a marriage must be. One of the surest ways for a tradesman to fall into ruin, according to Defoe, was for him to take on the diversions of the gentry. "When I see young shopkeepers keep horses, ride a hunting, learn dog-language, and keep the sportsman's brogue upon their tongues," Defoe wrote in *The Complete English Tradesman* the following year, "I am always afraid for them" (I, 98).

The financial collapse of Roxana's "fool husband" affords Defoe the occasion to draw the same moral as in the episode of the ruin of Moll's second husband, the "gentleman-tradesman." Defoe tries to caution his readers about the dangers involved in their careless pursuit of pleasure and luxury, which can only end in bankruptcy. He prepares for the ruin of Roxana's husband by first having her older bother, a merchant, fail for "running on too rashly in his adventures" (I, 6). The fall of Roxana's husband, however, is presented almost as a case study. In *The Complete English Tradesman* Defoe was to outline the pattern of failure embodied in Roxana's husband: "To gentlemen of fortunes and estates, who are born to large possessions, 'tis certainly lawful to spend their spare hours on horseback with their hounds or hawks, pursuing their game . . . [To] the prudent tradesman . . . nothing of pleasure or diversion can be innocent to him, whatever it may be to another, if it injures his business, if it takes either his time, or his mind, or his delight, or his attendance from his business" (I, 104–105). Even after he has sold off his brewery and paid his debts, the fool husband does not learn his lesson;

he continues to live "as he did before," that is, he maintains his horses and hounds and huntsmen, riding out to the forest every day "a-hunting" while his "money decreased apace" (I, 8). When his funds are all but exhausted, he runs off "in a handsome furniture . . . having an embroidered housing, a case of pistols, and other things" (I, 12). He apes the life of the wealthy and leisured gentry to the last, leaving behind only the vestiges of the genteel diversions which accounted for his ruin, his "hunting-horn . . . and his hunting-saddle."

Roxana suddenly finds herself an abandoned wife without funds and with five little children. Defoe, who in his own life certainly experienced "differing fortunes," in less than half a year knowing "the difference between the closet of a King, and the dungeon of Newgate," is eminently qualified to portray the desperate feelings of his heroine, who is experiencing a fall in fortune from one social extreme to the other:

They saw me in rags and dirt, who was but a little time before riding in my coach; thin, and looking almost like one starved, who was before fat and beautiful. The house, that was before handsomely furnished with pictures and ornaments, cabinets, pier-glasses, and everything suitable, was now stripped and naked, most of the goods having been seized by the landlord for rent, or sold to buy necessaries; in a word, all was misery and distress, the face of ruin was everywhere to be seen . . . (I, 16)

Defoe designs this moving passage to serve a double purpose. First, it stands as a vivid and compelling reminder to his middle-class readers of what they may experience in their homes if they and their families fall victim to the trend of emulating the extravagant and luxurious living practiced by the upper classes. Defoe can present such a forceful case in no small part because he himself experienced on more than one occasion the disaster he here describes as befalling Roxana or earlier described as befalling Moll and her "gentleman-tradesman" husband. Second, Defoe now has swept away all the comforts and security of Roxana's bourgeois upbringing; she is at this point, like Moll Flanders, reduced by circumstance to a state of desperation and necessity. As her maid Amy counsels, "honesty is out of the question when starving is the case" (I, 28).

At the nadir of her fortunes, Roxana has the sanction of the law of nature in becoming the mistress of her landlord ("But poverty was my snare; dreadful poverty!" — I, 40). With her "gentleman" she lives very "gallantly," accompanying him to France, where she can have an equipage and live in genteel fashion. Roxana succinctly states the net result of her turning whore, "Before I was poor . . . now I was not only provided for, but very rich" (I, 55). And when her lover is murdered, she finds herself suddenly restored to her former fortunes, being "possessed of almost ten thousand pounds sterling" (I, 59). In a remarkably short career Defoe endows his heroine with a considerable fortune; but she is not like Moll Flanders, who wants only a settled and genteel way of living. Roxana now aspires to something higher than that.

In France Roxana attracts the notice of a prince, and despite obvious differences in "quality" between them, the prince persuades her that her "beauty" exalts her to an "equality" (I, 63). She wastes no time in putting her beauty to use; she changes into a new dress ("une dishabille") and the prince succumbs to her charms, promising her, as she goes to bed with him, "Now you shall be a princess" (I, 70). Roxana knows she cannot justify her actions to her readers; she can only explain that while "poverty and want is an irresistible temptation to the poor, vanity and great things are as irresistible to others" (I, 70). For Roxana, to be courted and loved by a prince who promises her "great things" is an irresistible temptation. Moll became a whore because her head was turned at the prospect of becoming a gentlewoman through marriage to an eldest son destined to inherit his family estate; Roxana already is a whore, but she clearly is tempted by the promise of becoming "a princess" in her liaison with the prince. Defoe, however, makes it clear that Roxana had no monetary motive, as Moll did. Roxana admits, "I had now no poverty attending me; on the contrary, I was mistress of ten thousand pounds before the prince did anything for me" (I, 71).

Roxana is irresistibly drawn to the fine things and the extravagant way of living that only a prince or other person of the highest quality can offer. She is charmed and dazzled by her new circumstances ("As he loved like a prince, so he rewarded like a prince" — I, 77). As the mistress of a prince, Roxana lives like a "princess," showered with luxurious gifts: jewels and money and clothes — "clothes, such as the Queen of France would not have disdained" (I, 77). The prince satisfies her every wish, showing her the beau monde as she requests (I, 93), and even according her the honor of meeting the King of France himself. It is not easy to abandon such a style of life once one has grown accustomed to it, let alone when one is inclined to such a life in the first place.

In the careers of Moll Flanders and Colonel Jacque, Defoe had for the most part depicted the problems of necessity attending the evil acts of his heroine and hero. In the career of Roxana, however, he aimed at a portrayal of the effects of avarice — and vanity — attending the wickedness practiced by his heroine. "Every station of life has its snares attending it," Defoe wrote in *The Complete English Tradesman*, and these he divided simply into two basic temptations: "1. Necessity tempts the poor man; 2. Avarice tempts the rich." Of the two temptations, there was no doubt in Defoe's mind about the far greater culpability of avarice. " 'Tis not criminal to be poor; necessity is no offence till it makes itself a snare . . . but avarice is a crime in its nature; 'tis a devil in its very kind, born of hell, and infused in the very soul itself" (II, 21–22). In Roxana's rapid rise to the apex of luxury and extravagant living, Defoe recorded for his readers the sin of avarice taking root in his heroine's soul.

Roxana is mistress to her prince for eight years, in which time she enjoys virtually every privilege and pleasure commonly associated with the life of a princess, including a fabulous Grand Tour of two years' duration among the highest society. In spite of her "affluence" and her "good fortune," Roxana cannot forget that she "had been rich and poor alternately," and she adopts a crass business-like attitude to her career as a mistress, realizing that it is supported only by her beauty ("the great article that supported my interest"), which in time was certain to depreciate. Her "business," therefore, is "to take care that I should fall as softly as I could" because "like the mistresses of great men," she can expect to be dropped eventually (I, 118).

When the prince does terminate their relationship, Roxana is "fully satisfied" (I, 124). She takes stock of her situation:

[I] had now no more temptation of poverty, or of the powerful motive which Amy used with me — namely, comply and live, deny and starve; I say, I had no poverty to introduce vice, but was grown not only well supplied, but rich; and not only rich, but was very rich; in a word, richer than I knew how to think of, for truth of it was, that thinking of it sometimes almost distracted me, for want of knowing how to dispose of it, and for fear of losing it all again by some cheat or trick, not knowing anybody that I could commit the trust of it to. (I, 124)

The paradox of Roxana's affluence is that it does not make her secure and easy, as she had hoped; rather it makes her fret about how to preserve her wealth. Her predicament is not unlike that of Colonel Jacque, when as a little boy he finds himself with a little money and is perplexed at how to keep it secure, first holding it in his fist, then tying it up in a dirty rag, and finally almost losing it in the trunk of a hollow tree. Defoe appreciated as few writers of his age the anxieties attending wealth as well as poverty ("Oh, the weight of human care! I, a poor beggar-boy, could not sleep so soon as I had but a little money to keep" — I, 25). If Colonel Jacque could experience such profound anxiety over his four guineas and eleven shillings, how much more acute the anxiety of Roxana over her princess' wealth. Avarice, Defoe suggests, is the work of the devil and carries its own punishment.

In her agitation over the security of her wealth, Roxana turns for help to a Dutch merchant in Paris, who proves himself her "deliverer" and a man "of substance and of honesty" (I, 125). But Roxana cannot even express her gratitude because her wealth has become so much of an obsession that it rules all her thoughts and she cannot act like a woman because of it. Instead of settling down to enjoy her wealth, she strikes out on a new career: "Now I was become, from a lady of pleasure, a woman of business, and of great busines too, I assure you" (I, 147).

Defoe leaves no doubt that Roxana could at this point in her life again have chosen to settle into a secure and affluent married life. Her first "fool husband" has been reported dead and she is now "a real free woman" (I, 149). Amy counsels that Roxana set herself up in a coach and snare herself a nobleman who will make her a "duchess," but she rejects this advice on the specious grounds that it is better to be a mistress than a wife. Amy's advice is well-taken, and Roxana knows it: "a wife appears boldly and honourably with her husband, lives at home, and possesses his house, his servants, his equipages, and has a right to them all, and to call them her own; entertains his friends, owns his children, and has the return of duty and affection from them, as they are here her own, and claims upon his estate, by the custom of England, if he dies and leaves her a widow" (I, 149). Roxana's reflections on the bright side of marriage read like a page out of Defoe's *Family Instructor* or *Religious Courtship*; they make a much more attractive alternative to the life of a whore or a woman of business.

The Dutch merchant, who has much to recommend him, wants to marry Roxana. He is wealthy in his own right and thus is not a fortune seeker. He is a gentleman by his manner and bearing, "bred among people more polite and more courteous than is esteemed the ordinary usage of the Dutch" (I, 159). He has demonstrated his honesty and devotion to her by attending to her business affairs in Europe, and now he expresses his love. But to all this she remains "inflexible." Roxana does eventually let the Dutch merchant lie with her, not out of love or affection or even pleasure, but out of commercial interests: "I, that was infinitely obliged to him before, began to talk to him as if I had balanced accounts with him now" (I, 163). Roxana in her "woman of business" way of calculating considers "the favour of lying with a whore was equal, not to the thousand pistoles only, but to all the debt I owed him for saving my life and all my effects" (I, 163). Roxana's terminology in describing the affair is the language of trade; she no longer is a woman in her own right; she has become an incarnation of the commercial spirit, "a man-woman" (I, 194), as she is later to describe herself aptly to Sir Robert Clayton.

Roxana has been corrupted by wealth. Even after she discovers herself pregnant by the Dutch merchant and he again comes forward with an honorable proposal of marriage, appealing even from totally unselfish motives ("as you are a Christian and a mother, not to let the innocent lamb you go with be ruined before it is born" — I, 178), she refuses, and for no cogent reason save the irrationality and wickedness that seizes people when their wealth is their primary, if not exclusive, concern. In refusing the Dutch merchant, Roxana catalogues what she turns her back on — and while pregnant at that:

I had one of the honestest, completest gentlemen upon earth at my hand . . . He had offered . . . to quit all his pretensions to my estate, and give it up to my management, having a plentiful estate of his own. Here I might have settled myself out of reach even of disaster itself; his estate and mine would have purchased even then about two thousand pounds a year, and I might have lived like a queen . . . and, which was above all, I had now an opportunity to have quitted a life of crime and debauchery . . . and to have sat down quiet in plenty and honor, and to have set myself apart to the great work . . . I mean that of repentance. (I, 180)

Roxana's rejection of everything a person of her religious and well-educated bourgeois background could conceivably hope for, including the opportunity to repent of her past transgressions, is calculated by Defoe to serve as an *exemplum* ("a memorial") for his readers on the evil consequences of avarice, on "how dangerously we act when we follow the dictates of an ambitious mind" (I, 183).

In the next phase of Roxana's career in London Defoe accomplishes two important things. First, he portrays her dazzling life among London high society, a course that naturally takes her to Court, where she is pictured among all the splendor and sinfulness generally associated in the Puritan mind with the Cavalier reign of Charles II; in fact, she even succeeds in capping her career at Court by becoming a mistress of the king himself. Second, through Roxana's life in London, Defoe presents a dramatic condemnation of the profusion and loose living among members of the gentry and nobility, not only in the time of Charles II but also in his contemporary London, where ostentation and extravagance were in evidence everywhere. Despite the obvious anachronism of the account in the novel, Defoe was offering his readers what amounted to a reflection of their times, a reflection that was as certain to concern them as it alarmed Defoe.

In London Roxana seeks the assistance of "the famous Sir Robert Clayton" in putting her fortune to work. The appearance of Sir Robert Clayton in the novel has been something of a puzzle to Defoe scholars; he is the only person who figures in the story under his own name. Two questions arise: why did Defoe place him in the novel under his own name and what function was he supposed to serve? First of all, Sir Robert Clayton was a prototype of those *novos homines* who rose to wealth and power in the latter half of the seventeenth century. Humbly born, he started as a scrivener and eventually accumulated a prodigious personal fortune from banking and moneylending. Defoe significantly mentions Sir Robert Clayton in his *Tour*, which came out the following year, as a lively example of those mighty merchants "whose beginnings were small, or but small compar'd, and who have exceeded even the greatest part of the nobility of England in wealth." Given Defoe's reading audience, it is not difficult to deduce the reason he chose a familiar figure like Sir Robert to handle Roxana's business interests. "Sir Robert," Roxana notes appropriately, is "a man thoroughly versed in arts of improving money, but thoroughly honest" (I, 192). Sir Robert's function simply is to improve Roxana's fortune, which he does very cleverly and successfully; he not only secures for her safe mortgages and other securities forming a "handsome estate of a thousand pounds a year" (I, 187) but also raises the interest she receives on her investments from five to six percent, which to Roxana "was a very satisfying article" (I, 192).[1]

Roxana's relations with Clayton further highlight her avarice. She is not content to accrue profits even from the favorable and reasonably safe investment opportunities afforded by the financial world of London and the seasoned investment counsel of Sir Robert Clayton. Sir Robert outlines a scheme whereby Roxana may raise her fortune "to a prodigious height" if only she would live "frugally" and every year for twelve years reinvest her earnings. Roxana rejects the proposal on the grounds that she is still a young woman, is "used to live plentifully, and with a good appearance," and knows not "how to be a miser" (I, 191). She cannot be content with waiting twelve years; she is impatient to have her money. While Sir Robert does his best to advance her fortune through the assorted channels of finance, Roxana resorts to a swifter and surer way of amassing money: "But Sir Robert knew nothing of my design, that I aimed at being a kept mistress, and to have a handsome maintenance; and that I was still for getting money, and laying it up too, as much as he could desire me, only by a worse way" (I, 193). Like Moll, Roxana must have a "handsome maintenance"; but Roxana requires more than Moll and can be satisfied only by luxurious living and a title. As a kept mistress Roxana will consort with the gentry and nobility at the Court of Charles II; but before Defoe shifts the scene he has one more important use for Sir Robert Clayton.

As John Robert Moore has commented, Sir Robert Clayton could easily be omitted from the story altogether without any loss to the plot, yet Defoe accords him no less than one-fiftieth of the story, mentioning him by name at least twenty-four times and, most important, making him the central figure in a passage running six pages — "probably the longest single passage in the book in which no action is going forward." [2] The high point of this passage unquestionably is Roxana's protracted and carefully exampled relation of Sir Robert's advice on the advantages of marrying a prosperous merchant or tradesman:

Sir Robert said, and I found it to be true, that a true-bred merchant is the best gentleman in the nation; that in knowledge, in manners, in judgment of things, the merchant outdid many of the nobility; that having once mastered the world, and being above the demand of business, though no real estate, they were then superior to most gentlemen, even in estate; that a merchant in flush business and a capital stock is able to spend more money than a gentleman of £5000 a year estate; that while a merchant spent, he only spent what he got, and not that, and that he laid up great sums every year; that an estate is a pond, but that a trade was a spring; that if the first is once mortgaged, it seldom gets clear, but embarrassed the person for ever; but the merchant had his estate continually flowing; and upon this he named me merchants who lived in more real splendour and spent more money than most of the noblemen in England could singly expend, and that they grew immensely rich.

He went on to tell me that even the tradesmen in London, speaking of the better sort of trades, could spend more money in their families, and yet give better fortunes to their children, than, generally speaking, the gentry of England from £1000 a year downward could do, and yet grow rich too.   (I, 193–194)

Sir Robert's remarks stand out boldly, like a purple patch, in the novel. Defoe apparently got carried away with enthusiasm for his subject in this passage, which reads less like sound marital advice relevant to the action than a spirited panegyric to the merchant and trading class of England. This kind of information coming from the mouth of an eminent London figure like Sir Robert Clayton, who certainly knew more about this subject than anyone, must have been inspiring to Defoe's middle-class readers.

The partisan bourgeois tone shows Defoe consciously pitching his comments to his audience, as he had done with such success earlier in the pages of the *Review*. Sir Robert had died in 1707, but he was still very much remembered; and his account stands as an effective and sustained piece of interpolated propaganda on the glory and greatness of the middle class compared to the waning historical superiority of the upper classes. Defoe was shortly to pursue this theme more openly and more appropriately in such works as the *Tour*, the *Complete English Tradesman*, and the *Plan of the English Commerce*.

Roxana does not follow Sir Robert's sage advice. She moves on instead "to act in a new sphere" (I, 196), the Court, which is pictured as "gay and fine" but "wicked." As Roxana observes, "if the sovereign gave himself a loose ["the King had several mistresses"], it could not be expected the rest of the court should be all saints" (I, 196). In Roxana's career at Court, Defoe sets forth the traditional Puritan position that the debauched state of the nation is ultimately traceable to the loose morals and bad manners of the upper classes, which are set above the rest of the people not to abuse their privileges but to set a worthy example.

In the heat of the Puritan reform movement of the 1690's, when Jeremy Collier began the renovation of the English stage, Defoe lent his pen to the movement with *The Poor Man's Plea*, in which he argued:

'Twas the kings and the gentry which first again degenerated from that strict observation of moral virtues, and from thence carried vice on to that degree it now appears in. From the Court vice took its *progress* into the country; and in the families of the gentry and nobility it harbour'd, till it took heart under their protection; and made a general sally into the nation; and we the poor commons, who have been always easy to be guided by the example of our landlords and gentlemen, have really been debauch'd into vice by their examples. And it must be the *example of you the nobility and gentry of the kingdom* that must put a stop to the flood of vice and profaneness . . . or it will never be done.[3]

Roxana's life at Court and among the members of the upper classes offers a graphic illustration of the corrupting examples set by these people for the nation. Defoe even transfers some of the extravagant and lascivious entertainments of the upper classes to Roxana's London apartments, where she holds luxurious parties for her high society guests, who enjoy her masquerade dances (she is depicted by Defoe as performing an exotic and erotic Turkish dance on one occasion) and her gaming tables. Roxana prospers on the vices of her clientele.

Defoe was sharply critical not only of the loose morals but also of the luxury and profusion of the nobility and gentry. He had warned his countrymen about the "luxury and extravagancies of the English nobility and gentry" early in the century, when he mounted a sustained campaign in the pages of his *Review* to point up the consequences of this alarming national trend. The commercial middle class responded to the demands created by the upper classes for luxury items and new trades mushroomed almost overnight, trades which depended on the "destructive follies" of the upper classes. Such trades, however, were unnatural and unreliable for a thriving and stable national economy, according to Defoe, and as they favored the importation of sumptuary goods at the expense of national manufactures, they jeopardized the balance of trade of the nation. The only satisfaction Defoe and his middle class could derive from this trend was to observe "how many of these great and noble families have been impoverish'd by the luxurious way of living . . . and how have the estates of these great families been swallow'd up by the commonalty and tradesmen, who are now richer all over the nation than men of blood, families and inheritance, put them all together." Still, Defoe was concerned about the effects of this trend on the trade of the nation and the manners of society; for this national vice of luxury could infect the middle classes, especially if they emulated the patterns of their social betters in earnest.[4]

When in her fifties, Roxana reviews her career. She remarks, "necessity first debauched me, and poverty made me a whore at the beginning, so excess of avarice for getting money and excess of vanity continued me in the crime" (II, 17). By this time in her life, however, "avarice could have no pretence" because she is now worth £50,000, with "£2500 a year coming in upon very good land securities" (II, 17–18). Only her "vanity" remains a viable motive, but it is closely allied to her avarice in that she seeks acceptance among the most exclusive of social circles, the nobility. When Amy informs her that her former paramour, the prince, has said that if he could find her, he would marry and make a "countess" of her this time, Roxana becomes excited at the prospect. Amy well knows her mistress' "weakest part" — Roxana "loved great things" (II, 51). She is so taken with the idea of becoming the wife of a nobleman that all her former objections to marriage are instantly dispelled: "The thoughts of being surrounded with domestics, honoured with titles, be called her Highness, and live in all the splendour of a court, and, which was still more, in the arms of a man of such rank . . . all this, in a word, dazzled my eyes, turned my head, and I was as truly crazed and distracted for about a fortnight as most of the people in Bedlam" (II, 54). Roxana is portrayed as totally infatuated with the prospect of becoming a member of the nobility through marriage, even though it means, as Amy points out, going to a remote part of Europe and learning "the devil's language, called High Dutch." But, as Roxana sums up her motivation, "I, that was so willing once to be mistress to a king, was now ten thousand times more fond of being the wife to a prince" (II, 59). For the first time in her life Roxana is actually in a position to become a full-fledged member of the aristocracy of Europe by marriage, and she seizes at the opportunity greedily.

Roxana's attempt at satisfying her "vanity" and love of "great things" by marrying the prince is frustrated, however. At the last moment he turns penitent and rejects his former life, an action that Roxana derides. But in the end Roxana still realizes her ambition for a title of nobility when another former paramour, the Dutch merchant, again proposes marriage. Defoe uses this proposal to comment at some length on conditions in England that permit wealthy merchants to buy titles and set themselves up as gentlemen and men of quality:

He told me that money purchased titles of honour in almost all parts of the world, though money could not give principles of honour, they must come by birth and blood; that, however, titles sometimes assist to elevate the soul and to infuse generous principles into the mind, and especially where there was a good foundation laid in the persons . . . that as to England, he had nothing to do but to get an act of naturalization in his favour, and he knew where to purchase a patent for baronet — that is to say, to have the honour and title transferred to him; but if I intended to go abroad with him, he had a nephew, the son of his eldest brother, who had the title of a count, with the estate annexed, which was but small, and that he had frequently offered to make it over to him for a thousand pistoles, which was not a great deal of money, and considering it was in the family already, he would, upon my being willing, purchase it immediately. (II, 62)

Such a narration must have been as satisfying to Defoe's middle-class readers as the passage by Sir Robert Clayton cited earlier. It also is not without its charm to the ears of Roxana: "I was not a little tickled with the satisfaction of being still a countess, though I could not be a princess" (II, 63). As it turns out, Roxana manages to become "a princess in High Dutch" by being made both "a lady in English and a countess in Dutch" (II, 64).

The novelty and pleasure of a title are experienced as naturally and fully by Roxana as they were by Colonel Jacque. Defoe knew the psychology of his characters and of his readers because he knew himself and his own satisfaction in adopting the title of gentleman. He knew that his readers shared his social ambitions and he could assume their interest in and appreciation of Roxana's reaction to her new title:

I was now my Lady——, and I must own I was exceedingly pleased with it; 'twas so big and so great to hear myself called "her ladyship," and "your ladyship," and the like, that I was like the Indian king at Virginia, who, having a house built for him by the English, and a lock put upon the door, would sit whole days together with the key in his hand, locking and unlocking, and double-locking, the door, with an unaccountable pleasure at the novelty; so I could have sat a whole day together to hear Amy talk to me, and call me "your ladyship" at every word . . . (II, 68)

With her title of "my Lady ——" Roxana's second motive is satisfied. She is now so vastly wealthy as not to consider her avarice; she is a titled lady of quality and so need aspire to "great things" no longer. Roxana and her husband can look forward to an assured annual income from the interest of their combined estates of no less than £4,000. They go to Holland to assume their titles of the Count and Countess de ——.

At this stage of her long and spotted career Roxana can well reflect with unsurpassed satisfaction on her success in life. She has achieved everything that she had ever really coveted: unprecedented wealth and titles of nobility. Her marriage to the

Middle-Class Gentility in Defoe's Fiction

Dutch merchant (the "best husband in the world" — II, 86) even brings to pass the happy prediction of Sir Robert Clayton that if she married a "true-bred merchant" she would have the "best gentleman in the nation," a man who, with a fortune in business investments, would be able to maintain her "like a queen" (I, 193–194). In Holland she is not only maintained like a queen, living in "magnificence" and with an abundance of fine things and servants, she is also actually a "countess," riding about town in a handsome equipage with her own coronet emblazoned on the sides. "I was now in the height of my glory and prosperity" (II, 87), she notes approvingly. None of Defoe's heroes or heroines had ever risen to such an eminence socially and financially.

Yet after having brought Roxana to the summit of success, Defoe proves unable either to justify her success and have her become a sincere penitent or to record her fall and so destroy the fortune she has so cunningly amassed. He apparently found himself on the horns of a dilemma as he came to the end of the novel. His uneasiness of mind over Roxana's career is evident from the abrupt and disjointed closing paragraphs:

> I can say no more now, but that, *as above,* being arrived in Holland with my spouse and his son, *formerly mentioned,* I appeared there with all the splendor and equipage suitable to our new prospect, *as I have already observed.*
>
> Here, after some few years of flourishing and outwardly happy circumstances, I fell into a dreadful course of calamities, and Amy also; the very reverse of our former good days. The blast of Heaven seemed to follow the injury done the poor girl by us both, and I was brought so low again, that my repentance seemed to be the only consequence of my misery, as my misery was of my crime.   (II, 166–167)

This so-called conclusion, with its moral tag, reads like a coda. Defoe's own dissatisfaction with the way the story was turning out is further to be discerned in Roxana's final years in Europe, which are crowded with confused feelings of guilt and anxiety. Her daughter Susan serves as a combination "Fury" and Puritan conscience haunting Roxana and her maid Amy. But the story by this time is no longer controlled by Defoe; he cannot write a clear dénouement with Susan as catalyst and he cannot even bring himself to finish the novel satisfactorily.

The Fortunate Mistress marks the sudden end to Defoe's major period as a writer of fiction. Why he should so suddenly stop writing about the lives of his ambitious characters and their quests for money and position is perhaps in large part explainable by the incomplete ending to Roxana's life. Defoe became involved personally in the career of Roxana, as he had become involved with his other heroes and heroines and their ambitions to better themselves in society through the dynamics of economic individualism. Defoe tried to check himself by occasional moralizing and by reminders ("But I am not to preach, but to relate" — I, 52), but he was not entirely successful in these endeavors. His fascination with the process whereby Roxana accumulates her wealth caused him to lose his perspective — the remarkable scene between Roxana and her Dutch merchant husband, when they parade their respective holdings and wealth for the benefit of their partner (II, 82–83), is lovingly detailed by Defoe and reaches a pitch unequaled in the pages of his novels.[5] Defoe's preface to the novel discloses his awareness that the story looks too attractive as it stands ("It is true she met with unexpected success in all her wicked course"), and all he can do by way of justifying her career to his middle-class Puritan readers is to assure them that "the pleasure of her wickedness was not worth the repentance" (xiv). But that is not how the story tells it or demonstrates it. The repentance theme is never developed by Defoe and the closing pages deteriorate noticeably, with the ending coming as a penitential second thought rather than evolving out of the action. Clearly the novel did not turn out the way he had intended it.

By 1724 Defoe surely realized that he was, as a devout Puritan, dealing with a difficult and dangerous medium that induced him to give his teeming imagination free play. The themes he dealt with were, as he knew, harmless in themselves and of vital interest to his readers. But was prose fiction the best vehicle for expressing them? Without question Defoe's imagination in *The Fortunate Mistress* was beginning to dwell on the perverse side of life, and he probably was disturbed by it. Consider the unexplained and erotic scene where Roxana forces her faithful maid Amy to lie with the landlord: "I fairly stripped her, and then I threw open the bed and thrust her in" (I, 49). As if this demoralized act were not enough, Roxana remarks how she "stood by all the while" Amy and the landlord have intercourse, thus deriving the depraved satisfaction of seeing her maid debauched before her eyes and so becoming "a whore too" (I, 50). Roxana arranges for the landlord to lie with Amy several more times — ruling out the possibility that the first action was not a premeditated and perverse act of wickedness — until Amy finally is made pregnant. Such incidents as this or Roxana's lascivious Turkish dance or even the dark and guilt-ridden atmosphere Defoe manages to generate in the closing yet inconclusive pages of the story, where the murder of a daughter is plotted and perhaps executed, all these revealing signs suggest, in short, that Defoe no longer was able to control his imagination or his material, and being a good Puritan he decided not to tempt the devil any longer. He ceased writing imaginative biographies in which he identified with his creations not wisely but too well.[6]

Some light can be shed on Defoe's troubled state of mind about writing novels if we consider his *Political History of the Devil,* which appeared in 1726. In this work Defoe's Puritanism and his belief in the significance of dreams and apparitions are given full expression. One revealing passage suggests how his own imagination probably was getting out of control by the time he was writing of Roxana's career: "I knew a person who the devil so haunted with naked women, fine beautiful ladies in bed with him . . . and all in his sleep; so that he seldom slept without some such entertainment; the particulars are too gross for my story, but he gave me several accounts of his night's *amours,* and being a man of virtuous life and good morals, it was the greatest surprise to him imaginable." This experience apparently impressed Defoe singularly, for he related it again the following year in *An Essay on the History and Reality of Apparitions.* He interpreted such erotic fantasies in orthodox Puritan fashion as the work of the devil: "I take dreams to be the second best of the advantages the *devil* has over mankind . . . by dreams he may be said to get into the inside of us without opposition." When he discerned the devil gaining access to his imagination in his own writing, as in the episodes cited in his last novel, he responded in the only way possible for a person of his religious training. As he admonished his readers in his long treatise on the devil: "I say, 'tis a great part of human wisdom to know when the *devil* is acting in us and by us, and when not; the next and still greatest part would be to prevent him, put a stop to his progress, bid him go about his business, and let him know he should carry his designs no farther in that manner . . . in short, to turn him out of doors, and bring a stronger power to take possession." Defoe doubtless followed this stern advice in his own career as a writer of prose fiction, and in 1724 he abandoned his reliance on his imagination for the "stronger power" of his reason.[7]

As Rudolf G. Stamm has argued persuasively, Defoe was always a writer in the Puritan tradition, even during his intensely creative period as novelist. He could balance the conflicting impulses of the artist to create a fictive world and of the Puritan preacher to deal only with the phenomenal world, which was to be apprehended and interpreted in the Puritan framework. He was able to satisfy the artist in himself by convincing his readers, and perhaps also himself, that he was not writing stories of fiction but of fact, not romances but histories. That helps us to understand why he relied so heavily on his own experiences and personal feelings in his stories, and why he inevitably resorted to self-dramatizations in writing about the careers of his heroes and heroines, into whose lives he was able to project himself so easily. Hence his remarkable sense of sympathy and understanding for the ambitions and frustrations and fears of his characters.[8]

Defoe was himself, like Crusoe, suspended between the new mercantile spirit of the "merchant adventurers" and the old traditional order of the seventeenth century, a tradition of men like Richard Baxter or Samuel Annesley in divinity and John Bunyan in literature. It was under the influence of these men that he grew up while preparing himself for a career in the dissenting ministry. But it was under the influence of those *novos homines* of the mercantile order of the late seventeenth and early eighteenth century that he became a London merchant and an exponent of England's destiny in trade. This tension between the two orders is traceable in Defoe's entire career.

The apparent absence of any obvious artistic development in Defoe's writing career has led critics to conclude that he wrote strictly by trial and error. "Even within the wonderful years 1719–1724," Alan D. McKillop writes, "it is impossible to arrange his major works of fiction in a sequence that will clearly show development by artistic self-discovery." In large part this criticism certainly is justified. But surely the fact that Defoe in 1724 suddenly broke off his career as a writer of fiction must tell us something about his "artistic self-discovery"; else why abandon a kind of writing that was, on the whole, so commercially successful? Defoe was astute enough as a Puritan and as an artist to realize that his fictions were leading him to excesses of the imagination over which he could not exercise the same control as in his other forms of writing, or as in his earlier works of prose fiction.[9]

From 1722 on Defoe's hold on his imagination in describing the lives of his characters was growing noticeably lax. Walter De La Mare has noted that "Defoe's passion as a writer of fiction was this craving to mimic life itself, and, in his later books, preferably its wrong and seamy side." [10] We can see the first indications in *Moll Flanders* and *Colonel Jacque,* in which the immorality of the marriage themes is justified only by the thin veneer of moralizing commentary and the final repentance of the characters. Still, when writing about people like Moll and Jacque, he knew from first-hand experience the basically middle-class milieu in which they operated and had their values shaped. But when he came to write *The Fortunate Mistress,* he was dealing with a character and a world beyond his familiar middle-class realm of experience, and a heroine about whom he obviously felt ambiguous. Roxana turns her back on her middle-class background and strikes out for the corrupt world of high fashion and high society, a world and a way of life antithetical to Defoe's. The result was that Defoe had to rely more on imagination than on experience when treating Roxana's career. In depending so heavily on his imagination, he became aware that he could not, like a true Puritan, pass off this story as "laid in truth of fact" and therefore "not a story, but a history" (xii). For his conscience's sake, Defoe needed to make this assertion, but the usual assurance behind the assertion is missing, and he apparently knew it because he could not bring himself to finish the story. Defoe's dilemma was that he could neither square the story of Roxana's life with the Puritan view of such a life as history nor bring himself to dismiss the claims his heroine made on him as a successful entrepreneur and social climber. Unable to resolve the dilemma, he left the novel as it stands.

His experience with this novel, however, did alert him to the problems he was bound to encounter if he continued to write prose fiction. This was without question his most significant "artistic self-discovery" in those creative years of 1719 to 1724, and it offers us at least one cogent explanation for his sudden abandonment of the novel. From 1724 on Defoe returned to the more reliable medium of expository prose to develop further his ideas and themes. In 1725 Defoe wrote the first version of his *Complete English Tradesman,* wherein he was able to combine his interest in the Puritan life with his interest in the dynamics of economic individualism. No longer having to worry about the unreliability of the imagination, he could rely again on his personal experiences and serve God and Mammon at the same time in his writings. Defoe's great career as the champion of the middle class was a natural extension of his career as writer of fiction.

Part III. The Tradesman as Gentleman

Chapter 10. The Complete English Tradesman: Gentility and Trade

King Charles II, who was perhaps the prince of all kings that ever reigned in England, that best understood the country and the people that he governed, used to say, *That the tradesmen were the only gentry in England.* His Majesty spoke it merrily, but it had a happy signification in it. — Defoe, *The Complete English Tradesman*, I, 304

Defoe abandoned the writing of fiction with the unfinished story of Roxana in 1724, but he continued his outpouring of books and pamphlets. His major works of the next few years show him preoccupied with two mighty and related themes. In the three volumes of *A Tour thro' the Whole Island of Great Britain* (1724, 1725, 1727), the two volumes of *The Complete English Tradesman* (1725, 1727), and the volume of *A Plan of the English Commerce* (1728), Defoe presented his observations and advanced his ideas on trade in England as well as the claims to a new status by the tradesmen of England.

The first volume of the *Tour* appeared on May 21, 1724, only three months after the publication of *The Fortunate Mistress.* Defoe's interest in the theme of middle-class gentility grew over the five-year period in which he wrote novels. In the *Tour* Defoe dealt with this favorite theme factually, not imaginatively. In the author's preface to the first volume he assured his readers that no less than "seventeen very large circuits" and "three general tours over almost the whole English part of the island" formed the basis for the work and that he described nothing "but what he has been an eye-witness of himself." [1]

The transition from *The Fortunate Mistress* to the *Tour* came easily to Defoe. He had planned to publish an account of his observations on England in the form of a travel book for some time, and in 1722 he is believed to have made his last extensive journey through England, supposedly to check doubtful notes and make final revisions for his projected *Tour.* [2] His rich assortment of personal experiences as a traveler over a period of many eventful years was unique. So far as we know, no other living person had anything approaching Defoe's immediate and comprehensive sense of his country and his society; for when he traveled, he sought out everything that might be of relevance to a man of his many-faceted interests: economist, journalist, projector, reporter, government agent, historian, poet, novelist, merchant-trader. Nothing, in short, was likely to escape his notice. But of most immediate interest to Defoe would be evidence of the remarkable effects of trade on the nation and the middle class.

The final journey Defoe took through England in 1722 apparently had a profound effect on him. He became even more confident that England was not only the most prosperous and thriving mercantile power in all the world but also that its wealth and growth were largely owing to the efforts of the middle-class businessmen. Defoe was excited by what he saw and he naturally was eager to share his vision of this new nation with his countrymen in general and his fellow tradesmen in particular. But he wisely decided against writing the *Tour* under his own name, and so limiting its impact on a wider audience; he wrote rather as a "Gentleman" and "a member of the Church of England," casting the work in the form of a guidebook, a kind of early eighteenth-century Baedeker which described places and people of interest to all classes of society. The *Tour* did become a favorite with all kinds of readers; no less than eight distinct editions of the first volume appeared between 1724 and 1778 (I, viii).

Behind his mask of a "Gentleman" Defoe was able to survey England with the sharp and appraising eye of a tradesman. We therefore see him in the *Tour* carefully noting all the arresting examples that can be found in support of the contention that the middle class was vying successfully with the upper class in its overall manner of living. Defoe was especially impressed by the newness and brisk growth evident everywhere in the fashionable suburbs of London. He marveled at "the increase of buildings" in the towns of Newington, Tottenham, Edmonton, and Enfield, all of which stood in a line north of London so that "they seem to a traveler to be one continu'd street," but with this significant exception: "the new buildings so far exceed the old, especially in the value of them, and the figure of the inhabitants, that the fashion of the towns is quite altered" (II, 2). What pleased Defoe was the knowledge that much of this new building and fashion stemmed from the influx of successful citizens and tradesmen from London.

What Defoe witnessed in his many travels around the outlying areas of London was the revolutionary process of suburbanization, a phenomenon connected in England with the rise of the middle class. In the 1720's he was able to see the impact of this process of suburbanization on the age, particularly the middle class, and he responded to the trend warmly: "There is not any thing more fine in their degree, than most of the buildings this way [north of London]; only with this observation, that they are generally belonging to the middle sort of mankind, grown wealthy by trade, and who still taste of London; some of them live both in the city, and in the country at the same time: yet many of these are immensely rich" (II, 2). For the vastly wealthy merchants there was the option of maintaining both a house in London and a house in the country for holidays and weekends; but such a style of life, offering the best of both worlds, was not available to many of "the middle sort of mankind."

A more common pattern of life, and one more suited to the lives of tradesmen, was to have an attractive home in a fashionable town close to London and commute to work by coach every day. Such a way of life already was becoming a popular practice among the successful members of the middle class. They settled in such counties as Essex, Middlesex, and Surrey, where, Defoe noticed, "villages are increased in buildings to a strange degree, within the compass of about 20 or 30 years past at the most" (I, 6). Defoe's eye instinctively picked out the signs of wealth and fashion exhibited by these middle-class suburban families, both in their handsome houses and their equally handsome coaches.

The pursuit of wealth, if successful, led to the pursuit of leisure and pleasure by the middle class. The qualifications of money and an agreeable appearance were all that one needed to enjoy the diversions of people of quality. In Tunbridge, for example, Defoe informed his readers, "you have all the liberty of conversation in the world, and any thing that looks like a gentleman, has an address agreeable, and behaves with decency and good manners, may single out whom he pleases" (I, 126); but, he cautioned, "without money a man is nobody at Tunbridge, any more than at any other place" (I, 127). Defoe's middle-class readers, like his middle-class heroes and heroines, knew that appearances were important and money necessary in furthering their social ambitions, and once they acquired the means to live like quality, they knew how to satisfy their ambitions. Defoe recorded in the *Tour* that even in such genteel resort towns as Epsom wealthy tradesmen and their families were finding opportunities for combining business with pleasure during the summer season:

The greatest part of the men . . . may be supposed to be men of business, who are at London upon business all the day, and thronging to their lodgings at night, make the families, generally speaking, rather provide suppers than dinners; for 'tis very frequent for the trading part of the company to place their families here, and take their horses every day to London, to the Exchange, to the Alley, or to the warehouse, and be at Epsom again at night; and I know one citizen that practis'd it for several years together, and scarce ever lay a night in London during the whole season. (I, 161)

Defoe here, in essence, was describing a revolutionary leisure pattern among middle-class businessmen and their families. Wealth and leisure were transforming the style of life of the English middle class.

Most of all, Defoe was overwhelmed by the sight of all the lavish estates that graced the riverbanks from Richmond to London — "Beautiful buildings, charming gardens, and rich habitations of gentlemen of quality" in such splendor that not even the region around Paris could compare with them in beauty. Added to these vast estates were the many "houses of retreat" ("gentlemen's mere summer-houses, or citizen's country-houses") where nobility and gentry were intermingled with affluent merchants and tradesmen. All this was fresh evidence that successful merchants could purchase the home or estate of a nobleman or landed gentleman and members of the upper class could ally themselves through marriage with prosperous merchant families. Defoe never let pass an opportunity to point out to his readers that the middle ranks were becoming a part of the beauty and splendor of the nation. In Surrey, for example, he paused to respond to "all this variety, this beauty, this glorious show of wealth and plenty" displayed by both the upper and affluent middle classes in their homes and grounds outside London; he reflected on this resplendent show, interpreting it as "really a view of the luxuriant age which we live in, and of the overflowing riches of the citizens, who in their abundance make these gay excursions, and live thus deliciously all summer" (I, 168). Clearly the England Defoe surveyed in his *Tour* was a stirring sight, both to a "true-born Englishman" proud of his country and to a "complete English tradesman" equally proud of his calling, both of which Defoe was par excellence.

Everywhere there were abundant signs attesting to the rising wealth and prominence of the middle class. In Essex he noted with satisfaction that "there are several very considerable estates purchas'd, and now enjoy'd by citizens of London, merchants and tradesmen, as Mr. Western an iron merchant, near Kelvedon, Mr. Cresnor, a wholesale grocer." He went on to record the names of other such middle-class estate owners, and under the guise of his persona of "Gentleman," he injected such partisan remarks with the mien of a disinterested observer: "I mention this, to observe how the present increase of wealth in the city of London, spreads itself into the country, and plants families and fortunes, who in another age will equal the families of the ancient gentry, who perhaps were bought out" (I, 15) — hardly a comforting thought for the nobility and gentry but the sweetest prospect for the merchants and tradesmen to contemplate.

These encouraging signs were not restricted to London and its environs. In the inland manufacturing and trading towns and in the seaport shipping towns, like distant Plymouth, the same trend was very much in evidence, although not as strikingly as around London. Defoe found Plymouth "populous and wealthy, having . . . several merchants, and abundance of wealthy shop-keepers, whose trade depends upon supplying the sea-faring people." Although Plymouth did not have many gentlemen per se ("I mean those that are such by family, and birth, and way of living"), it was clear to him that the town was developing its own kind of gentlemen ("men of value, persons of liberal education, general knowledge, and excellent behavior" — I, 231), who with the advantages of wealth would in time become a breed of gentlemen in their own right. What Defoe saw evolving in Plymouth, he saw all over England.

The overall purpose of the *Tour*, according to the author's preface, "is a description of the most flourishing and opulent country in the world," and judging from Defoe's account of the England he saw with his own eyes and over a period of many years, his description is neither forced nor hyperbolic. He unquestionably was convinced of the growing greatness and affluence of the nation, as his preface indicates: ". . . the improvement, as well in culture, as in commerce, the *increase* of people . . . the *increase* of buildings, as well in great cities and towns, as in *new* seats and dwellings of the nobility and gentry, also the *increase* of wealth, in many eminent particulars" (I, 1; italics mine). Defoe saw everywhere change and growth and improvement. In his preface to the second volume the following year, he observed: "New foundations are always laying, new buildings always raising, highways repairing, churches and public buildings erecting . . . so that as long as England is a trading, improving nation, no perfect description . . . can be given" (I, 252). Defoe's tone is optimistic and assured; his eye finds countless indications of material prosperity; he is gratified to see all these improvements resulting from trade. So long as England is a trading nation, England will be an improving nation. That was his motto, and in the dynamics of that motto rested his hope and the hopes of his middle class.

In many ways Defoe's tone in the *Tour* bears an uncanny resemblance to the strident optimism and faith in progress voiced by Thomas Babington Macaulay about a century later — and for good reasons. The England Defoe described in the 1720's was a harbinger of the England Macaulay was to describe with such smug satisfaction for his countrymen some hundred and more years later. Defoe saw in miniature the mighty industrial empire of Macaulay's age. Despite the difference in their eras, they both had the same vision of England. If Macaulay is, as Matthew Arnold remarked, the "apostle to the Philistines," then Defoe stands prominently at the head of that apostolic succession. And, in the estimate of G. D. H. Cole, that is precisely how we must see him: "Defoe is, indeed, the first great apologist of the English middle class" (I, xiii).

Defoe's *Tour* stands alone as the most graphic personal account of the condition of England, economically and socially, in the first quarter of the eighteenth century, a period that eludes a precise description because it was, as Defoe observed, a period of transition. England at the time was neither an agricultural country, even though she was able to feed herself and agriculture constituted her most important single livelihood, nor was she yet an industrial country, even though a large and swelling part of the population lived by her manufactures and overseas trade and commerce. As Defoe noted in his prefaces to the *Tour*, England in the 1720's was in a state of flux; but the direction England was taking because of trade left no doubt in his mind about the future condition of the nation. Though he obviously could not anticipate the Industrial Revolution that was to come later in the century, he could and did anticipate the central role that trade and manufacturing were to play in the industrial England that was fast coming into being.

The salient social and economic observation emerging from Defoe's descriptions in the *Tour* was the rapid and unchecked rise to national prominence of the mercantile middle class. This was attributable to the economic development of the nation through expansion of trade and manufactures in all parts of England. London, to be sure, still dominated the business scene, but, as Defoe noted, population centers were shifting all the time because of the mushrooming industries. The wool industries were already flourishing in the north, as were the coal trades and some manufactures. Birmingham and Sheffield, for example, were becoming centers for the metal industries and hardware; Derby, Nottingham, and Leicester were specializing in the hosiery trades. "It is surprising to find how many places by the seventeen-twenties," M. Dorothy George observes, "were already noted for the industries which are still among their staple products." Roads were poor and the canal system lay in the future, but the beginnings were decidedly promising, and seaports like Bristol, Liverpool, Glasgow, and Plymouth were growing in size and importance to handle this traffic in goods and materials. If England was able to feed herself because of agriculture under the control of the upper class, she was also able to clothe and in large part furnish herself from industry and commerce under the control of the enterprising middle class. The traditional control and historical supremacy of the nobility and gentry were being seriously challenged. One historian has even gone so far as to sum up the shifting society of the age by stating, "The aristocracy of eighteenth century England was really little more than a wealthier middle class." [3]

Defoe's extensive travels and varied experiences enabled him to observe and understand the stirrings that were gradually transforming the face of the English landscape as they were transforming the structure of English society. It is evident from the general tenor of the *Tour,* as well as from specific passages, that Defoe became inspired with a great sense of purpose during this time. Consider the passage where he abruptly breaks off his descriptive narration to address the reader directly:

I shall sing you no songs here of the river in the first person of a water nymph, a goddess (and I know not what) according to the humor of the ancient poets. I shall talk nothing of the marriage of old Isis, the male river, with the beautiful Thame, the female river, a whimsy as simple as the subject was empty, but I shall speak of the river as occasion presents, as it really is made glorious by the splendor of its shores, gilded with noble palaces, strong fortifications, large hospitals, and public buildings; with the greatest bridge, and the greatest city in the world, made famous by the opulence of its merchants, the increase and extensiveness of its commerce; by its invincible navies, and by the innumerable fleets of ships sailing upon it, to and from all parts of the world.   (I, 173–174)

The prose is definitely Defoe's, but the sentiments might well be Macaulay's. The voice is that of the assertive *bourgeoisie.* Defoe shows himself to be under the spell of his subject, which will allow no room for water nymphs and mythology and such other idle stuff as formed the subject of the "ancient poets." The emerging new England, as seen by Defoe, was modern and mighty and dynamic. The future of this England rested with the men of the middle class.

Since the future greatness of England lay in trade and the men of trade, Defoe next addressed the tradesmen, particularly the young apprentices who were just starting out in business. On September 7, 1725, three months after the appearance of the second volume of the *Tour,* he published the first volume of *The Complete English Tradesman,* a work initially of ten epistolary sections aimed primarily at beginning tradesmen. As he saw the enthusiastic reception of this effort, he was encouraged to expand the volume and eventually he issued two volumes in 1727, the first volume aimed at apprentices and the second at experienced tradesmen. The final two-volume edition was intended by Defoe to be in every way a "complete" manual for the English trades-man, covering every important topic "from his first entering business, to his leaving off."

In *The Family Instructor,* Defoe had hoped to instruct his middle-class readers in the management of their home and reli-gious life; now, in *The Complete English Tradesman,* he hoped to guide them in the management of their business and social life. In his books on religion he had drawn on his early religious training and home life; now in his manual for tradesmen he drew on his varied business experiences. The flat quality of De-foe's religious writings contrasts sharply with the enthusiasm of his writings on business. He simply could not project himself into the role of preacher and religious instructor with quite the same "gust" as he could act the role of apostle of trade and apologist of the middle class. In *The Complete English Trades-man* he wrote openly as one tradesman to other tradesmen.

As early as 1692, when writing his *Essay upon Projects,* Defoe envisioned the kind of responsible role men of business might play in the affairs of England, already then becoming a complex trading nation. He at that time proposed the establishment of what he called a "Court Merchant," a court of six eminent mer-chants appointed by authority of Parliament and empowered to hear and rule on cases dealing with trade as a court of equity. The "project" not only made good sense, it showed that Defoe foresaw the growth and importance of trade, and that men of trade were themselves best qualified to deal with such matters. By the time he came to write his *Complete English Tradesman* he was more convinced than ever that men of trade must assume a national role. He saw that the "wise, sober, modest tradesman, when he is thriven and grown rich, is really a valuable man; and he is valued on all occasions" (II, 237). The seasoned and wealthy tradesman, when he retires from business, "has more opportunity of doing good than almost any other person" because his special "experience and knowledge of business" qualify him more than

"men of ten times his learning and education." Defoe had always argued in favor of practical education over mere book
learning, and now in his tradesman he portrays a new kind of
ideal senior citizen, a man who, on a modest and local scale, performs the very work Defoe earlier ascribed to the projected
"Court Merchant." The retired tradesman is to be valued as a
"natural magistrate" where he lives; for he can best serve as
"general peacemaker of the country, the common arbitrator of
all trading differences, family breaches, and private injuries; and,
in general, he is the domestic judge, in trade especially" (II,
237–238). Defoe has modified his idea of one board of six eminent
merchants residing in London as the "Court Merchant"; now he
envisions mature tradesmen in all the reaches of England assuming the duties of arbitration and general peacemaking on a
local level.[4]

Charmed as he was by the ideal tradesman, he was greatly concerned about the realities of trade and the adverse effects it had
on tradesmen. He therefore felt obliged to comment at length on
the tradesman's "particular personal conduct in his prosperity,"
especially the contemptible figure cut by a "purseproud tradesman" (I, 227). The purse-proud tradesman is the reverse of the
tradesman as natural magistrate, and Defoe uses him as a kind of
"character" to point up to his fellow tradesmen the stereotype
with which they may commonly be associated and by which they
may be condemned. A tradesman cannot simply be catapulted
into the company of gentlemen, despite the so-called sanction of
his wealth, without first having learned to act like a gentleman.
The purse-proud tradesman embodies some of the worst features
of the acquisitive ethic and its effect on men in business. Defoe's
concern, however, is broader than that; he is eager to have tradesmen as a class be presentable because they must be prepared to
assume their place in society as a dignified and respected body.

Defoe was fully aware of the mobility of his society: "the rich
tradesman once left, having converted his money into solid rents,
laid the tradesman down and commenc'd gentleman" (II, 168).
But the process of accumulating wealth was often a sordid one,
and the most honest men had to compromise their consciences
on occasion to succeed in business — just as Defoe's heroes and
heroines all had to bow to the "necessity" of their careers. "Cus-

tom, indeed, has driven us beyond the limits of our morals in many things," Defoe observes ruefully, "which trade makes necessary, and which we can not now avoid" (I, 234). No one can withstand the pressures of business; everyone succumbs eventually to the "necessity" of engaging in "trading lies" and other disagreeable practices when transacting business. He even singles out the principled Quakers who "for a time stood to their point . . . resolving to ask no more than they would take, upon any occasion whatsoever"; but, he concludes, "time and the necessities of trade made them wiser [and] have brought them off of that severity" (I, 227). He knew his fellow tradesmen faced the same pressures almost daily in their business careers as did his fictitious creations in his novels. When one spends the better part of one's life in such an atmosphere, it is not easy to cease such practices and suddenly emerge a gentleman. Part of Defoe's purpose in *The Complete English Tradesman* was to prepare tradesmen for their transition to gentlemen after they have prospered, and to make the transition more smooth and natural.

Defoe's *Complete English Tradesman*, then, was not only a practical manual on how to succeed in business but also a conduct book designed to dignify the profession and to polish the men who practice it. In the early chapters directed at apprentices, he sought to prepare them for a broader career than the running of a shop or the transaction of modest business. His obvious care in telling apprentices how to write letters, how to suit their style to their subject, how to learn about different countries, how to master modern languages, how and with whom to converse profitably, all these matters and more show that he endeavored to make of trade a highly knowledgeable calling, and of the "complete" tradesmen a versatile class capable of assuming new roles beyond those of their initial calling.

Above all, Defoe did not want tradesmen to pattern themselves indiscriminately on the gentry and nobility, the consequences of which were as disastrous as the pattern was ridiculous:

Tradesmen neglect their shop and business to follow the track of their vices and extravagances: some by taverns, others to the gaming houses, others to balls and masquerades, plays, harlequins, and operas . . .
    This is an age of gallantry and gaiety, and never was the city

transpos'd to the court as it is now: the play-houses and balls are now fill'd with citizens and young tradesmen, instead of gentlemen and families of distinction; the shop-keepers wear a different garb now, and are seen with their long wigs and swords, rather than with aprons on, as was formerly the figure they made. (I, 55)

Defoe certainly appreciated as well as anyone the itch of his fellow tradesmen not only to become but also to act like the gentry. His thoughts on "vices and extravagancies," on "balls" and "masquerades," he summed up in his treatment of the careers of Moll's "gentleman-tradesman" and Roxana's "fool husband" and Roxana herself; such things were to be eschewed. He realized that a slavish emulation of the upper classes resulted only in excesses that were to a Puritan immoral and to a tradesman ruinous. Tradesmen ought to mind their businesses and make money, and when they become wealthy they ought to act like model citizens. Trade, to Defoe, was the source of a new species of gentry.

Defoe had an abiding interest in genealogy. He had put his genealogical knowledge to good use in his defense of King William in *The True-Born Englishman,* and he apparently continued collecting genealogies attesting to the intermixture of noble and landed families with those of merchants and tradesmen or tracing families which owed their illustrious stations to beginnings in trade. Whenever an opportunity presented itself, he delighted in parading his choice pieces of genealogical information and similar findings before his readers. The *Tour* contains capsule histories and *obiter dicta* on the titles and estates of distinguished men. In his description of the countryside between Chelmsford and Boreham, in Essex, Defoe, for example, embarks on a digression to mention something he knows will be of immediate interest to his middle-class readers:

[Here] lives the Lord Viscount Barrington, who tho' not born to the title, or estate, or name which he now possesses, had the honour to be twice made heir to the estates of gentlemen, not at all related to him, at least one of them, as is very much to his honour mention'd in his patent of creation. His name was Shute, his uncle a linnen draper in London . . . He chang'd the name of Shute, for that of Barrington, by an Act of Parliament, obtain'd for that purpose, and had the dignity of a baron of the kingdom of Ireland conferr'd on him by the favour of King GEORGE. His lordship is a Dissenter, and

seems to love retirement. He was a Member of Parliament for the
town of Berwick upon Tweed.   (I, 15)

Defoe, we notice, is careful to present all the relevant facts for
his readers: his lordship was not born to his title or estate or
even his name; but now he is a retired nobleman, despite his
middle-class background — and a Dissenter, too. The digression
is a pointed piece of propaganda. Apparently Defoe devoted a
more than passing interest during his many trips through England to collecting such comforting case histories.

In *The Complete English Tradesman* he continued to share
with his middle-class readers genealogical evidence to support the
claim that gentility and trade were not incompatible but that, indeed, they were complementary. His purpose is altogether clear
in the chapter devoted to the dignity of trade:

First, our tradesmen are not, as in other countries, the meanest of
our people.
Secondly, some of the greatest and best and most flourishing families
among not the gentry only, but even the nobility, have been rais'd
from trade, owe their beginning, their wealth, and their estates to
trade; and I may add
Thirdly, those families are not at all ashamed of their original, and
indeed have no occasion to be ashamed of it.   (I, 305–306)

To support his thesis he cites the names of some of these "best
and most flourishing families" among the gentry and nobility
who owe their fortunes to trade. Unlike other European countries where trade and tradesmen were treated as "mechanic" and
inferior, England traditionally has had a respect for trade. That
is why Defoe can argue that in England a "gentleman-tradesman
is not so much nonsense as some people would persuade us to
reckon it"; because as trade increases so does the wealth accruing
to the trading classes, "and the wealth of our tradesmen is already
so great, 'tis very probable a few years will show us still a greater
race of trade-bred gentlemen than ever England yet had." Nor
does Defoe envision these "gentlemen-tradesmen" being respected
only in England, for he writes with assurance that "the English
tradesman may in a few years be allowed to rank with the best
gentlemen in Europe" (I, 313–314).

Defoe repeatedly attempted to reconcile the interests of the nobility and gentry with those of the merchants and tradesmen through a common investment in trade. "It is indeed one of the curiosities of English life from the Fifteenth to the Nineteenth Centuries," according to G. M. Trevelyan, "that, although the landed gentry looked down on the mercantile class as a lower order of society, many of the landed families had not only acquired their estates by money made in trade, but continued from generation to generation to invest in mercantile and financial adventures of every kind." Certainly no writer of his age saw this "curiosity" more clearly or endeavored more strenuously to make the gentry see it than Defoe. It was one thing to talk of the *ancien régime* in France, with its jealously guarded line of cleavage between *noblesse* and *bourgeoisie,* for which there was at least an indisputable historical precedent; but in England of all countries, where so many of the gentry and nobility "are raised by and derived from trade," such distinctions are without precedent and can at best be vainly derivative. Since trade afforded anyone the opportunity to amass a fortune, "it was easier in England," according to H. J. Habakkuk, "for a man of humble birth and great fortune to acquire considerable landed property and a title." [5] Defoe saw how trade in the early eighteenth century was transforming the fortunes of the middle class, and he could conclude triumphantly: "Trade is so far from here being inconsistent with a gentleman, that, in short, trade in England makes gentlemen, and has peopled this nation with gentlemen" (I, 310).

Despite the clarity of Defoe's vision and the cogency of his argument historically, the nobility and landed gentry apparently persisted in their prejudiced refusal to acknowledge the claims of trade and tradesmen. In 1728 Defoe felt compelled in *A Plan of the English Commerce* to convince the upper classes of their folly in denying the trading interests of the nation. [6] He returns to the *ab origine* argument of *The True-Born Englishman* to demonstrate that ultimately "tradesmen and the gentry should never cap pedigrees, since the most noble descendants of *Adam's* family, and in whom the primogeniture remained, were really *mechanics*" (p. 5). Defoe, of course, here uses the term "mechanic" in its neutral meaning of someone who makes or fixes things. By the early eighteenth century, however, the term had assumed derogatory connotations and was used to refer to anyone engaged in

demeaning employment of any kind; the term accordingly assumed the opprobrious associations of "vulgar, low, base." To
call a tradesman "mechanic" in Defoe's time was doubly offen-
sive: it reflected on his occupation as being of a low or inferior
form of work, and it also reflected on him personally as being a
coarse or vulgar sort of person. Defoe naturally did not like to see
tradesmen abused by so invidious a sentiment, then still in vogue
among the gentry and nobility, which ranked tradesmen with the
"commonalty" as a kind of "mechanics." Not only was such a
sentiment an affront to the class he identified with, it was also an
affront to him personally and to his claims as a gentleman. He
had a personal interest in defending the "trading part" of English
society.

We know how strongly Defoe felt about this matter from the
persistence and care with which he presses his attack:

. . . if they would look a little nearer, they would see themselves not
by practice only degenerated into trading men, but even their fortunes, nay, their very blood mingled with the mechanics, *as they call
them;* the necessity of the circumstances frequently reconciles the
best of the nobility to these mixtures; and then the same necessity
opens their eyes to the absurdity of the distinctions which they had
been so wedded to before.

It is with the utmost disgrace to their understanding that those
people would distinguish themselves in the manner they do, when
they may certainly see every day prosperous circumstances advance
those mechanics, *as they will have them called,* into arms, and into
the rank of the gentry; and declining fortunes reduce the best
families to a level with the mechanic.   (p. 9)

Defoe's mocking use of the term "mechanics" undoubtedly was
aimed at taunting the gentry, particularly those members whose
declining fortunes had reduced them to a low level. But his self-
conscious use of the term (*"as they will have them called"*) also
discloses his acute sensitivity about it, a sensitivity that recalls his
prickly reaction to being called "illiterate" during his days as Mr.
Review; for to be called "illiterate" or "mechanic" derogated
from his personal claims to gentility as well as from the claims of
his middle class.

The Defoe of the 1720's, however, writing as the champion of
trade and the trading part of the nation, was a markedly more
assured and inspired writer than the Defoe writing for the Tory

government as Mr. Review some twenty years earlier. He was still human and could react on occasion to sentiments which threatened his self-image as a true gentleman, but on the whole he was now supremely confident about the glorious future for trade and commerce in England and the implications this future held for the middle class. A somewhat closer look at his language, especially its metaphoric texture, reveals that his favorite themes of trade and gentility were now presented optimistically and persuasively, even though he had nothing radically new to say. His role as apologist simply was to be as repetitious and as forceful as possible. Defoe's fund of ideas was never large, but he had an uncanny facility for stating them freshly and vigorously to his audience.

Defoe's central metaphor for describing the declining fortunes of the gentry and nobility and the commensurately rising fortunes of the merchants and tradesmen was *"an estate is but a pond, but trade is a spring."* The figure obviously caught his fancy, for he relied on it as a kind of formula to explain economic and social shifts between the upper and middle classes early in the eighteenth century, notably the 1720's. In *The Fortunate Mistress* he had Sir Robert Clayton sum up his disquisition to Roxana on the advantages of marrying a successful merchant over a landed gentleman with the explanation, "an estate is a pond, but . . . trade was a spring" (I, 193). In a similar passage in *The Complete English Tradesman* a year later he again pointed out that members of the lower gentry (£100–£300 a year) cannot even live as splendidly as a shoemaker in London, who "shall keep a better house, spend more money, clothe his family better, and yet grow rich too." This paradoxical phenomenon he explained as follows: *"an estate's a pond, but a trade's a spring;* the first, if it keeps full, and the water wholesome, by the ordinary supplies and drains from the neighbouring grounds, 'tis well, and 'tis all that is expected; but the other is an inexhausted current, which not only fills the pond, and keeps it full, but is continually running over, and fills all the lower ponds and places about" (I, 310). Defoe saw in trade a natural supremacy over the rents and produce of the landed estates; it was only a matter of time before England's national economy would be converted from that of a primarily agrarian society, as represented by the Tory landed gentry, to a dominantly mercantile society, as represented by the men of industry and trade — and the Whig party now in power under the dynamic leadership of Robert Walpole. In his *Plan of the English Commerce* of 1728 he could write confidently, "How many shop-keepers, ware-house-keepers, and wholesale traders . . . drapers, iron-mongers, salters, haberdashers . . . spend 500 pounds a year . . . and lay up 500 pounds a year more, while a gentleman of a thousand pounds a year estate can hardly bring both ends together at the close of the year . . . ?" The natural economic law operating behind this happy trend he saw simply as *"an estate is* but *a pond,* but *trade is a spring"* (p. 75). It is owing to "the manufacturers and the shop-keepers" of England, in his estimate, that "trade is raised up to such a prodigy of magnitude" (p. 76).

By the late 1720's, however, Defoe was very much conscious of his advancing years. Just before publishing *A Plan of the English Commerce* in 1728, he published a pamphlet entitled *Augusta Triumphans,* a work designed, as the subtitle stated, "To Make London the Most Flourishing City in the Universe." The pamphlet marked a return to the heady projecting spirit behind the *Essay upon Projects,* published more than thirty years before, but Defoe now wrote with a decided note of urgency: "I have but a short time to live," he reminded his readers, "nor would I waste my remaining thread of life in vain." [7] Defoe knew his days were numbered by 1728; he was sixty-eight years old and his usually robust health was failing fast. Yet he felt that he had some last few important things to say before he died, and in his remaining time he wrote with an unmistakable sense of purpose, as is clear from his *Plan of the English Commerce.*

In *The Complete English Tradesman* he had drawn a neat metaphoric opposition between the diseased and declining gentry and the robust and rising tradesmen. Defoe showed that the "excessive high living" of the upper class had "of late grown so much into a disease" that many families witnessed their estates sunk deeply into debt or even ruin. Around London he found "the ancient families worn out by time and family misfortunes, and the estates possessed by a new race of tradesmen, grown up into families of gentry, and established by the immense wealth gained . . . behind the counter" (I, 308). The contrast he outlined for his readers is obvious enough: the gentry are worn out, old, bankrupt; the tradesmen are a new race, young, wealthy. This general pattern is borne out further by the new dwellings on the outskirts of London, as Defoe noted in the *Tour* and reemphasized in the *Tradesman* by inviting his readers to witness the "many noble seats . . . erected within few miles of this city by tradesmen, or the sons of tradesmen, while the seats and castles of the ancient gentry, like their families look *worn out* and fallen into *decay*" (I, 309). Indeed, when a tradesman fails, he can rise again, like a "phoenix," as Defoe himself had risen on more than one occasion; but the gentry and nobility are doomed by their vanity and pride, which prevent them from redeeming their estates through trade. Only a reconciliation with the trading classes can enable them to redeem or rejuvenate their conditions.

Defoe knew he struck at the upper classes' most vulnerable point by so focusing on their failing economic position, and in the *Plan of the English Commerce* he hoped to humble the gentry and nobility by demonstrating in detail how their pride and luxury have all but beggared them and wasted their once thriving estates. Pleasure is the pursuit of the upper class and trade of the middle class, according to Defoe, but with this all-important consequence: "where the trade is, there are the people, there the wealth, there the great markets, and the large towns; and in a word, there the ready money: for it is the trade that has made the common people rich, as pride has made the gentry poor" (p. 60). In tracing for his readers this so-called "Revolution of Trade" (pp. 36f) back to the Renaissance, he resorts to the same facile formula to explain the causes behind the flourishing state of the middle class and the degenerate state of the upper class in England: "the frugal manufacturers . . . lay'd up money, and grew rich; and the luxurious and purse proud gentry . . . grew vain, gay, luxurious . . . [and in time] grew poor and necessitous, till the former began to buy them out" (p. 37). Such was the pattern in the Renaissance, and now in the early eighteenth century Defoe derives a smug satisfaction from the repetition of this historical process: "now we see the nobility and ancient gentry have almost everywhere sold their estates, and the commonalty and tradesmen have bought them: so that now the gentry are richer than the nobility, and the tradesmen are richer than them all" (p. 38). The present plight of the upper classes Defoe views as fitting and proper punishment for their vices of pride and luxury; the middle-class tradesmen, on the other hand, are deservingly rewarded for their virtues of industry and frugality. It makes for a pretty middle-class Puritan moral.

Actually, of course, Defoe's account of the situation is an egregious oversimplification. He fails to take into consideration, among other things, the severe burden of taxes borne by the nobility and gentry to finance the numerous and costly wars waged by England since the Restoration. Like all good propaganda pieces, however, Defoe's survey contains just enough truth to make the interpretation plausible. His survey of the contemporary scene regarding the sale of estates is exaggerated but essentially accurate; according to H. J. Habakkuk, "in the two or three decades after 1715 a large number of estates were sold." And as successful merchants and tradesmen and manufacturers were able to purchase estates, they were also able to establish themselves as people of quality. Defoe saw them "coming every day to the herald's office to search for coats of arms of their ancestors"; and if they found no family arms in existence, they "would begin a new race" (I, 311), as Defoe did himself.[8]

Looking beyond London, he envisoned the broader implications of this opposition between the trading and the landed interests for the future condition of England:

Look to the lands, and consequently to the estates of the gentry, the manufacturing counties are calculated for business, the unemploy'd counties for pleasure; the first are throng'd with villages and great towns, the last with parks and great forests; the first are stored with people, the last with game; the first are rich and fertile, the last waste and barren; the diligent part of the people are fled to the first, the idler part are left at the last; in a word, the rich and thriving tradesmen live in the first, the decaying wasting gentry in the last. (pp. 67–68)

Defoe's overall vision of England, like Disraeli's a century later, is of two nations, not yet simply the rich and the poor, as they were to become, but a vision basically in keeping with his metaphoric pattern of rise and fall, growth and decay, spring and pond: the "rich and thriving tradesmen," already busily transforming England into the great industrial and manufacturing nation she was to become in the nineteenth century, and the "decaying wasting gentry," blindly persistent in maintaining their lands as anachronistic sixteenth- and seventeenth-century pleasure preserves. In effect, the style of living maintained by the gentry was pernicious because it did not encourage industry, productivity, employment and wealth; on the contrary, it wasted resources and curbed the growth of England as a trading nation.

By the 1720's Defoe sensed that the gentry and nobility were not only losing ground to the middle classes economically, but were also relinquishing their historical role of leadership in the affairs of the nation. In *The Complete English Tradesman,* he could contend with some confidence that "the English tradesmen may in a few years be allowed to rank with the best gentlemen in Europe" because of their outstanding service in the late war with France under Queen Anne, in which they served as soldiers "who went from the shop, and behind the counter, into the camp, and who distinguished themselves there by their merits and gallant behaviour" (I, 312–314). The gentlemen of a nation historically provided the officers for armies in time of war, and the war with the French showed up the weaknesses of the English gentry and nobility while exhibiting the strengths of the trading class. In 1708 Defoe already had written in his *Review* that "of all the nations now at war, *England* has the fewest of her nobility and gentry in the field, I mean compared to the great number of gentlemen we have in this nation" (V, 406). The nobility and gentry had become debilitated and ineffectual by their selfish pursuit of idle and loose pleasures. Fortunately for England, according to his appraisal of the problem, the tradesmen were able to assume the necessary role of leadership as officers and soldiers in the armies. They had proved their mettle on the battlefields of Europe; now they would prove their mettle in the affairs of England.

Trade was to form the great reservoir from which England's new leaders were to be drawn. Defoe's concern for "completeness" in his tradesmen suggests that he came to regard them as the important national force. In *The Complete English Tradesman* he remarked that "after a generation or two the tradesmen's children, or at least their grand-children, come to be as good gentlemen, statesmen, parliamentmen, privy-counsellors, judges, bishops, and noblemen, as those of the highest birth and the most ancient families" (I, 310). It was most unusual but not impossible for a wealthy merchant or tradesman to exploit the "rotten borough" system, and by buying the estate of a "borough lord" buy himself a seat in Parliament as well. The door, at least, was not shut tight to all, as in European countries, and the mere fact that one or two merchants could in this way buy themselves seats in Parliament was enough to excite the imaginations of the others.[9] And since trade, as he argued repeatedly, "is the readiest way for men to raise their fortunes and families" (I, 306), the tradesmen must be "complete" in preparation of their new roles in society.

Trade, however, was to Defoe a vast ocean, a mighty river, big enough to accommodate all who are willing to sail upon it, be they of the middle or upper class. The future of England unmistakably lay in trade, as the more far-sighted and sensible members of the gentry and nobility realized, and as Defoe in the *Plan of the English Commerce* again reminded his readers:

1. The ancient families, who having wasted and exhausted their estates, and being declin'd and decay'd in fortune by luxury and high living, have restor'd and rais'd themselves again by mixing blood with the despis'd tradesmen, marrying the daughters of such tradesmen as, being overgrown in wealth, have been oblig'd for want of sons to leave their estates to their female issue . . .

2. And thus the decay'd estates of the nobility and gentry have been restored, and their family wounds heal'd by the daughters of the richer tradesmen; so on the other hand, by the tradesmen themselves, or by their sons, the numbers of the families of the gentry have been recruited, when sunk out of rank and lost in poverty and distress.   (p. 61)

Defoe liked to dwell on these encouraging signs; they pointed to the possibility, even necessity, of an eventual acceptance of trade and tradesmen by the gentry and nobility, particularly if such an interchange and intermingling between the two classes continued. Defoe saw trade as the major cause of social change: "Trade, in a word, raises ancient families when sunk and decay'd, and plants new families, where the old ones are lost and extinct" (p. 63).

Defoe was confident that the interests of trade and the middle class would ultimately prevail. The gentry and nobility would probably never entirely relinquish their prejudices against trade;

but without a great deal of money, the kind of money that could only be made from trade, they could not continue to flourish. Thus, England would in time "have very few families of gentlemen left" because "families are as effectually extinct, and lost, and as much forgotten, when the heirs are left in misery and poverty, and the estate sold from them, as if they were sunk into the grave" (pp. 61–62). Without money, birth and blood were empty pretensions. And as an ancient estate was sold to a wealthy tradesman, a new kind of gentleman rose to replace the bankrupt old gentleman:

The estate (of one thousand eight hundred pound *per annum*) is purchased by a citizen, who having got the money by honest industry, and pursuing a prosperous trade, has left his books and his warehouses to his two younger sons, is retir'd from the world, lives upon the estate, is a justice of the peace, and makes a complete gentleman. His eldest son, bred at the university, and thoroughly accomplish'd, is as well receiv'd among the gentry in the county, and upon the valuable fund of his true merit, as if he had been a gentleman by blood for a hundred generations before the Conquest.   (p. 62)

Such a tradesman turned gentleman caught Defoe's fancy. He was eager to have the tradesman prepared for this important social transition, as is evident from his *Complete English Tradesman*. "Completeness" was of direct concern to tradesmen because a "complete tradesman" could in time become a "complete gentleman."

Having rounded off his discussions of trade and commerce in *The Complete English Tradesman* and the *Plan of the English Commerce,* Defoe in 1729 began *The Compleat English Gentleman,* in many ways a companion to the preceding volume on trade, and the capstone to his treatment of gentility.

Chapter 11. The Compleat English Gentleman: The Born and the Bred Gentleman

I say there are gentlemen by birth and gentlemen by education, and I insist that the last is the better of the two; for he is the best and truest original of a gentleman, and has been so, of all the families of gentlemen in England; or else they have no originals at all. — Defoe, *The Compleat English Gentleman*, pp. 48–49

Before Defoe came to write his formal treatise on *The Compleat English Gentleman* at the close of his life, he was at work in the latter part of 1728 and early part of 1729 on a book entitled *Of Royall Educacion*. Although it survives as a fragment of less than four chapters, the intent of the book is clear from the headnote to the first chapter: "Of the reason and necessity of good education, the importance of it . . . in the children of princes and noblemen, as also of all persons of rank, either for quality or employment." Defoe did not complete this book, perhaps, as Professor Moore suggests, for fear that his treatise might be read in a political light, as bearing in some direct way on "the most dangerous subject in England at that time — the long and bitter quarrel between George I and the Prince of Wales over the care of the royal grandchildren." [1] Defoe had all his life been interested as well in the concept of the bred gentlemen, especially during the 1720's, and he accordingly attempted to salvage what he could of his original design by undertaking to write a more comprehensive book that would embrace both the born and the bred gentleman — or, more familiarly, the respective claims of the upper and middle classes to true gentility.

Defoe knew he could not hope to win a hearing from the gentry and nobility if it were known the book was written by Daniel Defoe; consequently, he resorted to a favorite device, the persona of a gentleman, which he had used to great advantage in disseminating his more unpopular sentiments in the past. In *Mist's Journal*, for example, he prefaced his attack on the self-interest of Whig and Tory statesmen with this assurance: "From the privilege of my birth and education, I have had frequent opportunities of conversing with people of the first condition." [2] In the *Tour* he characterized himself a "Gentleman" and a member of the Church of England. The device of the mask was a common and effective vehicle for communicating one's ideas to a large and varied audience. As Dr. Johnson was to remark in the final *Rambler* paper: " 'A mask,' says Castiglione, 'confers a right of acting and speaking with less restraint, even when the wearer happens to be known.' " [3]

In *The Compleat English Gentleman* Defoe is quick to reassure his readers at the outset that he is not just another leveler ("I am far from levelling the clown and the gentleman") but a gentleman addressing himself to fellow gentlemen ("I have the honour to be rank'd, by the direction of Providence, in the same class").[4] The use of the persona of a gentleman was, however, as much a restraint to Defoe as it was a decoy for his upper-class readers. Fortunately there survives in the manuscript copy of the work a first draft of an incomplete introduction that offers us a valuable insight into his true feelings about his subject. The original title of the treatise, *The True Bred Gentleman*, clearly indicates where Defoe's primary interest lay, and the opening paragraph of this introduction reveals his unconcealed attitude toward his upper-class readers: "Nothing in the world can be more preposterous, and yet nothing of the kind is more warmly espoused and dogmatically insisted upon, than the gross notions of nobility and gentility, as they are at this time entertained among [us]" (p. xii). Such a tone, however, could only antagonize the upper classes; hence Defoe's reliance on the persona of gentleman as not only the best means of addressing an unsympathetic upper-class audience but also a reminder to himself to moderate his tone lest his passionate feelings on the subject vitiate his arguments. Indeed, Defoe takes care throughout the text not to offend his upper-class readers unnecessarily. He even addresses them directly: "The gentlemen of England will have no room to be offended at this work; it is neither written to expose or insult them, much less to wrong and abuse them" (p. 88).

We know that Defoe wrestled at length with the problem of how best to convey his thoughts on the subject of gentility because he attempted at least three introductions for *The Compleat English Gentleman* and apparently was not satisfied with any of them, for he did not complete even one.[5] In this second introduction Defoe makes clear his intention to reconcile the conflict of interests between the upper and middle classes concerning gentility by subsuming both the "born gentleman" and the "bred gentleman" under the rubric of the "complete gentleman" (p. 3). In essence, however, he is merely elaborating the themes he recently treated in *The Complete English Tradesman* and *A Plan of the English Commerce,* wherein he sought to reconcile the upper and middle classes through a common concern in the commerce and trade of the nation. He still holds essentially to that plan, but now he seeks to formulate it in more detail and in terms of the writings on gentility in England.

The second introduction summarizes neatly Defoe's basic position in *The Compleat English Gentleman.* "The born gentleman is a valuable man," Defoe states, only if he is "bred up as a gentleman ought to be, that is, educated in learning and manners suitable to his birth" (p. 3). On the other hand, gentility cannot be denied a person simply because he lacks noble birth and an ancient lineage. Defoe contends that even "the son of a mean person furnish'd from heaven with an original fund of wealth, wit, sense, courage, virtue, and good humor, and set apart by a liberal education for the service of his country . . . must be allowd . . . into the rank of a gentleman"; and though he be but the first of his line to become such an "accomplish'd gentleman," there is no reason why he cannot himself "raise a *roof tree* (as the ancients call it) of a noble house and of a succession of gentlemen as effectually as if he had his pedigree to show from the Conqueror's army or from a centurion in the legions that landed with Julius Caesar" (p. 4). Defoe's "difficult case" in the treatise reduces itself to this: how to describe and discuss the "compleat gentleman" in a way that will "reconcile the ancient line to . . . the modern line" (p. 4)?

Defoe's intention can perhaps be most easily understood if considered within the framework of the history of English courtesy literature. In the earliest major treatise in English on the subject, the anonymous *Institution of a Gentleman* of 1555, gentlemen are divided into three classes: (1) "Gentle gentle," (2) "Gentle ungentle," and (3) "Ungentle gentle." The "Gentle gentle" category accommodates those gentlemen directly descended of gentle blood and accomplished in gentle manners and arts. In the "Gentle ungentle" category are those gentlemen descended of gentle blood but marked in their behavior by "corrupt and ungentle manners." Last and most significant is the "Ungentle gentle" category, comprised of a new species of gentleman who, though "born of a low degree," has distinguished himself "by his virtue, wit, policy, industry, knowledge in laws, valiancy in arms, or such like honest means, becometh a well beloved and high esteemed man, preferred then to great office . . . and so grown rich, doth thereby advance and set up the rest of his poor line or kindred; they are the children of such one commonly called gentleman." The author of the *Institution* goes on to remark that in England at this time there are "very many" such gentlemen in the "Ungentle gentle" category and they "are now called upstarts, a term lately invented." Although the class of gentlemen in the middle of the sixteenth century still constituted an exclusive caste, and there was a natural distrust of "upstart" newcomers, works like the *Institution* do show how the class recruited outstanding members of society to itself, even though these new gentlemen did not have the traditional qualifications of birth and blood.[6]

"Blurred as class lines became during the sixteenth century, and new as many of England's prominent families were," Ruth Kelso concludes, "the idea that gentility meant fundamentally gentle birth is never lost." The century became increasingly uneasy, however, about defining gentility solely in terms of direct noble descent because of the *ad absurdum* flaw of the argument on which such claims to exclusiveness were founded; since everyone traced his ancestry to Adam and Eve, everyone ultimately was of "mechanic" birth. The author of the *Institution of a Gentleman,* for example, quoted the nub of the problem as follows: "When Adam delved and Eve span, who was then a gentleman?" This unsettling "old objection of the common people" was repeated in variant forms throughout the century, as indeed it had been since the fourteenth century.[7]

The Born and the Bred Gentleman

Following the fashion set forth in the *Institution of a Gentleman*, the sixteenth and seventeenth centuries classified gentility as "nobility native," based on birth and blood, or as "nobility dative," derived from royal conferral for outstanding achievements, as in the case of the "Ungentle gentle." Since "nobility dative" required only royal action, it could be attained by the receipt of permission to bear arms from the College of Heralds, which, at least theoretically, involved royal action in that the College of Heralds acted in the name of the Crown and issued coats of arms by right of the king. In fact, the connection between a coat of arms and the concept of gentility became so close as the century progressed that by 1586 a treatise entitled *The Blazon of Gentry* defined a gentleman simply as one who bears arms.[8]

The consequences of this system of distinguishing gentlemen are not difficult to determine. Soon the door to status as a gentleman was open to almost anyone who could pay the price for armorial bearings. By the end of the sixteenth century, as Miss Kelso notes, "the College of Heralds had fallen into evil repute, for the sale of coats of arms was notorious, and the devices were stolen from old families without shame or designed to suit the whims of buyers to the utter confusion and degradation of the honorable sign language of chivalric days." This abuse of "nobility dative" brought about a radical shift in the traditional concept of gentility by the beginning of the seventeenth century. Sir Thomas Smith, a conservative writer on heraldry and gentility, wrote:

Ordinarily the king doth only make knights and create barons or higher degrees: for as for gentlemen, they may be made good cheap in England. For whosoever studieth the laws of the realm, who studieth in the universities, who professeth liberal sciences, and to be short, who can live idly and without manual labor, and will bear the port, charge and countenance of a gentleman, he shall be called Master, for that is the title which men give to esquires and other gentlemen, and shall be taken for a gentleman.

Gentlemen were being "made good cheap in England" because of the opportunities to buy arms and social standing.[9]

Defoe certainly was no stranger to these liberalizing and vulgarizing trends in the history of gentility and courtesy literature in England. His interest in genealogy had made him keenly aware that the traditional qualifications for gentility, birth and blood, were no longer as valid or as strictly adhered to as they once were, and he tried to exploit this weakened position on behalf of the middle class.

Defoe's treatment of gentility, as set forth in the introduction to *The Compleat English Gentleman*, significantly omits any discussion of birth and blood, so prized by the gentry and nobility, and focuses on breeding and learning, which would serve to qualify members of the middle class for the rank and title of true gentlemen. In a word, Defoe follows the historical trend from the sixteenth century on: "Ungentle gentle," as stated in the *Institution* of 1555, or "nobility dative," as first stated by Robert Glover's *Catalogue of Honour* in 1610 and vulgarized in practice throughout the late sixteenth and seventeenth centuries.[10] Defoe wanted to further these favorable and liberal trends in his treatise, but since he was writing for a hostile upper-class audience, he had to conceal his intentions and conform superficially with the conservative ideals upheld by the nobility and gentry.

The influence of the conservative position among writers on gentility even by the third decade of the eighteenth century, when Defoe was composing his work on the subject, was still considerable. The tenor of Defoe's arguments clearly indicates his assumption that most of his upper-class readers regard only the "born" gentleman as fit for the title, whatever his failings of character and deficiencies of learning; birth and blood still seem to be the touchstones of gentility. Making a conscious effort not to outrage his readers at the outset, he defines a gentleman in terms of contemporary usage: "Our modern acceptation of a *Gentleman* . . . is this, A person BORN (for there lies the essence of quality) of some known or ancient family, whose ancestors have at least for some time been rais'd above the class of mechanics" (p. 13).

Despite his persona of a gentleman, Defoe cannot resist the temptation of exposing the absurdity of his conservative position when logically extended: "I wonder our modern pretenders to the title of gentility should lay so much stress upon what they call a long descent of blood" because, he observes, "the highest families begun low, therefore to examine it too nicely, is to overthrow it all" (p. 13). He confronts the upper classes with the basic argument discussed throughout the sixteenth century by writers on gentility ("When Adam delved and Eve span, who was then a gentleman?"). He also finds it hard to restrain himself when dealing with "the jargon of the heralds." Obviously experiencing great difficulty in controlling his point of view, Defoe restrains himself repeatedly and attempts to ridicule by indirection the position he ostensibly represents: "Not therefore to search too far where the thing will not bear the inquisition, I shall take it as the world takes it, that the word *Gentleman* implies a man of family, born of such blood as we gentlemen, such ancestors as liv'd on their estates, and as must be suppos'd had estates to live on, whether the present successor be poor or rich" (pp. 15–16). Defoe's persistent exposure of the weakened economic position of the upper classes was his way of strengthening the case of the middle classes, which were growing in wealth and power all the time. The conflict between what Defoe really feels and what, in compliance with "the language of the times," he must avow is clear in passages like this: "So I must join, for the present purpose, with these people that value themselves on their unmix'd blood, and call them gentlemen, tho' they want a pair of shoes, and the ladies who scorn to marry a tradesman however rich, wise, learned, well-educated or religious, tho' at the same time they have little or nothing to support the character of their birth, and perhaps, no means to subsist" (pp. 17–18). The Defoe who unmistakably breaks through the persona is Mr. Review or Defoe the tradesman. Finally he cannot control himself and bursts out: "Unhappy humour! truly ridiculous, and indeed preposterous!" (p. 18). Such outbursts suggest why Defoe, an old and ill man, was having difficulty in writing this work. Not even the mask can keep the old man's feelings entirely under control, and the text as it survives, though a revealing statement of his real sentiments, lacks the polish and consistency of a finished work.

Defoe had hoped to postulate a modified modern ideal of the complete gentleman for his age. To accomplish this end, he first had to show why the conservative ideal no longer was adequate and how the class of "born" gentlemen had fallen into disrepute. He states his case plainly:

But setting up a new class truly qualified to inherit the title, turn the ancient race into the woods . . . notwithstanding all the trappings of their antiquity, high birth, great ancestors, and boasted family fame, 'till they learn to know themselves, 'till their understandings return, and 'till they can be brought to confess that when learning, education, virtue and good manners are wanting, or degenerated and corrupted in a gentleman, he sinks out of rank, ceases to be any more a gentleman, and is *ipso facto,* turn'd back among the less despicable throng of the *plaebeii.* That when it is thus . . . they lose all pretence of right to the quality they bore, forfeiting their claim of blood they really ought to rank no otherwise than according to merit.   (p. 18)

In essence, Defoe does away with the traditional trappings of gentility and quality by ignoring blood and birth entirely and concentrating almost exclusively on merit. Under such a scheme even the eldest sons of families of the gentry and nobility, if they failed to meet the requirements of "learning, education, virtue and good manners," would lose their right to the title of true gentlemen by default; whereas the sons of wealthy tradesmen and merchants, if they possessed these qualities and the means to live like gentlefolk, would qualify as the "new class" fittest to be called gentlemen.

Defoe's ideal gentleman is in the best tradition of courtesy literature: "a person of merit and worth; a man of honour, virtue, sense, integrity, honesty, and religion, without which he is nothing at all" (p. 21). No mention, significantly, is made of birth or ancestry; the stress is entirely on the qualities of gentility. Defoe knows that he cannot question a gentleman's rank. With an estate and a distinguished family name, one cannot be called plebeian; but without certain characteristics of heart and mind, one cannot merit the title of a true or complete gentleman. He makes a point of drawing this distinction for his readers: "Well did King *Charles* II. say, *he could make a knight, but could not make a gentleman*" (p. 25). Defoe's underlying strategy in *The Compleat English Gentleman* is to unite the "born" and the "bred" species of gentlemen, the "ancient" and the "modern" lines, through a proper appreciation and emulation of the qualities of the ideal gentleman.

Much of the first half of the existing text of *The Compleat English Gentleman* is a catalogue of the failings of the "born" gentlemen of England. The persona of the gentleman enables

Defoe to accomplish this end most effectively: "Do not *we English gentlemen* think, that to be a good sportsman is the perfection of education, and to speak good dog language and good horse language is far above Greek and Latin; and that a little damming and swearing among it makes all the rest polite and fashionable" (p. 38, italics mine). He can support such censures by recording supposedly actual conversations that he, as a gentleman, has had with typical city and country gentlemen. By this means he can, for example, offer a caricature of the early eighteenth-century country squire: He "enjoys his espous'd brutality, hunts, hawks, shoots, and follows his game, hallows to his dogs, damns his servants, dotes upon his horses, drinks with his huntsman, and is excellent company for two or three drunken elder brothers in his neighbourhood; and as here is his felicity, so here is the utmost of his accomplishments" (p. 39). Defoe can continue in this vein, castigating the ignorance and the boorishness of the country gentry, because he is writing as a gentleman looking at his social equals, not as a social inferior.

Defoe also resorts to the dramatic dialogue, a technique he first used to sustained advantage in his *Family Instructor* of 1715. By 1729, after his period as novelist, he had so perfected this literary device that he could convey economically and forcefully the shortcomings of eldest sons among the gentry through a colloquy between a typical eldest son, who is destined to inherit the title and family estate, and a typical younger brother, who earns the title of gentleman by his education and breeding. The eldest brother embodies the point of view of the unenlightened conservatives by countenancing only birth and blood as fit prerequisites for gentility; the younger brother, on the other hand, embodies the liberal and modern notion that gentility must be merited by education and breeding or be forfeited. As Defoe's mouthpiece, the younger brother consistently confronts his older brother with the untenability of his position, while the boorish older brother, in turn, is made to appear all the more foolish by his myopic views and gross manners. Defoe uses these heated exchanges to demonstrate dramatically that in every respect the "gentleman by education" is superior, both in principle and in practice, to the "gentleman by birth" (pp. 48f).

Careful not to arouse the gentry and nobility unnecessarily

while presenting his case, he offers his upper-class readers models with which they can readily identify. The two brothers represent extreme positions, but they are both, intentionally, members of the upper class by birth and blood; thus Defoe is certain not to alienate his readers by asking them to identify with someone whom they undoubtedly would think beneath their station, like a merchant's or tradesman's son. The eldest brother is portrayed as "heir to an estate of about 3000 pounds a year, and expected to be chosen Parliament man" (p. 44). He is also the prototype of the hunting squire, and he appears at the coffee-house, appropriately, "with the French horn in his hand" (p. 44). The younger brother is drawn as his foil in every way, having been "bred at the university," where he had "acquir'd a good stock of learning," which he rounded into a "liberal education" (p. 43). The essential point that emerges from the opposition and exchange between the two brothers is the vital importance of education to any claims of gentility, and the unseemly figure one cuts before the world for the lack and abuse of it.

We know from Defoe's writings that he consistently regarded education as of paramount importance to the life and career of all human beings, both high and low. Only the previous year, in *Of Royall Educacion,* he had undertaken to demonstrate that "wise and prudent education of children, of what degree soever they are, is undeniably an advantage to the children themselves . . . even in the meanest rank or degree of men," but most significant for "children of highest rank" (p. 8). In *The Compleat English Gentleman* he planned to resume his discussion of this all-important subject. His intent is easily inferred from a scratched-out heading to the second chapter: "That the ignorance and the bad education of gentlemen of quality and fortune is nowhere in Christendom so entirely neglected as in this nation, and some of the consequences of it" (p. 59n). What he had undertaken to prove for royalty in particular the preceding year, he now attempted to prove for the English gentleman, both "born" and "bred," in general.

"The proposition is plain," Defoe argues, *"that our English gentlemen are not men of learning"* (p. 96). The paradox of this sorry situation is that those men who pride themselves upon being the "best of the race" are indeed no better than "fools," and not because of any deficiencies of nature but simply "for want of teaching" and, more important, lack of the desire to learn. Because they maintain that book learning is strictly for scholars, and practical learning for mechanics, the upper classes are proficient at nothing but idle pleasures like hunting and drinking. These pernicious prejudices against education encourage so-called gentlemen to be ignorant and debauched and, worse still, to take pride in such failings.

Defoe attributes the blame for this condition largely to the parents and their willful neglect of a proper education for their children. At the time he was writing, the general attitude among the members of the gentry and nobility was still one of fashionable contempt for learning, a contempt soon adopted by the young, who were taught to respond to queries about their studies as follows: "School, Sir? I don't go to school. My father scorns to put me to school. Sure I an't to be a trades-man; I am to be a gentleman: I an't to go to school" (p. 98). It was this kind of sentiment, so well reproduced here, that Defoe sought to correct.[11]

Defoe also satirizes the equally fashionable but meretricious display of learning affected by some "born" gentlemen. He again utilizes the device of the dramatic dialogue to emphasize his point. In this case, he creates Sir A.B., "a gentleman of a great estate and of a mighty ancient family, belov'd in the country where he lives to an extravagance" (p. 122). Sir A.B. is the epitome of the popular ideal of the country gentleman: wealthy, honest, beloved by his tenants. His interlocutor in the dialogue is a city gentleman, "a man of letters" who has lived much abroad and is sophisticated in the ways of the *beau monde*. In the dramatic exchange between the two Defoe exposes the incredible ignorance of the country gentleman and the false values of culture of the city gentleman, both of whom are designed as representatives of their respective classes. Sir A.B. cannot even read or write with any facility; he must rely on his servants for the composition and reading of even his personal correspondence. Despite his lack of literacy, he has a vast room set aside to house his library, the contents of which suggest the libraries of country squires around 1700: "a great Bible, the register of the house . . . three mass books . . . the old ballad of Chevy Chace . . . an old base viol, two fiddles, and a music book . . . four or five folio Common Prayer Books . . . and the old Book of Martyrs" (p. 135).[12] When his city friend asks why he never added to his father's library, he answers honestly that he saw no point in it since he "never read any." But his worldly counterpart from the city remonstrates, "O but, Sir, no gentleman is without a library. 'Tis more in fashion now than ever it was" (p. 135).

In so satirizing the fashion of gentlemen keeping up showy personal libraries, despite their contempt for any kind of book learning, Defoe put his finger on a seemingly widespread vogue among the upper classes. The city friend of Sir A.B. views the library not as a collection of knowledge but solely as "a handsome ornament" (p. 136). And so apparently did others. The following year, for example, the Edinburgh *Echo* printed an anonymous letter from a servant girl describing the library of a wealthy baronet. The girl at first was impressed by the vast number of "choice books curiously bound, gilt and letter'd," but soon she noticed that no one ever went into the library except when it was displayed to guests on evenings when the baronet and his wife were entertaining. Eventually it dawned upon this servant girl that "a study is as necessary in a nobleman or gentleman's house, altho' he does not read, as a chappel, tho' he never hears prayers." [13] Probably no one discerned more clearly than Defoe that both country and city gentlemen were much more eager to acquire books than to open them. This fashion, like so many other vain practices, he attributed to the disesteem of the upper classes for knowledge and a liberal education.

But Defoe saw in the general state of the gentry and nobility something of far more sweeping national significance than unread libraries or boorish behavior; he saw that the decline of the "born" gentlemen, caused by their ignorance and contempt for learning, was threatening the very liberty and leadership of the English nation. If gentlemen persuade their sons that it is degrading and dishonorable to go to school and become educated and disciplined, if they teach them to scorn knowledge and breeding, then, Defoe asks, "what hope can we entertain of the next age?" (p. 145). England's cherished liberty, historically upheld and protected by the nobility and gentry, will be seriously threatened:

Want of learning makes them easy, indolent, manageable, thoughtless, and extravagant. Want of learning makes them incapable, breaks their economy, and exposes them to a thoughtless luxury; the consequence of which is reduction of estates, necessitous circumstances, and even beggary; and the natural consequence of that is being subject to all manner of corruption, easily purchas'd for parties and faction, and by pensions and places to betray themselves and their country, and give up all to the craftsmen of the Court.   (p. 175)

Defoe's reasoning stems from his reading of human nature, which he often summed up simply as, "Give me not poverty lest I steal." He foresees that the gentry and nobility will by their present course be led into all manner of temptation and "necessity," which their pressed circumstances will not allow them to resist. Happily, the present government, according to Defoe, serves to safeguard the liberties of the people for the time being, but casting an eye to the future he can see "but a melancholy prospect for the safety of our posterity" unless the upper classes alter their regard for education.

Despite their miseducation, Defoe offers to the upper classes the same encouragement he had offered to fallen tradesmen in *The Complete English Tradesman* a few years earlier: *"Nil desperandum . . . while there are brains there is hope"* (pp. 185–186). He was well aware of the sterile nature of much of the grammar school and university training offered in the early eighteenth century. The curriculum was largely dominated by the study of Latin and Greek, and learning relied less on inquiry than on dull rote memorization. In his proposed program of studies, however, Defoe reassured his readers that he could make of a born gentleman a "man of learning . . . without the fatigue of the school, without hammering seven years at the Latin and the Greek, and without tormenting, loading, and overloading his memory with the mere dead weight of words" (pp. 187–188). The inferior subject matter at the schools was generally matched by an equally inferior level of instruction. Perhaps something of a characteristic pedagogical pose was struck by the Oxford don whose fondest wish it was "to emancipate himself from the slavery of pupils." [14] In any event, education was certainly antiquated, and Defoe hoped to rejuvenate the curriculum with a more modern and viable approach to learning, an approach derived in large part from his own course of studies some fifty years before at Morton's academy in Newington Green.

Defoe broke completely with the classical curriculum that had formed the core of virtually all previous programs of formal education. Instead of a lengthy and detailed study of Latin and Greek, he followed the lead of his mentor Charles Morton in establishing English as the language both for recitation and for instruction in all subjects. Also he shifted the course of studies from pure to applied knowledge, from pedantry to practical knowledge. "The knowledge of things, not words," according to Defoe, "make a scholar" (p. 212). In proposing these basic educational reforms he was not unique, although his position ranked him among the few truly enlightened theorists of the age, and the position he promulgated was in time to prevail.

The study of Latin and Greek was, in Defoe's eyes, a looking to the past rather than an awareness of the present or a looking to the future. Everything he saw about him in society convinced him all the more that "the moderns begin to gain upon the ancients extremely, and some parts of knowledge shine brighter in English than ever they did in Latin" (pp. 230–231). So long as the ancient traditions at the universities and grammar schools continued unmodified, so long as all pupils were forced to master Latin and Greek because the lectures were declaimed in Latin and the reading was mainly in the ancient tongues, learning would continue to be largely an onerous process, one which by its very severity discouraged rather than encouraged learning. The consequences of such an antiquated system of education were to confine the useful branches of science "to those only who can read and understand Latin," which, in Defoe's judgment, "is tying up knowledge to a few, whereas science being a public blessing to mankind ought to be extended and made as diffusive as possible" (p. 197).

Defoe's solution to this problem was simply to replace the focus on Latin and Greek with a focus on English. There were no contemporary justifications for teaching in the ancient languages, except the untenable ones of tradition or exclusiveness or polite pedantry. The world of practical affairs had convinced Defoe that in, for example, navigation, which required a sophisticated knowledge of astronomy, mathematics, and geography, a formal knowledge of Latin and Greek was irrelevant; "for where is there a sea-faring man in twenty that understands Latin, and yet some of them [are] the completest artists in the world" (p. 198). Let the study of Greek and Latin be the rightful province of the scholar, but let a man well read in English qualify as having received a liberal education suited for a gentleman. Defoe does not depreciate the value of the classical authors; quite the contrary, he merely argues that they be taught in translation and so be accessible to all: "if the philosophy, the geography, the astronomy of as well the ancient as the modern writers were made familiar to us, and all liberal arts and sciences taught in our mother tongue, it must be granted men might be made scholars at a much easier expence as well as of labour as of money than now, and men might be truly learned and yet kno' nothing of the Greek or the Latin" (pp. 209–210). Defoe's aim is to liberate the curriculum from the tyranny of the Greek and Latin mongers. He is unsparing in his denunciation of "such bigots to the languages to wrap up all learning in their swaddling clothes and determine the world to the bondage of their tyranny or to irretrievable ignorance" (pp. 215–216).

After the replacement of the classical languages by English for all recitation and instruction, the shift from mere scholarship and pedantry to practical and modern subjects follows naturally. The study of modern subjects obviously does not require ancient languages. As for the ancient classics, they will be read and taught in English with as much advantage to students as if they "had read them critically in the Latin and the Greek" (p. 225). As for the studies in English, Defoe shows the gentry that, their past deficiencies in education notwithstanding, "they have it in their power to instruct themselves in all manner of science and humane knowledge" (p. 217).

Defoe obviously was struck by the parallel between the problem in education faced by his age and the problem in education when he attended school a half-century earlier at Morton's academy. Defoe noted how Morton surmounted the problems posed by his age. According to his recollection, Morton had himself written a treatise "against the school learning and their locking up . . . all science in the Greek and Latin, compelling all their pupils to learn the sciences in those languages or not at all, and to perform all their public exercises in Latin or Greek" (p. 218). Morton's solution to the problem was to set up his academy, in which he sought to rectify the educational malpractices at the universities and grammar schools by adopting a method of instruction centered on English and emphasizing science as well as other modern subjects, like geography and modern languages, all of which "he taught in English" (p. 219). So impressed was Defoe by Morton's visionary approach to education that he can find no better tribute to his former mentor than to recommend the same kind of academies and curricula "at this time for the recovery of our younger gentry from that unhappy ignorance which the negligence of their opinionated ancestors and instructors left them in" (220).

It is clear that Defoe's design in *The Compleat English Gentleman* was two-fold: he endeavored to make learning fashionable again to the class of "born" gentlemen (the gentry and nobility) and to displace the pedantry of the classically-oriented universities with a practical curriculum more suited to the modern needs of a mighty trading nation like England. Men grounded in Greek and Latin, no matter how successfully mastered, would not weld a far-reaching mercantile empire out of England and her growing colonies; but men conversant with the world by their mastery of modern languages and science would be in a position to further the trading interests of the nation. By breaking up the monopoly of learning among those of a classical education, Defoe not only made education open to all who were literate but also made of the practically trained middle class a respectably educated body, from whose ranks could be recruited the best of the "bred" gentlemen who would join with the best of the "born" gentlemen in shaping the destiny of England as a world power.

By devoting the first part of his *Compleat English Gentleman* to a detailed demonstration of how deficient the "born" gentlemen were in education, manners, and over-all reputation, Defoe was prepared in the second part to launch into a presentation of his main thesis: the importance of recruiting new blood into the class of gentlemen, thereby establishing a bold new national concept of "the compleat gentleman" which incorporated the best of "the ancient line [with] . . . the modern line." He makes his appeal to his upper-class readers in the light of the recent growth in England in "law, trade, war, navigation, improvement of stocks, loans on public funds, places of trust, and abundance of other modern advantages and private ways of getting money" so that "a great number of families" have accumulated immense fortunes and purchased equally "immense estates" in a relatively short period of time, with the result that England is now faced with a social phenomenon "difficult to describe and not less difficult to give a name too" (p. 257). He presents the rise of the middle class to national prominence as an incontestable yet puzzling fact, and rather than risk alienating his upper-class readers by ascribing to this parvenu class the prized title of gentlefolk at the outset, he wisely defers the matter of identifying and describing these families until later.

Playing to the prejudices of his audience, Defoe readily acknowledges all the stereotyped characteristics of the merchant or tradesman who amassed the family fortune. He may well bear the trappings of a gentleman: wealth, fine clothes, liveried servants, coach and four — "perhaps, coach and six" — and a wig and sword, but despite his possessing "all the ensigns of grandeur that a true bred gentleman is distinguish'd by," the man still carries the air of "the stock jobber, the 'Change Alley broker, the projector" about him and so only passes for the poor "shadow of a gentleman" (pp. 258–259). Defoe was realistic enough in his assessment of his fellow tradesmen to realize how difficult it was for a person to spend all his life behind the counter or in a warehouse and then suddenly quit the life of trade and begin to act like a true gentleman. This concern was evident earlier in his *Complete English Tradesman,* particularly in the passages where he wrote of the tradesman's "personal conduct in his prosperity" and the contemptible example set by a "purse-proud tradesman" (I, 227f). Now in *The Compleat English Gentleman* he concedes to his readers that tradesmen grown wealthy often may be "purse-proud, insolent, without manners." Moreover, a man who has dedicated his life to the acquisition of money cannot resist the temptation to make even more money; therefore, these *nouveau riche* tradesmen may exude the "usual air of a sharper and a bite" as they discover they can no more leave off "ravening after money . . . than . . . an old whore leave off procuring" (p. 258).

But after conceding this much, Defoe is prepared to concede no more. He can see that the man who made the fortune might justifiably be barred from the class of true gentlemen, but there is absolutely no reason to exclude the man's "politer son, and the next age quite alters the case":

Call him what you please on account of his blood, and be the race modern and mean as you will, yet if he was sent early to school, has good parts, and has improv'd them by learning, travel, conversation, and reading, and above all with a modest courteous gentleman-like behaviour: despise him as you will, he will be a gentleman in spite of all the distinctions we can make, and that not upon the money only, and not at all upon his father and family, but upon the best of all foundations of families; I mean a stock of personal merit, a liberal education, a timely and regular discipline and instruction, and a humble temper early form'd and receptible of the best impressions and subjected to the rules and laws of being instructed.　　(p. 258)

Defoe's strategy of stressing the qualities that constitute a gentleman in the first part of *The Compleat English Gentleman,* and his concomitant de-emphasis of ancestry and birth, has set the stage for his affirmative and assured stance in the second half when he treats the "bred" gentleman. He attempts to strike something of a compromise in his position. He defers to the prejudices and interests of both the middle and upper classes by acknowledging, on the one hand, some of the more prominent failings of the men of business, whose lives are taken up with the pursuit of money, and, on the other hand, the faults of the gentry and nobility, whose ignorance and boorish behavior detract from their social standing. Defoe wisely sought to reconcile the two classes not through the prejudiced and intransigent fathers but through the "politer sons" who, be they "born" or "bred," will have the advantages of a proper education and upbringing. The complete English gentleman Defoe envisoned was a man who prided himself not on the chance circumstance of being born rich or a gentleman of rank, but on his own achievements in perfecting the qualities of gentility: education, manners, and morals.

There remains, however, one intensely personal aspect of Defoe's discussion of education in *The Compleat English Gentleman* worth noting. The wounds inflicted on Defoe's gentlemanly self-esteem by his enemies and social betters during his troubled period as Mr. Review never quite healed. He was always acutely sensitive whenever his education was derided, for such attacks clearly were intended to derogate from his standing as a gentleman in the technical sense of the word, a standing he guarded with jealous care. In *Applebee's Journal* of October 30, 1725, he had seized upon a minor debate of the time about what constitutes a man of learning to write a thinly veiled defense of his own education: "I remember an author in the world, some years ago, who was generally upbraided with ignorance, and called an 'illiterate fellow' by some of the *beau monde* of the last age. He was run down in this manner by some that, upon enquiry, had a much clearer title to the character of a blockhead by a great deal than himself; but his enemies were noisy, and the man was negligent of his own defence." Defoe here refers to the time Swift impugned his learning in 1710 in the *Examiner*. Swift's remarks, although made only in passing, obviously hurt Defoe's pride more sharply than the numerous taunts he suffered at the hands of his rival journalists, such as Tutchin or Browne or even Leslie. Defoe was anything but "negligent" when he defended his education and countered by attacking Swift's — indeed, he devoted two complete and consecutive issues of the *Review* to this personal matter. Yet the very fact that he should still have it on his mind fifteen years after it occurred is ample proof that Defoe continued to be sensitive about his education and could never stop defending himself and his standing as a gentleman before the world.

In this particular issue of *Applebee's Journal* he again felt compelled to parade his learning before his readers to convince them — and perhaps also reassure himself — of the justness of his claims to an education befitting a gentleman, even though he personally lacked the traditional "gentlemanly" prerequisites of a classical education, notably complete proficiency in Latin and Greek:

In short, I found he understood the *Latin*, the *Spanish*, the *Italian*, and could read the *Greek*, and I knew before that he spoke *French* fluently, — *yet this man was no scholar.*

As to science . . . I heard him dispute . . . upon the motions of the heavenly bodies, the distance, magnitude, revolutions, and especially the influences of the planets, the nature and probable revolutions of comets, the excellency of the new philosophy, and the like; *but this man was no scholar.*

In geography and history, he had all the world at his fingers' ends . . . He knew not only where everything was, but what everybody did in every part of the world; I mean what business, what trade, what manufacture was carrying on in every part of the world; and had the history of almost all the nations of the world in his head, — *yet this man was no scholar.*[15]

In the *Review* Defoe had informed Swift that he was "pretty well master of five languages," although at that time he perhaps prudently failed to specify which five they were. Judging from the way he always over-reacted when his knowledge of the classical languages was questioned, we can safely assume that his knowledge of them was not all that he might have liked — or all he thought adequate to qualify him as an equal to such classically-educated men as Swift. What made him most uneasy about his education was that it was acquired not at a university like Oxford or Dublin but at a dissenting academy.

In the next number of *Applebee's Journal* which he wrote, Defoe made his intention clear by comparing an education in practical affairs like his with the accomplishments of "a profound scholar, [who] . . . had been eight years fellow of a college in *Cambridge* . . . had written a book upon the pointings of the Hebrew, and had made some learned amendments to the Greek grammar; [who] . . . spoke the Latin better than the English; and, in short, [who] was known and valued for a man of extraordinary learning." The outcome of this comparison is predictable. Such a scholar Defoe dismisses with hearty contempt as "a LEARNED FOOL"; whereas his own learning, by contrast, is rendered all the more attractive and impressive.[16] In so deriding the university-educated pedant, Defoe was obviously trying to minimize the importance of a university education as a qualification for a gentleman and also to point up the value of his own education at Morton's academy.

This need for reassurance and self-justification evidently remained with Defoe the rest of his life, for he returned to the subject of his learning four years later while composing his *Compleat English Gentleman*. Again Defoe defends his learning and accomplishments, this time stating his case more forcefully in a dramatic dialogue between two gentlemen on the familiar question, "Will nothing make a man a scholar but Latin and Greek":

"There's Mr. ——, a gentleman who you know very well, and we all think him an extraordinary person."

"Why," said I, "is not Mr. —— a scholar? I wish I were as good a scholar as he, I would desire no better stock of learning." (p. 199)

Defoe here indulges himself in a delicious irony, Mr. ——, that gentleman of learning and "extraordinary person," being none other than a transparent disguise for Defoe himself. Despite the levity ensuing from his little contrivance of Mr. ——, this anonymous gentleman's accomplishments are enumerated in full seriousness:

1. He speaks French as fluent as the English. He speaks Spanish and Italian and something of the Sclavonian [sic] . . . and he also has something of the Portuguese: and yet he is NO SCHOLAR.

2. He is as good a proficient in experimental philosophy as most private gentlemen . . . yet he is NO SCHOLAR.

3. He is a master in geography, has the situation of the world at his fingers' ends . . . yet he is NO SCHOLAR.

4. He is as well skill'd in all astronomical knowledge, the motions and revolutions of the heavenly bodies as most masters in that science . . . but he is NO SCHOLAR.

5. He is a master of history, and, indeed, I may say he is an universal historian . . . but he is NO SCHOLAR.

6. For his own country he is a walking map; he has travell'd thro' the whole island, and thro' most parts of it several times over; he has made some of the most critical remarks of several parts of it . . . and yet this man forsooth is NO SCHOLAR. (pp. 200–201)

It is instructive to compare this unmistakable *apologia* with Defoe's previous defense in *Applebee's Journal*. They both follow the same overall format and rely heavily for their effect on the rhetorical figure of *epiphora* ("yet he is NO SCHOLAR"). In both efforts Defoe underscores the unreasonableness of the age in its requirements for men of learning; but the attack is less on scholars as such than on the exclusive claims to learning by the universities and their privileged upper-class graduates. Defoe passionately defends his lack of proficiency in the classical tongues by defining a "scholar in their sense" as a "mere pedant, and Greek and Latin monger" (p. 201). His position on education in *The Compleat English Gentleman* is as much personal defense as objective assessment.

The significant point that emerges from this discussion of education and gentility is the crucial distinction between "a man of polite learning and a mere scholar: the first is a gentleman and what a gentleman should be; the last is a mere bookcase, a bundle of letters, a head stuffed with the jargon of languages . . . in a word, all learning and no manners" (p. 203). What more clever way of defending one's qualifications for the title of gentleman than to set oneself up as a kind of model for gentlemen to emulate? In essence, this is precisely what Defoe does in discussing the accomplishments requisite for a "man of polite learning" or, more directly, "what a gentleman should be." He turns to advantage the handicap of a dissenting academy education by ridiculing as "pedantry" the classical learning of the universities and praising his own practical and liberal education as most suitable to a complete gentleman.

Defoe's confidence in the claims of the "bred" gentleman to national prominence and social acceptability rested firmly on the limitless wealth and opportunities resulting from trade. "The heralds and the critics in blazonry and the rights of blood shall adjust it," Defoe concludes confidently, "this is certain, that as trade, especially in this country, raises innumerable families from the dust, that is to say, from mean and low beginnings to great and flourishing estates, so those estates exalt these families again into the rank or class of gentry" (p. 266). He senses the revolutionary shifts in English society because of the growth of trade and the trading class: "It must be acknowledg'd that the wealth and estates of these rising families is very particular in this age, more than ever it was before" (p. 266). Defoe's final vision of his England made him feel assured about the favorable future for his middle class.

For some reason Defoe never completed the second part of *The Compleat English Gentleman*. The writing breaks off abruptly after a preliminary discussion "of the fund for the increase of our nobility and gentry in England, being the beginning of those we call Bred Gentlemen" (p. 256), as the author's headnote to the first chapter of the second part reads. Since most of this chapter contains much the same information he had already presented in greater detail in *The Complete English Tradesman* and *A Plan of the English Commerce* a year or so before, he may have realized that he was largely repeating himself and stopped writing for the moment. This would help to explain the incomplete state of the surviving manuscript in the British Museum. Even with the help of the persona of a gentleman, his control of his material was not sure, and inconsistencies in tone throughout the text suggest that parts of the treatise would have needed additional revisions before it could have been published. In fact, a letter from Defoe to John Watts, his printer, dated September 10, 1729, corroborates such an explanation: "I have revised it [the manuscript] again and contracted it very much, and hope to bring it within the bulk you desire or as near it as possible . . . I will endeavour to send the rest of the copy so well corrected as to give you very little trouble." [17]

In spite of whatever difficulties Defoe encountered in writing and revising the manuscript for *The Compleat English Gentleman*, and the incomplete state of the surviving manuscript, his central thesis in the work is unmistakably clear, as is his unshakable belief in the certainty of its coming to pass: the son of the complete English tradesman in Defoe's mind ultimately is none other than the complete English gentleman as seen in the ideal of the "bred" gentleman. Without question the "bred" gentleman, when compared with the "born" gentleman, is "the better of the two" (pp. 48–49); and if the world was not yet prepared to accept this for a fact in the 1720's, Defoe had every confidence it would, of necessity, do so in the near future. England was, after all, the mightiest trading nation in all the world, and trade made gentlemen in England. Even though the treatise was never completed and had to wait more than a century and a half for its appearance before the world in 1890, the themes of gentility and trade which had occupied Defoe's mind all his life had their appropriate conclusion in *The Compleat English Gentleman*.

Chapter 12. The Final Years
of Daniel Defoe, Gentleman

I am to suppose, if a tradesman is leaving off, it is with the usual saying of the rich men that withdraw from the world, *That he may enjoy himself; that he may live in quiet and peace at the latter end of his days, without noise and without hurry.* And how can that be done when the remaining disputes of twenty years standing continue unsettled, and all the little brangles of forty years trade hang upon and haunt him to the last? — Defoe, *The Complete English Tradesman*, II, 213

By the mid-1720's, Defoe's life had assumed a physical comfort and financial ease unusual for him since his fiasco with the *Shortest Way* in 1703. He was living stylishly again in the manner suitable to a gentleman. In a personal account left by Henry Baker, who became Defoe's son-in-law by marrying his favorite daughter Sophia in 1729, we have a clear picture of Defoe's life in Stoke Newington in 1724, when Baker first made his acquaintance. Defoe, according to Baker, "had newly built there a very handsome house, as a retirement from London, and amused his time, either in the cultivation of a large and pleasant garden, or in the pursuit of his studies, which he found means of making very profitable." Retired comfortably from the bustle and crowding of London, living graciously in a spacious new house with adjoining garden and pleasure grounds, reasonably secure from financial worries, widely known for his many books and pamphlets, and happily devoting much of his energies to matters of great personal interest (the themes of trade and gentility) instead of political journalism, Defoe had indeed arrived at a new high point in his vicissitudinous fortunes. This period is aptly described by Thomas Wright as "the happiest period of Defoe's life," with the possible exception of 1689–1691, when he cut so promising and dashing a figure in London as a "merchant adventurer" and an "Athenian" wit.[1]

Defoe's life at Stoke Newington was that of a gentleman, and he undoubtedly designed it to be so. The splendid house he had built for himself fronted on Church Street, as did the buildings which housed his horses and his coach. In cultivating his "large and pleasant garden" he was not only emulating the example set by his beloved King William, who introduced "the love of gardening" into England, but also the fashionable pursuit of "the English gentlemen of late years." It was Defoe, we recall, who assisted Queen Mary during happier times in planning the magnificent gardens for Kensington Palace. This new period of peace and moderate prosperity also afforded him the opportunity to pursue his special studies in his library. Unlike the showy city gentlemen's or sparse country gentlemen's libraries ridiculed by him in *The Compleat English Gentleman*, his library was a comprehensive and truly outstanding collection of books, ranging from ancient works to contemporary tracts, and revealing the diverse interests of an insatiably curious man. When Defoe's library was sold after his death, an announcement for a catalogue of its contents was published for prospective buyers in *The Daily Advertiser* on November 13, 1731, stating that the library belonged to "the late ingenious Daniel De Foe, Gent., lately deceas'd," and contained books "relating to the history and antiquities of divers nations" as well as "several hundred scarce tracts on parliamentary affairs, politics, husbandry, trade, voyages, natural history, mines, minerals, &c." Given Defoe's possessions and pursuits in 1724 and after, it is easy to see why young Henry Baker's head was turned by what he saw on his frequent visits to the Defoe home. Although Baker admitted he "knew nothing of Mr. Defoe's circumstances," he was very much impressed by "his very genteel way of living" and assumed Defoe must be a man of means.[2]

Defoe's writings on gentility and trade in the middle and late 1720's, his *Tour, Complete English Tradesman, Plan of the English Commerce,* and *Compleat English Gentleman,* all owe something of their inspiration and confidence to his own genteel and secure circumstances as a kind of suburban gentleman living in Stoke Newington. Defoe no longer had to base his thesis that tradesmen could become gentlemen on an historical argument or a pious hope; he was now himself once more a living example of the tradesman as "phoenix," capable of rising time and again until he finally succeeded in establishing himself as a gentleman. It is not likely that he could have written his major works as apologist of the middle class, and the trading interests they represented, with that distinctive assurance and verve were he not so financially and physically secure. His life, like the lives of Moll Flanders and Colonel Jacque, had been a continuous quest for security and gentility, and now, like his fictive heroine and hero, he could in his old age enjoy his "settled way of living." [3]

Defoe's abiding ambition to establish a family name that would last is evident at this time from his concern to insure the financial security of his family. He had always shown an uncommon interest in insurance. His own involvement with maritime insurance culminated in his first bankruptcy in 1692. In the *Essay upon Projects*, which he wrote soon thereafter, he outlined a variety of sensible insurance schemes, including an office of insurance, a pension office, and friendly societies. Extant records of policies on his property in Stoke Newington testify to Defoe's belief in the importance of insurance. In 1721 he took out a fire insurance policy estimated at £400 from the London Assurance, a policy he held for about five years. The records of the Sun Fire Insurance Office Limited reveal that he held insurance in the amount of up to £700, for on January 7, 1728, a premium of fourteen shillings was paid by "Daniel De Foe of Stoke Newington, Gent. on his dwelling house." [4]

Defoe's other business dealings corroborate his concern for the financial security of his family. In 1722, for example, he sold some stock he held in the South Sea Company in order to invest £1,000 in the surer security of a ninety-nine-year lease on Kingswood Heath, in the borough of Colchester, Essex. Noticing that the property contained "extraordinary good tile clay," he could not resist the temptation of re-establishing the thriving factory he had owned in former days at Tilbury. He entered into a mysterious sort of partnership with a John Ward of Colehill, who had become the tenant of the Kingswood Heath property in 1724, the aim of the partnership being to set up a brick and pantile works on the property. A factory actually was started but the venture never materialized, and the partnership between Defoe and Ward ended in an inconclusive litigation between the two men in the Court of Chancery.

Also in 1724 Defoe engaged in a series of trading enterprises on a modest scale. The records of a Chancery suit reveal that he was trading in such consumable commodities as honey, cheese, bacon, and oysters in that year; and for all we know he may well have been involved in other such activities. Apparently the tradesman in Defoe was irrepressible, even in Mr. De Foe of Stoke Newington, Gent. We know that in 1727 he paid off the mortgage which completed the purchase of the lease of Kingswood Heath, an estate which increased so steadily in value that Defoe's daughter Hannah was able to derive from it a secure income up to the time of her death in 1759.[5]

Part of Defoe's concern for the financial well-being of his family no doubt was also prompted by his advancing years and failing health. When Henry Baker first came to visit him at his home in 1724, he saw a man well over sixty and "afflicted with the gout and stone." Old age was encroaching on Defoe's usually robust constitution. Age and illness apparently began to prey upon his mind, and in the preface to his *Protestant Monastery* in 1727 he abandoned his usual composure for a personal interjection: "Alas! I have but small health . . . being now in my sixty-seventh year, almost worn out with age and sickness. The old man cannot trouble you long." Even though Defoe was naturally given to self-dramatization, it is certain that he suffered intermittent periods of acute pain from his gout and stone, and to be confined to bed or chair must have been exceedingly trying for such a habitually active and energetic man. Baker mentioned in his account that "sometimes Mr. Defoe's disorders made company inconvenient." These discomforts were not mitigated with time; if anything they probably became more virulent. In December of 1727 a distressed Sophia wrote to Henry Baker, to whom she was then engaged, that her father suffered from "a violent sudden pain which spreads itself all over him." She is not fearful that the illness will be fatal, but she is melancholy at the prospect that "it is a messenger from that grand tyrant which will at last destroy the (to me) so-much-valued structure." [6]

Defoe none the less wrote on manfully, despite his declining health and increasing years, composing an amazing number of topical pamphlets as well as more substantial works. But the strain of all this exertion was proving excessive, and around the middle of 1729 his health broke down completely. On September 10, 1729, he wrote to John Watts, his printer, apologizing for holding the manuscript of *The Compleat English Gentleman* "for . . . so long." "But I have been exceeding ill," he explains. He promises to send the rest of the revised manuscript soon, but he was never to keep that promise.[7]

Just at the time when in his old age Defoe was becoming accustomed to the comforts and security of "his very genteel way of living," he found his estate and his very person threatened by the most familiar nemesis of his career, an obdurate creditor — in this particular case a creditrix by the name of Mary Brooke. The background of Mrs. Brooke's claims on Defoe is long and involved in legal technicalities, but since it bears on his last years so directly, it is worth summarizing. After suffering his first bankruptcy, Defoe in 1695 made a composition ("for time only") with his many creditors, including a Samuel Stancliffe, from whom Defoe had borrowed money for his civet-cat fiasco in 1692. In time the estate of Samuel passed to his brother, James Stancliffe. After suffering his second bankruptcy, Defoe in 1704 was obliged to compound with his creditors again, included among whom was James Stancliffe (both as a creditor of Defoe in his own right and as administrator of his brother's estate, to which he fell heir). Stancliffe agreed to act as trustee for Defoe in this second composition with his creditors, and Defoe turned over to him all his goods and effects, which Stancliffe in his capacity of trustee was to divide among the various creditors, himself included, in full satisfaction of Defoe's outstanding debts to them all. Supposedly there was enough in the estate Defoe turned over to Stancliffe to effect a full and final settlement. As trustee Stancliffe was authorized by Defoe not only to divide his estate among the creditors but also to collect for him all receipts and releases from the creditors. But before he could settle all these affairs and turn over to Defoe these papers discharging him of all debts, James Stancliffe died, intestate. The administration of his estate was assumed by Samuel Brooke, a weaver, who noticed the unsettled question of Defoe's composition but, according to Defoe, accepted his explanation and even agreed to discharge him. When Brooke died the estate passed to his wife, who at first assured Defoe she would carry out her husband's promise to discharge him but then changed her mind and laid claim to supposed large sums that he still owed to the principals of the estate, Samuel and James Stancliffe. At the start of 1728 she seems to have initiated legal proceedings against Defoe in the Court of the King's Bench.[8]

The crowning irony of this final encounter with creditors is that Mrs. Brooke's claim was not based on anything recent or indeed anything Defoe owed her directly, but rather on some long forgotten and since settled (although not in a conclusive legal way) composition with creditors dating back no less than thirty-five years. Prophetically, Defoe had written in "Of Projectors" in 1692, "when, by the errors of a man's youth, he has reduced himself to such a degree of distress as to be absolutely without three things, money, friends, and health, he dies in a ditch." [9] The truth of this prediction was striking home in 1730; the errors of his projecting youth were returning to reduce him to "distress" in his old age.

In response to Mrs. Brooke's suit he filed a countersuit in the Court of Chancery, hoping thereby to delay proceedings. He was understandably apprehensive about the safety of his estate, and took steps to safeguard his property as well as he could by assigning most of it to his son Daniel, Jr., a merchant of Cornhill, in St. Michael's. Mrs. Defoe also held considerable property in her own name. In April 1730 he filed a second bill of complaint in Chancery against Mrs. Brooke's suit in which he stated that defendants had of late begun actions against him in both the Courts of the King's Bench and Exchequer for recovery of alleged debts dating back to the unsettled business with Samuel and James Stancliffe. Pressed from several sides, Defoe's only hope now was to stall proceedings against him. This stratagem, however, failed.

In the early summer Defoe could already foresee the inevitable. Mrs. Brooke's suit was sure to engulf the family estate in disastrous ruin. Rather than risk being forced to pay large sums of money for alleged debts incurred many years ago, and so deplete the family estate he had been so carefully building and protecting in recent years, Defoe appears to have come to a momentous decision: he would not allow his family fortunes to be jeopardized under any circumstance. Defoe apparently decided, in spite of his infirmities, to choose the braver course of a self-imposed exile from his family to elude the prosecutions of Mrs. Brooke and any other creditors who had or might come forward. He had worked too hard and too long for the good name and secure fortunes of his family to see all his efforts come to nothing at the end of his life.

In the summer of 1730 Defoe fled from his home in Stoke Newington and went into hiding. Three times before in his checkered career he had known the terrors of concealment from his persecutors: in 1692, in 1703, and in 1715. The pattern was, if anything, all too familiar. As he had observed in *Robinson Crusoe,* "How strange a chequer-work of Providence is the life of man" (I, 173). Now a sick and aged man, he had to turn his back on all he had spent a lifetime working and writing for: a suburban house with a well-stocked library, a large garden, and a coach and four — in short, his "very genteel way of living." Thus insuring the protection of the family property, Defoe went into hiding for the fourth and final time in his life. It was a characteristic action, at once desperate and brave — not unlike his triumph over the terrors of the pillory.

The last word we have from Defoe came on August 12, 1730, when he wrote a long letter to his son-in-law Henry Baker while in close concealment "about two miles from Greenwich, Kent." We know that Defoe had been especially careful in isolating himself from his remark that Baker's letter, which he acknowledges gratefully, was ten days in reaching him:

. . . [the delay of your letter] depriv'd me of that cordial too many days, considering how much I stood in need of it to support a mind sinking under the weight of affliction too heavy for my strength, and looking on myself as abandon'd of every comfort, every friend, and every relative, except such only as are able to give me no assistance.
. . . it would be a greater comfort to me than I now enjoy, that I could have your agreeable visits with safety, and could see both you and my dear Sophia, could it be without giving her the grief of seeing her father *in tenebris,* and under the load of insupportable sorrows. I am sorry I must open my griefs so far as to tell her it is not the blow I recd from a wicked, perjur'd, and contemptible enemy that has broken in upon my spirit, which as she well knows has carried me on thro' greater disasters than these. But it has been the injustice, unkindness, and, I must say, inhuman dealings of my own son, which has both ruin'd my family, and, in a word, has broken my heart; and as I am at this time under a weight of very heavy ill-

ness, which I think will be a fever, I take this occasion to vent my
grief in the breasts who I know will make a prudent use of it, and
tell you that nothing but this has conquered or could conquer me.
Et tu! Brute. I depended upon him, I trusted him, I gave up my two
dear unprovided children into his hands; but he has no compassion,
but suffers them and their poor, dying mother to beg their bread at
his door, and to crave, as if it were alms, what he is bound under
hand and seal, besides the most sacred promises, to supply them
with; himself, at the same time, living in a profusion of plenty. It is
too much for me. Excuse my infirmity, I can say no more; my heart
is too full. I only ask one thing of you as a dying request. Stand by
them when I am gone, and let them not be wrong'd.[10]

As he had done so often in his life, Defoe dramatizes his over-
whelming emotions; but there can be no question about his
sincerity: he lays bare his heart, relying on the relation of his
pathetic plight as a necessary catharsis ("I take this occasion to
vent my grief"). In seeing himself as *"in tenebris,"* he seems to
call to mind, either consciously or unconsciously, a former time
of affliction he endured when imprisoned in Newgate, where his
Review was conceived *"in tenebris."* But then he was a robust
man of middle age, and not as now worn out with age and illness.

The picture of Defoe that emerges from the letter is that of
a broken old man. It is important to note, however, that his
spirit was not broken by the blow directed at his comfortable
existence by Mrs. Brooke ("a wicked, perjur'd, and contemptible enemy") and her specious suit, although that certainly precipitated his present predicament. The "inhuman dealings" of
his own son Daniel have broken the old man's heart, and understandably so; for it was on him that Defoe based all his hopes
of safeguarding the good name and property of the family, and
now to his uncontrollable despair he sees everything he had
striven so hard to secure, even risked his own safety and sacrificed
his own comforts to insure, undone by his son ("I depended upon
him, I trusted him").

As Dr. Johnson observed to Mrs. Thrale, "In a man's letters,
you know, Madam, his soul lies naked, his letters are only the
mirrour of his breast, whatever passes within him is shown un-
disguised in its natural process." [11] Defoe's final letter is a kind
of last will and testament by an old and ill man who senses that
death is near ("I only ask one thing of you as a dying request").

The realization that he will never see his family again fills him with sadness:

It adds to my grief that it is so difficult to me to see you. I am at a distance from London in Kent . . . At present I am weak, having had some fits of a fever that have left me low. But those things much more.

I have not seen son or daughter, wife or child, many weeks, and kno' not which way to see them. They dare not come by water, and by land there is no coach, and I kno' not what to do.

. . . I am so near my journey's end, and am hastening to the place where the weary are at rest, and where the wicked cease to trouble; be it that the passage is rough, and the day stormy, by what way soever He please to bring me to the end of it, I desire to finish life with this temper of soul in all cases: *Te Deum Laudamus.*

.   .   .   .

It adds to my grief that I must never see the pledge of your mutual love, my little grandson. Give him my blessing . . . Kiss my dear Sophy once more for me; and if I must see her no more, tell her this from a father that loved her above all his comforts, to his last breath.

The very fact that Defoe must write to his son-in-law about his deepest emotions instead of to one of his own sons, either Daniel or Benjamin, indicates how fully the old man realizes that there can be little hope of his name being carried on in a new and distinguished line of Defoe gentlemen. He must unburden himself to Henry Baker and to his beloved Sophy, and he closes his parting letter, significantly, "Your unhappy, D.F.," not D. De Foe. His only consolation he finds in his faith as a Puritan (*"Te Deum Laudamus"*).

The combined effects of illness and grief were too much for him; within eight months of writing his *cri de coeur* letter to Baker, Defoe was dead. He died on April 24, 1731, alone, in a lodging house in Ropemaker's Alley, St. Giles, Cripplegate. The cause of death was recorded as "lethargy." Moving from hiding place to hiding place during his period of concealment, Defoe somehow had managed to make his way back to the parish of his birth before he died; in fact, he died ironically enough in a place merely two hundred yards from Fore Street, where he was born.[12]

On April 26 Defoe's body was laid to rest in Tindall's Burying-ground, in time to become known generally as Bunhill Fields, "the Nonconformist Campo Santo," as Southey termed it later.

It was an altogether fitting place for the former ministerial student to be buried, among Puritan worthies like John Bunyan; and on the very spot where Defoe reckoned the Great Plague pit was located. At the time of his death he seems to have been so little known that the record of his burial in the register at Tindall's reads incorrectly, "Mr. Dunbow, Cripplegate." Fortunately the register of his parish of St. Giles, Cripplegate, recorded the information accurately and also accorded him the title he prized above all else: "1731. Daniel Defoe, gentleman. To Tindall's. (Lethargy.) April 26." Defoe would have approved of the entry. It consummated, in his death, the personal quest of his life.[13]

Notes

Abbreviations

Aitken
: *Romances and Narratives by Daniel Defoe*, ed. George A. Aitken (London: J. M. Dent & Co., 1895), 16 vols.

CEG
: Daniel Defoe, *The Compleat English Gentleman*, ed. Karl D. Bülbring (London, 1890)

CET
: Daniel Defoe, *The Complete English Tradesman* (London, 1727), 2 vols.

Dottin
: Paul Dottin, *Daniel De Foe et ses romans* (Paris and London: Oxford University Press, 1924), vol. 1

Lee
: William Lee, *Daniel Defoe: His Life, and Recently Discovered Writings* (London, 1869), 3 vols.

Letters
: *The Letters of Daniel Defoe*, ed. George H. Healey (Oxford: Clarendon Press, 1955)

Moore
: John Robert Moore, *Daniel Defoe, Citizen of the Modern World* (Chicago: University of Chicago Press, 1958)

Morley
: *The Earlier Life and Chief Earlier Works of Daniel Defoe*, ed. Henry Morley (London, 1889)

Shakespeare Head Ed.
: *The Shortest Way with the Dissenters and Other Pamphlets by Daniel Defoe*, Shakespeare Head Edition (Oxford: Basil Blackwell, 1927)

Sutherland
: James Sutherland, *Defoe*, 2nd ed. (London: Methuen & Co., 1950)

Tour
: Daniel Defoe, *A Tour through England & Wales*, introduction by G. D. H. Cole (Everyman ed.), 2 vols.

Trent
: William P. Trent, *Daniel Defoe: How to Know Him* (Indianapolis: Bobbs-Merrill Co., 1916)

Wilson
: Walter Wilson, *Memoirs of the Life and Times of Daniel De Foe* (London, 1830), 3 vols.

Wright
: Thomas Wright, *The Life of Daniel Defoe*, rev. ed. (London: C. J. Farncombe & Sons, 1931)

Notes

In quoting from Defoe and other contemporary works, including modern scholarly editions that reproduce the original texts, I have sought to modernize the spelling, punctuation, and capitalization whenever possible; but I have also sought to retain the idiom of the originals. The place of publication for all works is London unless otherwise specified.

CHAPTER 1. A CRUCIAL DECISION: MINISTER OR MERCHANT?

1. *Review*, VI, 341. All references to the *Review*, parenthetically in the text or in the notes, are to the Facsimile Text Society reprint of *Defoe's Review*, ed. Arthur Wellesley Secord (New York, 1938); the Roman numeral cites the volume of the *Review* in this edition.

2. A. G. Matthews, *Calamy Revised* (Oxford, 1934), pp. ix–xv, lxx–lxxii; David Ogg, *England in the Reign of Charles II*, 2nd ed. (Oxford, 1956), I, 197–218; G. N. Clark, *The Later Stuarts, 1660–1714*, 2nd ed. (Oxford, 1955), pp. 16–24; Moore, pp. 13–19.

3. Dottin, pp. 14–15; Sutherland, p. 11.

4. *Review*, II, 500; [IX], 115.

5. Moore, p. 11; Sutherland, pp. 13–16; Wright, p. 6; Dottin, pp. 16–18; Lee, I, 6–7.

6. Quoted in Wilson, I, 7.

7. *Review*, II, 498.

8. *The Present State of the Parties in Great Britain* (1712), pp. 288–289.

9. *Review*, VIII, 614; see also VI, 573.

10. Matthews, *Calamy*, pp. 13–14; Edmund Calamy, *A Continuation of the Account of the Ministers . . . Ejected and Silenced . . . by or before the Act of Uniformity* (1727), I, 65–73.

11. *The Character of the Late Dr. Samuel Annesley, By way of Elegy* (1697) in Defoe's *A True Collection of the Writings of the Author of the True Born English-man* (1705), I, 113–115.

12. Matthews, *Calamy*, p. 198; Calamy, *Account of Ministers*, II, 814–815; Moore, pp. 30–32, 39.

13. Calamy, *Account of Ministers*, I, 198; also Matthews, *Calamy*, pp. 356–357.

14. John Dunton, *The Life and Errors of John Dunton* (1818), I, 123. There is substance to Dunton's encomium on Morton as a teacher: "In a word, Mr. Charles Morton (late of Newington Green) was that pious and learned man, by whose instructions my reverend and worthy uncle, Mr. Obadiah Marriat, was so well qualified for the work of the ministry" (p. 123). Morton's reputation commended him to the worthies of the Massachusetts Bay Colony, where he went in 1686 expecting to become president of Harvard College. We have a warm description of him in a letter from Henry Horsey of Newington Green to his brother in Cambridge, Massachusetts, in April 1681: "Mr. Charles Morton . . . is a person of great learning, and piety, and moderation, and of an excellent sweet natural

temper, of a loving and generous spirit"; see Samuel Eliot Morison, *Harvard College in the Seventeenth Century* (Cambridge, Mass., 1936), II, 476n.

15. *Present State of the Parties*, pp. 317–319.

16. Moore, p. 40; Sutherland, p. 20. In 1703 and 1704 Samuel Wesley wrote two pamphlets (*A Letter from a Country Divine to His Friend in London* and *A Defence of a Letter Concerning the Education of Dissenters in Their Private Academies*) in which he attacked the education at dissenting academies generally and Morton's at Newington Green, where he like Defoe was educated, particularly. In 1704 Defoe stepped forward to enter the controversy with a spirited defense both of the Dissenters' education and of "that learned gentleman" Morton with *More Short-Ways with the Dissenters*.

17. *Present State of the Parties*, p. 351.

18. The manuscript is in the Huntington Library, but Professor Healey kindly let me consult his photostat copy. The seven verse meditations which follow the sermons in the MS notebook were published as *The Meditations of Daniel Defoe*, ed. George H. Healey (Cummington, Mass., 1946).

19. *Meditations*, pp. vii–viii. Defoe employed the same kind of shorthand in the MS copy of his *Compleat English Gentleman*, which is in the British Museum.

20. Cotton Mather, *Magnalia Christi Americana* (Hartford, Conn., 1853), II, 139–140.

21. John Langdon Sibley, *Biographical Sketches of Graduates of Harvard University* (Cambridge, Mass., 1873), I, 186–191; Walter Wilson, *The History and Antiquities of Dissenting Churches and Meeting Houses . . . Including the Lives of Their Ministers* (1808), I, 225–228.

22. Matthews, *Calamy*, p. 128 — the statement is by Nathaniel Mather, Harvard class of 1647, who was in London in the 1680's; Mather, *Magnalia*, II, 140; *Present State of the Parties*, p. 352; Calamy, *Account of the Ministers*, I, 205.

23. The page references in parentheses that follow in the text are to Defoe's *Meditations*, ed. Healey.

24. *Present State of the Parties*, pp. 294–298, 316.

25. *CEG*, pp. 219–220.

26. *More Short-Ways with the Dissenters* (1704), pp. 5–6.

27. Calamy, *Account of the Ministers*, I, 211; *An Essay upon Projects* in Morley, p. 30.

28. Lew Girdler, "Defoe's Education at Newington Green Academy," *Studies in Philology*, L (Oct. 1953), 573–591, esp. 589; see S. E. Morison, *Harvard College in the Seventeenth Century*, II, 236–251, for a detailed examination of the content and influence of Morton's *Compendium*.

29. *Review*, VIII, 422. Some five years later James Foe, then a butcher in business on Fore Street, Cripplegate, gained his son entry as "a Freeman of the Butchers' Company" — see Arthur Pearce, *The History of the Butchers' Company* (1929), p. 180.

30. *The Shortest-Way with the Dissenters: . . . With its Author's Brief Explication Consider'd . . .* (1703), p. 2. For a representative example of Defoe's talents as a preacher, see his *A Commendatory Sermon Preach'd November the 4th, 1709* (first printed in *Review*, VI, 365–368) to com-

memorate the birthday of the late King William III; see also Wilson, III, 645–646n, for further indication of Defoe's interest in the church.

CHAPTER 2. LONDON MERCHANT AND ATHENIAN WIT

1. G. M. Young, *Victorian England, Portrait of an Age,* 2nd ed. (1957), p. 77.
2. David Ogg, *England in the Reign of Charles II,* 2nd ed. (Oxford, 1956), I, 127–128; Sutherland, p. 26; Morley, p. 40.
3. *CET,* II, pt. ii, 142; G. N. Clark, *The Later Stuarts, 1660–1714,* 2nd ed. (Oxford, 1955), p. 41.
4. Thomas Babington Macaulay, *The History of England,* ed. Charles Harding Firth (1913), I, 338. A list kept for revenue records of the number of ships entering the Thames shows 1,055 in 1672, 1,764 in 1685 — see Ogg, *Reign of Charles II,* I, 241n.
5. John Summerson, *Georgian London* (1945), chap. iv, "The Mercantile Stronghold"; also Norman G. Brett-James, *The Growth of Stuart London* (1935), chap. xv.
6. Macaulay, *History,* I, 340–341.
7. *The Diary of John Evelyn,* ed. E. S. de Beer (Oxford, 1955), IV, 343.
8. H. J. Habakkuk, "English Landownership, 1680–1740," *Economic History Review,* X (Feb. 1940), 5; Sutherland, pp. 28–29.
9. Moore, pp. 83–84.
10. Wright, p. 17; Moore, p. 45; H. J. Habakkuk, "Marriage Settlements in the Eighteenth Century," *Transactions of the Royal Historical Society,* XXXII (1950), 23–25 — all things considered, Defoe had done about as well for himself by this marriage as he could have hoped; for although mercantile wealth was rising rapidly in this period, probably more rapidly than national income, a merchant might hope to marry his daughter off with a substantial dowry to a member of the landed gentry, but a young merchant at best could hope to marry such a merchant's daughter, which was what Defoe did in marrying Mary Tuffley.
11. *Tour,* II, 14, 148.
12. *The Succession to the Crown of England, Considered* (1701), p. 32.
13. Arthur Pearce, *The History of the Butchers' Company* (1929), p. 180; see also P. H. Ditchfield, *Story of the City Companies* (New York, 1926), pp. 40f.
14. *Review,* VIII, 207; Moore, p. 64.
15. John Oldmixon, *The History of England, During the Reigns of King William and Queen Mary, Queen Anne, King George I* (1735), p. 37.
16. *Tour,* II, 10; Moore, p. 73.
17. Moore, p. 47; Daniel Lysons, Supplement to first ed. of *Historical Account of the Environs of London* (1811), p. 91; Wilson, I, 175.
18. *CET,* I, 143; Wright, p. 33; *Letters,* p. 124.
19. *CET,* I, 118.
20. *Reformation of Manners. A Satyr* (1702); *Review,* III, 415; *Robinson Crusoe Examin'd and Criticis'd,* ed. Paul Dottin (London and Paris, 1923), p. 73.
21. John Dunton, *The Life and Errors of John Dunton* (1818), I, 180; II, 425.

22. *Athenian Mercury* (1691), vol. II, no. 5, quest. 9; IV, 23, 9; III, 30, 12; II, 29, 6.

23. *Dictionary of National Biography*, XVI, 237.

24. [Elkanah Settle], *The New Athenian Comedy* (1693), pp. 4–5.

25. Dunton, *Life and Errors*, I, 193–195; see also Irvin Ehrenpreis, *Swift, The Man, His Works, and the Age* (Cambridge, Mass., 1962), I, 114–117.

26. Theophilus Cibber, *The Lives of the Poets* (1753), IV, 315. Dr. Johnson also relied on Cibber's *Lives* for his Dryden quotation on Swift's poetry; but for a confutation of this celebrated pronouncement, see Maurice Johnson, "A Literary Chestnut: Dryden's 'Cousin Swift,'" *PMLA*, LXVII (Dec. 1952), 1024–1034.

27. Charles Gildon, *The History of the Athenian Society* (1693), p. 3.

28. Robert Wolsley, preface to Rochester's *Valentinian* (1685) in *Critical Essays of the Seventeenth Century*, ed. J. E. Spingarn (Oxford, 1909), III, 12; Dunton, *Life and Errors*, I, 191–192.

29. *Review*, I, 369.

30. Clark, *The Later Stuarts*, pp. 166–179; David Ogg, *England in the Reigns of James II and William III* (Oxford: Clarendon Press, 1955), pp. 281–318, 350–362; *Review I*, 369; also VI, 223; William L. Payne, *Mr. Review, Daniel Defoe as Author of The Review* (New York, 1947), pp. 14–15. Also John Masefield, ed., *Defoe* (1909), p. xxv — "His sense of tragedy is so much tainted by his love of commerce, that it is hard to determine which his characters dread more, shipwreck or sentence to death. Defoe himself dreaded shipwreck the more. The most terrible thing ever seen by him was the loss of some West Indiamen in Plymouth Harbor. The thought that some of them may not have been insured 'affected him strangely' until the end of his life."

31. *CET*, II, 105.

32. Sutherland, pp. 34–42; also James Sutherland, "Some Early Troubles of Daniel Defoe," *Review of English Studies*, IX (1933), 275–290.

33. Moore, pp. 90–94.

34. Theodore F. M. Newton, "The Civet-Cats of Newington Green: New Light on Defoe," *Review of English Studies*, XIII (1937), 10–19.

35. *Review*, VIII, 754.

36. *Review*, III, 86–87.

37. Ogg, *Reign of Charles II*, I, 118–120; *Review*, III, 90; M. Dorothy George, *London Life in the XVIIIth Century* (1925), p. 307.

38. *Review*, III, 109–110.

39. *Review*, III, 90; *The Life & Strange Surprising Adventures of Robinson Crusoe* (in Aitken, vol. I), p. 177.

40. *CET*, I, 68.

41. *CET*, II, 96.

CHAPTER 3. FROM SUNDAY GENTLEMAN TO THE TRUE-BORN ENGLISHMAN

1. *CET*, II, 182–184.

2. Morley, p. 112 — all page references to Defoe's *Essay upon Projects* and *True-Born Englishman* are to the texts in Morley.

3. James Sutherland, "Some Early Troubles of Daniel Defoe," *Review of English Studies*, IX (1933), 286; *Review*, III, 399; Moore, p. 47.

4. Moore, pp. 90–94.

5. Morley, p. 26; *The Autobiography of Benjamin Franklin,* ed. Leonard W. Labaree *et al.* (New Haven, 1964), p. 58.

6. Morley, pp. 31–33. According to Defoe's rough reckoning, "about fifteen millions of pounds sterling, in ships and goods," were lost in "the first two or three years of the war."

7. Morley, pp. 112–123; *Review,* III, 75; IV, 100.

8. Wilson, I, 221–222.

9. *Tour,* II, 85; P. D. Mundy, "The Ancestry of Daniel Defoe," *Notes and Queries,* IV (June 1957), 242; Moore, pp. 8–9, 345.

10. *Review,* VII, preface.

11. Sutherland, pp. 2–3, 163; Moore, p. 293; Trent, p. 3; Dottin, pp. 74–75.

12. *Appeal to Honour and Justice* in Shakespeare Head Ed., p. 194; *Review,* VII, 527; VIII, 307.

13. *Appeal,* p. 194; Morley, p. 25; Moore, p. 74.

14. Morley, pp. 34, 27; *Review,* VII, 511, 570; VIII, 165.

15. *CET,* II, 191; *Tour,* I, 131.

16. We get a reliable impression of the magnitude of Defoe's operations at Tilbury from William Lee, one of the most indefatigable of Defoe's biographers, who personally visited the sight of Defoe's former factory. He reported in detail the success of his trip, during which he found not only samples of what he took to be Defoe's products "thrown into heaps" but also the entire pantile works "laid open, including the claypits, drying-floors, foundations of kilns, and other buildings." It was an operation of substantial size, and Defoe apparently was doing a brisk business as brick-maker — see Lee, I, 32. There is also a record of an account relating to the building of Greenwich Hospital which lists the payment of £20 to Daniel Foe, brickmaker, on March 6, 1697 — see Aitken, I, xvi.

17. *Letters,* p. 17; *Appeal,* p. 195; *Review,* IV, 319.

18. *Appeal,* p. 195; Morley, p. 178.

19. *Appeal,* p. 195.

20. Anthony Richard Wagner, *English Genealogy* (Oxford, 1960), p. 327.

21. G[uy] M[iege], *The New State of England Under Their Majesties K. William and Q. Mary* (1691), pt. ii, p. 226.

22. *A Second Volume of the Writings of the Author of the True-Born Englishman* (1705), preface.

23. For background see George Clark, *The Later Stuarts, 1660–1714,* 2nd ed. (Oxford, 1955), pp. 192–199; David Ogg, *England in the Reigns of James II and William III* (Oxford, 1955), pp. 459–464. For Defoe's own version of the affair see *The History of the Kentish Petition* (1701); also *The Consolidator* (1705) in Morley, pp. 358–361.

24. Wilson, I, 406; Trent, p. 40.

25. *Review,* VI, 368; *A Commendatory Sermon . . .* (1709), p. 7.

26. *An Enquiry into the Occasional Conformity of Dissenters, in Cases of Preferment* (1697), p. 17.

27. G. M. Trevelyan, *England Under Queen Anne* (1930), I, 49–59, 277–282.

28. *Review,* III, 399; *A Reply to a Pamphlet Entitled, the L--d H----'s Vindication of his Speech, &c* (1706), p. 7; *Letters,* p. 17.

29. *Letters, ibid.; Review,* II, 34. Defoe had informed Harley in 1704

that his loss from the ruin of his pantile works amounted to £2,500; in the *Review* in 1705 he estimated his loss at £3,000; and again in the *Review* in 1712 (VIII, 496) he spoke of his loss as totalling £3,500. Professor Moore finds in these differing estimates "no real discrepancy when we recall that claims and interest on claims were mounting steadily" (p. 286). The frequency with which Defoe returned to this time of his second financial ruin indicates how vividly the recollection of the event persisted in his mind and how he continued to recalculate the magnitude of his personal loss.

    30. *Observations on the Bankrupt's Bill* (1706), p. 35.

CHAPTER 4. PRISON AND PILLORY: BIRTH OF MR. REVIEW

    1. *Letters*, pp. 1–3.

    2. *Review*, III, 70; *CEG*, pp. 219–220.

    3. *Letters*, pp. 4–7.

    4. *An Essay on the History and Reality of Apparitions* (1727), pp. 220–222.

    5. Moore, p. 128; *Review*, [IX], 184.

    6. *Letters*, pp. 7–9; Moore, p. 131.

    7. *Hymn to the Pillory* in Shakespeare Head Ed., pp. 137, 151; Moore, pp. 139–142; *The True-Born Hugonot; Or, Daniel de Foe. A Satyr.* (1703), p. 25; Sutherland, pp. 96–97.

    8. *A Second Volume of the Writings of the Author of the True-Born Englishman* (1705), preface; *Review*, V, 466; VIII, 814; [IX], 158.

    9. *Review*, I, preface; III, 19; *Letters*, p. 11.

    10. *Letters*, p. 16; Sutherland, p. 106.

    11. *Review*, IV, 82; *Letters*, p. 159.

    12. *Review*, VII, 154, 212.

    13. *Review*, VIII, preface; Moore, p. 99, and "Chronological Outline," pp. 345–355.

    14. *Review*, II, 214.

    15. *Letters*, pp. 120, 124; *Review*, III, 399.

    16. Moore, pp. 97, 101–102; *Review*, V, 212.

    17. Trent, p. 3; Moore, p. 335; *CET*, I, 311. A check with the offices of the Garter King of Arms in London and Lord Lyon King of Arms in Edinburgh revealed no record of Defoe's receiving official permission to bear arms. Indeed, the arms Defoe had cut under his *Jure Divino* portrait have not been traceable in that particular form; perhaps they were devised by or for Defoe and he adopted them for his personal use in hopes of establishing a new line of gentlemen.

    18. *Letters*, pp. 241–242.

    19. *Letters*, pp. 86–87; Wright, pp. 117–119, 123; Defoe, *Jure Divino* (1706), Bk. XII, p. 5; Alexander Pope, "Epistle to Dr. Arbuthnot," in *Imitations of Horace*, ed. John Butt, Twickenham Ed., rev. (New Haven, 1961), p. 112n, 232, 233.

    20. *Letters*, p. 213; *Caledonia, A Poem in Honour of Scotland, and the Scots Nation* (Edinburgh, 1706); *A Tour thro' the whole island of Great Britain* (1727), III, pt. ii, 57–62; Wright, p. 332.

    21. *Review*, II, 135.

22. Wilson, II, 414–415; *Review,* II, 149–150; *The Present State of the Parties in Great Britain* (1712), p. 296.

23. *Review,* II, 21.

24. *Little Review,* II, 13–14. Dr. Browne urbanely answered Defoe's criticisms with "A Vindication . . . of Horace . . . from the Pretended Criticisms of Mr. De Foe, in his *Little Review*" (1705).

25. Moore, pp. 124, 234; Wilson, II, 416–417; *Review,* II, 297; III, 323; Alexander Pope, "Preface of 1717."

26. *The Consolidator* in Morley, p. 294. In the ensuing discussion of the exchange between Defoe and Swift I am indebted to the study of John Ross, *Swift and Defoe: A Study in Relationship* (Berkeley, 1941), esp. chaps. i and ii.

27. Jonathan Swift, *Bickerstaff Papers and Pamphlets on the Church,* ed. Herbert Davis (Oxford, 1957), pp. 112, 115.

28. Trent, p. 61; *Letters,* p. 358 — on Sept. 7, 1711, Defoe wrote Harley, "But as my being able to serve your Ldp and her Majty's interest consists much on my being concealed, I humbly submit it to your Ldp whether I should not rather attend in an evening." Defoe's under-cover activities as a spy necessitated his visiting Harley in secrecy.

29. Jonathan Swift, *The Examiner and Other Pieces Written in 1710–11,* ed. Herbert Davis (Oxford, 1957), p. 13, also xii.

30. *Letters,* pp. 291–292 (Defoe wrote Harley a letter from Edinburgh dated November 16, but a reference in the letter dates his arrival in Edinburgh as November 9); *Review,* VII, 449–451.

31. *Review,* VIII, 484.

32. *Review,* VII, 455.

33. For Defoe's reference to Swift, see *Mere Nature Delineated* (1726), p. 45.

34. George Sherburn, *The Restoration and Eighteenth Century (1660–1789), A Literary History of England,* ed. A. C. Baugh (New York, 1948), p. 857.

35. A. S. Turberville, *English Men and Manners in the Eighteenth Century* (Oxford, 1929), pp. 1–2; James Sutherland, *A Preface to Eighteenth Century Poetry* (Oxford, 1948), pp. 50–51; Leslie Stephen, *English Literature and Society in the Eighteenth Century* (1904, repr. 1947), p. 52.

36. Robert J. Allen, *The Clubs of Augustan London* (Cambridge, Mass., 1933), esp. chaps. ii and v.

37. Q. D. Leavis, *Fiction and the Reading Public* (1932), p. 106; Sutherland, *Eighteenth Century Poetry,* pp. 47–48; *Review,* II, 138; also William L. Payne, *Mr. Review: Daniel Defoe as Author of the Review* (New York, 1947), pp. 19–40.

38. Peter Smithers, *The Life of Joseph Addison* (Oxford, 1954), pp. 96–97; Joseph Addison, "The Late Trial and Conviction of Count Tariff," *Works* (1883), IV, 367–368.

39. *Letters,* pp. 430, 433–438; *Review,* VIII, 97; Trent, p. 108; also Lee, III, 411. In addition to a personal and political dislike for Steele, Defoe further was opposed to his involvement in the theater, both as playwright and manager. Oddly enough, even Steele's efforts to reform and moralize the stage were not supported by Defoe; see John Loftis, *Steele at Drury Lane*

(Berkeley, 1952), pp. 15–16 and Defoe's *The Fears of the Pretender Turn'd into the Fears of Debauchery* (1715); pp. 20–21.

40. John Gay, *The Present State of Wit* in *An English Garner*, ed. Edward Arber (Westminster, 1897), VI, 506. For information on the *General Postscript*, see William Henry Irving, *John Gay: Favorite of the Wits* (Durham, N.C., 1940), pp. 57–58.

41. *The Art of Sinking in Poetry*, ed. Edna L. Steeves (New York, 1952), pp. 27, 38, 118; *Advertisements from Parnassus* (1704) — quoted in Moore, p. 235.

42. Joseph Spence, *Anecdotes . . . from the Conversation of Mr. Pope*, ed. Samuel W. Singer (1820), pp. 258–259; Lee, III, 409–414.

43. Sutherland, *Eighteenth Century Poetry*, p. 42; Alexander Pope, *The Dunciad*, ed. James Sutherland, Twickenham Ed., rev. (New Haven, 1963), Bk. II, ll. 139–140, 383–386, and p. 437. The latest biographer of Savage makes an unconvincing case for the reliability of Savage's remarks about Defoe's bastard son; see Clarence Tracy, *The Artificial Bastard, A Biography of Richard Savage* (Cambridge, Mass., 1953), p. 107. A number of twentieth-century writers on Defoe have, however, given currency to this supposed scandal of Defoe's private life: Dottin, p. 80; William Freeman, *The Incredible De Foe* (1950), p. 122; Francis Watson, *Daniel Defoe* (1952), p. 86.

44. Payne, *Mr. Review*, p. 5.

45. *A Reproof to Mr. Clark, and a Brief Vindication of Mr. De Foe* (Edinburgh, 1710), pp. 7–8.

46. *A Reply to a Pamphlet Entituled, The L--d H----'s Vindication of his Speech, &c. By the Author of the Review* (1706), pp. 7–8 — the entire work is revealing of Defoe's regard for his character and social status; *CET*, I, 310.

47. *Review*, I, 44, 111.

48. *Review*, II, 381.

49. For background on contemporary readers of the *Spectator*, see *The Spectator*, ed. Donald F. Bond (Oxford, 1965), I, lxxxiii–xcvi; for a general survey of the stress on good breeding in a gentleman's education in this period, see George C. Brauer, Jr., *The Education of a Gentleman* (New York, 1959), pp. 134–154.

50. *Review*, II, 9; for brief background see George N. Clark, *The Wealth of England from 1496 to 1760* (1961), chap. vii and Edward Hughes, *North Country Life in the Eighteenth Century* (1952), chap. i.

51. *Little Review* (July 13, 1705), pp. 46–47. The phrase "a liberal education" meant different things to different classes. To Defoe it meant the kind of education he received at Newington Green Academy, with the emphasis on practical as well as scholarly knowledge and the instruction done in English. To polite authors of the age, like Pope, it meant a classical education modeled after the Greek and Latin curriculum of the grammar schools and universities. Writing to Caryll in 1711 about his *Essay on Criticism*, Pope remarked "not one gentleman in three score even of a liberal education can understand [it]" — *The Correspondence of Alexander Pope*, ed. George Sherburn (Oxford, 1956), I, 128.

52. *Review*, V, 406–407.

53. *Review*, III, 6–7; quote from *Essay upon Projects* in Morley, p. 33.

54. *CET,* I, 306; *Letters,* p. 17; *Appeal* in Shakespeare Head Ed., pp. 237–238.

55. *Appeal* in Shakespeare Head Ed., pp. 192, 238; Sutherland, pp. 211–213; cf. *The Fortunes and Misfortunes of the Famous Moll Flanders* (in Aitken, vols. VII–VIII), I, 125. — "It is true that sick-beds are the times when such correspondences as this are looked on with different countenances, and seen with other eyes than we saw them before: my lover had been at the gates of death, and the very brink of eternity; and, it seems, struck with a due remorse, and with sad reflections upon his past life of gallantry and levity . . . and he looked upon it now with a just abhorrence."

56. *Serious Reflections . . . of Robinson Crusoe* (in Aitken, vol. III), pp. 280–281; *Letters,* pp. 450–454.

57. *An Essay on . . . Apparitions,* pp. 220–222.

58. *Review,* [IX], 213–214; cf. *The Fortunate Mistress* (in Aitken, vols. XII–XIII), II, 68, where Defoe repeats the anecdote of the "Indian king at Virginia" for the same effect.

CHAPTER 5. FICTION AND THE AGE, 1714–1724

1. Leslie Stephen, *English Literature and Society in the Eighteenth Century* (1904, repr. 1947), pp. 24, 35; Basil Williams, *The Whig Supremacy, 1714–1760,* 2nd ed. (Oxford, 1962), pp. 150–164.

2. *Review,* VII, 98–99.

3. See J. H. Plumb, *Sir Robert Walpole, The Making of a Statesman* (1956), I, 18–24.

4. Edward Chamberlayne, *Angliae Notitia; or, the Present State of England* (1692 and 1700), p. 259, and (1707), p. 296 — quoted by Helen S. Hughes, "The Middle Class Reader and the English Novel," *Journal of English and Germanic Philology,* XXV (1926), 366–368.

5. Williams, *Whig Supremacy,* pp. 122–124; M. Dorothy George, *England in Transition, Life and Work in the Eighteenth Century* (Penguin Books, 1953), p. 147; also Paul Mantoux, *The Industrial Revolution in the Eighteenth Century,* rev. ed. (New York, Harper Torchbook, 1962), pp. 91–135 for useful background.

6. J. B. Botsford, *English Society in the Eighteenth Century* (New York, 1924), p. 192; *Tour,* I, 324; *Exchange Alley* quoted in John Loftis, *Comedy and Society from Congreve to Fielding* (Stanford, 1959), p. 94.

7. *Tour,* I, 326. Defoe had been a staunch advocate of the South Sea Company; see *An Essay on the South-Sea Trade* (1712).

8. R. H. Tawney, *Religion and the Rise of Capitalism* (New York, 1926), p. 207; Botsford, *English Society,* chap. v, esp. pp. 116f.

9. *Richard Steele's The Theatre 1720,* ed. John Loftis (Oxford, 1962), pp. 12, 126; reference to *The Conscious Lovers* is to Mermaid ed. of Richard Steele [*Plays*], ed. George A. Aitken (1894), pp. 335–337.

10. Robert J. Allen, *The Clubs of Augustan London* (Cambridge, Mass., 1933); Stephen, *Literature and Society in the Eighteenth Century,* pp. 100–102; Alexander Pope, "The Second Epistle of the Second Book of Horace," in *Imitations of Horace,* ed. John Butt, Twickenham Ed., rev. (New Haven, 1961), p. 169, ll. 68–69; Alexandre Beljame, *Men of Letters and the English*

Public in the Eighteenth Century, 1660–1744, English ed., trans. E. O. Lorimer, ed. Bonamy Dobrée (1948), pp. 365–381, xviii — the entire work, with Dobrée's introduction, is indispensable to an understanding of this period.

11. The considerable fortunes a publisher could amass in a comparatively brief time during this period can be seen in the career of William Taylor, publisher of *Robinson Crusoe*. The first volume of *Robinson Crusoe* netted Taylor more than £1,000, and although he died still a young man five years later, he left an estate "reputed to be worth between forty and fifty thousand pounds," according to *Read's Journal* of May 9, 1724. Jacob Tonson, Dryden's publisher, left a fortune of £80,000 at his death. See Beljame, *Men of Letters,* pp. 365–366; Lee, I, 293.

12. Quote from *Applebee's Journal* (July 31, 1725) in Lee, III, 410; Bonamy Dobrée, *English Literature in the Early Eighteenth Century, 1700–1740* (Oxford, 1959), p. 12; Ian Watt, *The Rise of the Novel* (Berkeley, 1957), chaps. i and ii.

13. Stephen, *Literature and Society in the Eighteenth Century,* pp. 133–134; Wilson, III, 428–429; Williams, *Whig Supremacy,* pp. 141–142 — also W. K. L. Clarke, *A Short History of the SPCK* (1919) and M. G. Jones, *The Charity School Movement* (Cambridge, 1938) for fuller discussions; for quote from Leslie see John T. Taylor, *Early Opposition to the English Novel* (New York, 1943), p. 4; for *Flying Post* quote see Sutherland, p. 236; Charles Gildon, *Robinson Crusoe Examin'd and Criticis'd,* ed. Paul Dottin (London and Paris, 1923), pp. 71–72.

14. *Review,* VI, 142; Watt, *Rise of the Novel,* pp. 49–50.

15. Stephen, *Literature and Society in the Eighteenth Century,* pp. 136–137; Dobrée, *English Literature,* pp. 4–5; Hughes, "The Middle Class Reader and the English Novel," p. 370.

16. Wilson, III, 425.

CHAPTER 6. MAJOR MIDDLE-CLASS THEMES

1. Ian Watt, *The Rise of the Novel* (Berkeley, 1957), pp. 63–65; *Review,* III, 9, 16; David Riesman, *The Lonely Crowd* (New Haven, 1950), pp. 94–95.

2. Max Weber, *The Protestant Ethic and the Spirit of Capitalism,* tr. Talcott Parsons (New York, 1958), chaps. iii and v — citations are to pp. 163, 180.

3. Robert K. Merton, *Science, Technology and Society in Seventeenth Century England, Osiris,* IV (1938), 596–597; R. H. Tawney, *Religion and the Rise of Capitalism* (New York, 1926), p. 241.

4. *Robinson Crusoe* (in Aitken, vol. I), pp. 2–3; subsequent references in the text are to this edition, with the Roman numeral citing the volume.

5. It is instructive to compare Crusoe's father's sermon on the middle state with the following passage by Defoe from the *CET,* II, 106–107: "I know no station of life, I mean in that we call the middle station of it, and among the sensible part of mankind, which is more suited to make men perfectly easy, and comfortable to themselves, than that of a thriving tradesman. He is below the snares of the great, and above the contempt of those that are call'd low. His business is a road of life, with few or no uneven places in it . . . He is a safe man, nothing can hurt him but himself."

Defoe here falls into the very same homiletic tone and uses the same central figure as Crusoe's father to persuade his middle-class trading audience that theirs is the best station of life. But in this instance Defoe does not empathize with the ambitions of a Robinson Crusoe and therefore can present the orthodox view of his Puritan readers. The tension portrayed between Crusoe *père* and *fils* is discernible in Defoe's own life and writings: in his imaginative prose fictions he identified closely with his heroes and heroines whereas in his didactic works he generally adopted a more orthodox and less intensely personal role as a Puritan.

6. *Coleridge's Miscellaneous Criticism*, ed. Thomas M. Raysor (Cambridge, Mass., 1936), p. 294; Bonamy Dobrée, *English Literature in the Early Eighteenth Century, 1700–1740* (Oxford, 1959), p. 414.

7. See H. J. Habakkuk, "England," in *The European Nobility in the Eighteenth Century*, ed. Albert Goodwin (1953), p. 16.

8. G. M. Trevelyan, *England Under Queen Anne* (1930), I, 28.

9. In this discussion of Defoe's colonial theme I am indebted to Maximilian E. Novak's *Economics and the Fiction of Daniel Defoe* (Berkeley, 1962), pp. 140–155.

10. *The Life, Adventures, & Piracies of the Famous Captain Singleton* (in Aitken, vol. VI), p. 108; subsequent references in the text are to this edition.

11. *A New Voyage Round the World* (in Aitken, vol. XIV), p. 14.

12. *The Fortunes and Misfortunes of the Famous Moll Flanders* (in Aitken, vols. VII–VIII), I, 85; subsequent references in the text are to this two-volume edition, with the Roman numeral citing the first or second volume of the work.

13. Boswell's *Life of Johnson*, ed. G. B. Hill, rev. L. F. Powell (Oxford, 1934), II, 312.

14. *General Public Acts, 3–5 George I (1716–19)*, pp. 183–188; Abbot E. Smith, *Colonists in Bondage* (Chapel Hill, 1947), pp. 110–135; James D. Butler, "British Convicts Shipped to American Colonies," *American Historical Review*, II (1896), 24–25.

15. *CET*, I, 380; cf. *Tour*, I, 67–68, for an example of Defoe's concern about the spotless reputation of merchants and traders.

16. *CET*, I, 311.

17. Education for the Puritan was also valued as the means to grace; see Merton, *Science, Technology and Society*, p. 427.

18. *Serious Reflections during the Life and Surprising Adventures of Robinson Crusoe* (in Aitken, vol. III), p. 2; subsequent references in the text are to this edition, with the Roman numeral citing the volume.

19. Richard Baxter, *The Poor Man's Family Book*, in *Works* (1830), XIX, 495; also E. D. Bebb, *Nonconformity and Social and Economic Life, 1660–1800* (1935), pp. 94–95.

20. In the *CET*, II, 43, Defoe offered essentially the same couplet as a consolation to tradesmen: "He that repents, and his crimes amend,/Stands next to him that never did offend."

21. Dobrée, *English Literature*, p. 415.

22. *The History and Remarkable Life of the truly Honourable Colonel Jacque* (in Aitken, vols. X–XI), II, 160; subsequent references in the text are to this two-volume edition, with the Roman numeral citing the first or second volume of the work.

23. *The Fortunate Mistress; or, A History . . . of the Lady Roxana* (in Aitken, vols. XII–XIII), I, 180; subsequent references in the text are to this two-volume edition, with the Roman numeral citing the first or second volume of the work.

24. Ernest A. Baker, *The History of the English Novel* (New York, repr. Barnes & Noble, 1957), III, 227.

CHAPTER 7. MOLL FLANDERS

1. *Essay upon Projects* in Morley, pp. 151–152.

2. Mark Schorer, "A Study in Defoe: Moral Vision and Structural Form," *Thought*, XXV (June 1950), 275–287; E. M. Forster, *Aspects of the Novel* (1949), p. 59; Dorothy Van Ghent, *The English Novel, Form and Function* (New York, 1953), pp. 33–43. For the controversy over irony, intentional or unintentional, in *Moll*, see, for example, Ian Watt. *The Rise of the Novel* (Berkeley, 1957), pp. 93–134; Howard Koonce, "Moll's Muddle: Defoe's Use of Irony in *Moll Flanders*," *Journal of English Literary History*, XXX (Dec. 1963), 377–394; Maximilian E. Novak, "Conscious Irony in *Moll Flanders*," *College English*, XXVI (Dec. 1964), 198–204.

3. Schorer, "A Study in Defoe," pp. 281, 284; M. Dorothy George, *London Life in the XVIIIth Century* (1925), chap. vi, "The Uncertainties of Life" — citation is to p. 269; also see Benjamin Boyce, "The Question of Emotion in Defoe," *Studies in Philology*, L (Jan. 1953), 45–58.

4. *The Great Law of Subordination Consider'd* (1724), preface and pp. 11, 14; *Everybody's Business is Nobody's Business* (1725), p. 14.

5. Watt, *The Rise of the Novel*, pp. 114–115.

6. *Essay upon Projects* in Morley, p. 148.

7. *CET*, I, 118; all further references in the text are to this edition.

8. G. M. Trevelyan, *England Under Queen Anne* (1930), I, 36; Jonathan Swift, "A Letter to a Young Lady, on Her Marriage," *Irish Tracts 1720–1723 . . .* , ed. Louis Landa (Oxford, 1948), p. 89.

9. *An Appeal to Honour and Justice* (1715) in Shakespeare Head Ed., p. 225.

10. Virginia Woolf, "Defoe" (1919), *The Common Reader* (New York, 1948), p. 130.

11. See Maximilian E. Novak, "The Problem of Necessity in Defoe's Fiction," *Philological Quarterly*, XL (Oct. 1961), 513–524.

12. Woolf, "Defoe," p. 130.

13. Van Ghent, *English Novel*, p. 42.

CHAPTER 8. COLONEL JACQUE

1. George Sherburn, *The Restoration and Eighteenth Century (1660–1789)*, *A Literary History of England*, ed. A. C. Baugh (New York, 1948), p. 854; for a useful discussion see William H. McBurney, "Colonel Jacque: Defoe's Definition of the Complete Gentleman," *Studies in English Literature*, II (Summer 1962), 321–336.

2. *Essay upon Projects* in Morley, p. 145.

3. Lee, I, 343; intro. to *Moll Flanders* (in Aitken), I, xvn; *Life . . . of Jonathan Wild* (in Aitken, vol. XVI), p. 237. Defoe also warned against the

attractive heroes made of criminals in popular dramas like *The Beggar's Opera* and *The Quaker's Opera*, wherein the hero "runs through such a scene of riot and success, that but too many weak minds have been drawn away, and many unwary persons so charmed with his appearance on the stage, dressed in that elegant manner, and his pockets well lined, they have forthwith commenced street-robbers or housebreakers"; see *Second Thoughts are Best* in *Works*, ed. Sir Walter Scott (Oxford, 1841), XVIII, 10; also *Augusta Triumphans* in *Works*, XVIII, 34.

4. John Masefield, ed., *Defoe* (1909), pp. xix, xxxi.

5. Mermaid ed. of Richard Steele [*Plays*], ed. George A. Aitken (1894), pp. 269–270.

6. *Review*, I, 77–79, 81–83, 97–99, 101–107, and Appendix; also John Robert Moore, *A Checklist of the Writings of Daniel Defoe* (Bloomington, 1960), p. 102.

7. In 1710 Defoe had introduced the same episode and moral about marital whoredom into his *Review* (VII, 451); he was "an enemy to dueling" because, as a Puritan, he regarded it "a sin against God," and as a person "the most unequal thing in the world" to stake one's life for "an affront."

CHAPTER 9. THE FORTUNATE MISTRESS

1. Sir Robert Clayton was regarded as one of the mightiest merchants of the Whig interest in London, a man prominent in the affairs of the city and, according to the historian David Ogg, "the best example of his age of this evolution of scrivener into banker" — *England in the Reigns of James II and William III* (Oxford, 1955), p. 87; *Tour*, I, 169.

2. John Robert Moore, *Defoe in the Pillory and Other Studies*, Indiana University Publications, Humanities Series No. 1 (Bloomington, 1939), pp. 44–49.

3. *The Poor Man's Plea* (1698) in Shakespeare Head Ed., p. 6.

4. *Review*, III, 37–38; *CET*, II, pt. ii, 151–152.

5. The marriage between Roxana and her Dutch merchant, in the apt analogy of Maximilian E. Novak, "is like the merging of two corporations" — *Economics and the Fiction of Daniel Defoe* (Berkeley, 1962), p. 133; see chap. vi for a generally suggestive and illuminating discussion of *The Fortunate Mistress*.

6. Bonamy Dobrée also perceives that *The Fortunate Mistress* is "different, not only that here Defoe moves in unfamiliar higher spheres, but because it has about it a slight flavour of the erotic" — *English Literature in the Early Eighteenth Century, 1700–1740* (Oxford, 1959), p. 424.

7. *The Political History of the Devil* (1726), pp. 360–363, 401; *An Essay on the History and Reality of Apparitions* (1727), p. 210.

8. Rudolf G. Stamm, "Daniel Defoe: An Artist in the Puritan Tradition," *Philological Quarterly*, XV (July 1936), 225–246, esp. 245; also see Benjamin Boyce, "The Question of Emotion in Defoe," *Studies in Philology*, L (Jan. 1953), 45–58, esp. 53.

9. Alan D. McKillop, *The Early Masters of English Fiction* (Lawrence, Kansas, 1956), p. 25. Professor Stamm believes that Defoe was able to deceive himself in *The Fortunate Mistress* as well as in the other novels about

what he was doing (see p. 245). My contention is that Defoe by 1724 finally realized what he was doing as a writer of fiction and, because of what happened to his imagination while writing *The Fortunate Mistress*, abruptly ended his story of Roxana's career and ceased writing novels.

10. Walter De La Mare, *Desert Islands and Robinson Crusoe* (1930), p. 37.

CHAPTER 10. THE COMPLETE ENGLISH TRADESMAN: GENTILITY AND TRADE

1. *Tour*, I, 3; subsequent references in the text are to this edition.
2. Moore, p. 354.
3. G. D. H. Cole, intro. to *Tour*, I, x–xi; M. Dorothy George, *England in Transition* (Penguin Books, 1953), pp. 37–38; H. J. Habakkuk, "England," in *The European Nobility in the Eighteenth Century*, ed. Albert Goodwin (1953), p. 18. For a useful survey see Edward Hughes, *North Country Life in the Eighteenth Century* (1952).
4. *An Essay upon Projects* in Morley, pp. 153–155.
5. G. M. Trevelyan, *England Under Queen Anne* (1930), I, 33; Habakkuk, "England" in *European Nobility*, pp. 16–17.
6. References in parentheses are to *A Plan of the English Commerce*, Shakespeare Head Ed. (Oxford: Basil Blackwell, 1928).
7. *Augusta Triumphans* in *Works*, ed. Sir Walter Scott (Oxford, 1841), XVIII, 2.
8. Habakkuk, "England" in *European Nobility*, p. 16.
9. Cole, intro. to *Tour*, I, x.

CHAPTER 11. THE COMPLEAT ENGLISH GENTLEMAN: THE BORN AND THE BRED GENTLEMAN

1. *Of Royall Educacion*, ed. Karl D. Bülbring (1895), p. 1; Moore, p. 220.
2. *Mist's Journal* (April 26, 1718) in Lee, II, 37.
3. Samuel Johnson, *Rambler* No. 208, in *Works* (Oxford, 1825), III, 463.
4. *CEG*, pp. 20–21; subsequent references in text are to this edition.
5. The second — and best — of the three incomplete introductions in the surviving British Museum manuscript copy has properly been affixed to the published text as the introduction by the editor, Karl D. Bülbring (*CEG*, pp. 3–10); it most accurately anticipates in tone and content the treatise itself.
6. *Institution of a Gentleman* (1555), also discussed by Bülbring in intro. to *CEG.*, pp. xxxv–xl. See also W. Lee Ustick, "The English Gentleman in the Sixteenth and Early Seventeenth Century," 2 vols., (unpub. diss., Harvard University, 1931), I, 117f. and John E. Mason, *Gentlefolk in the Making* (Philadelphia: Univ. of Pennsylvania Press, 1935), p. 37. The theses of Ustick and Mason, in large part surveying the same material, provide a valuable background to the evolution of ideals of gentility in England, although neither goes into any detail about Defoe's writings on the subject.
7. Ruth Kelso, "Sixteenth Century Definitions of the Gentleman in England," *Journal of English and Germanic Philology*, XXIV (July 1925), 370–382, esp. 371; Mason, *Gentlefolk in the Making*, pp. 303–304, note 22.

8. In her discussion Miss Kelso follows the distinction made between "nobility dative" and "nobility native" in Robert Glover's *Catalogue of Honour*, trans. Thomas Milles (1610); Sir John Ferne, *The Blazon of Gentry* (1586), p. 91.

9. Sir Thomas Smith, *The Commonwealth of England* (1612), p. 27 — quoted by Kelso in "Sixteenth Century Definitions," p. 377.

10. The theory of gentility in England from the sixteenth to the seventeenth century bears a marked change of emphasis from heredity and birth to education and personal worth; see W. Lee Ustick, "Changing Ideals of Aristocratic Character and Conduct in Seventeenth Century England," *Modern Philology*, XXX (Nov. 1932), 147–166.

11. For a useful survey of attitudes on the education of gentlemen in the seventeenth and eighteenth centuries, see George C. Brauer, Jr., *The Education of a Gentleman* (New York, 1959), pp. 52–103.

12. G. M. Trevelyan, *England Under Queen Anne* (1930), I, 28.

13 *Echo* quoted in R. M. Wiles, *Serial Publication in England Before 1750* (Cambridge: Cambridge University Press, 1957), pp. 11–12; see also the satirical portrait of "Lord Finical" in the *World* No. 64, quoted in Brauer, *The Education of a Gentleman*, p. 55.

14. Wooll, *Biographical Memoirs of S. Warton*, p. 305, cited in Edward Hughes, *North Country Life in the Eighteenth Century* (1952), p. 368.

15. Lee, III, 435–436.

16. Lee, III, 437–439 (Nov. 6, 1725).

17. *Letters*, p. 473.

CHAPTER 12. THE FINAL YEARS OF DANIEL DEFOE, GENTLEMAN

1. Lee, I, 439–440; Wright, p. 329.

2. For sketches and diagrams of Defoe's house and grounds at Stoke Newington, see Lee, I, 454; Wright, p. 336, also pp. 216, 329. *Tour*, I, 165–166, II, 10; Lee, I, 440.

3. Professor Moore interprets the spacious second house Defoe had built for himself in Stoke Newington — the "very handsome house" Baker noticed in his account — as "his own equivalent of Shakespeare's house at Stratford or Sir Walter Scott's at Abbotsford." Like Shakespeare and Scott, Defoe "hoped to establish a family name that would last" — see Moore, p. 335.

4. Bernard Drew, "The London Assurance — A Corporation Established by Royal Charter in 1720," *Notes and Queries* (Aug. 7, 1948), 342 — Professor Healey also let me see a letter from Mr. Drew dated Dec. 8, 1950, describing Defoe's Fire Policy No. 776; Moore, p. 305.

5. Moore, p. 326; Sutherland, pp. 251–252; James Sutherland, "A Note on the Last Years of Defoe," *Modern Language Review*, XXIX (1934), 140–141.

6. *The Protestant Monastery* (in Aitken, vol. XI), p. 190; Sutherland, p. 261.

7. *Letters*, p. 473.

8. Sutherland, "Last Years of Defoe," pp. 138–140.

9. *Essay upon Projects* in Morley, p. 44.

10. *Letters,* pp. 473–476.
11. *The Letters of Samuel Johnson,* ed. R. W. Chapman (Oxford, 1952), II, 228.
12. Moore, pp. 339–341.
13. C. E. Whiting, *Studies in English Puritanism* (New York, 1931), p. 450; Wilson, III, 610 and note.

Index

Index

276

Index

Index

Riesman, David, 125
Rochester, Earl of, 32, 93
Royal Society, The, 34, 35, 110
Ryswick, Treaty of, 49, 56

Sacheverell, Dr. Henry, 59
Saturday Club, 82, 88
Savage, Richard, 92
Schorer, Mark, 142, 143
Scriblerus Club, 82, 88, 90–91
Settle, Elkanah, 33
Shadwell, Thomas, 35
Sherburn, George, 86, 161
Smith, Sir Thomas, 227
Society for the Propagation of Christian
    Knowledge, 110, 118
South Sea Bubble, 112
South Sea Company, 112, 121, 248
Southey, Robert, 254
Spanish Succession, 56
Spectator, The, 8, 89, 95–96, 113–114, 116
Spence, Joseph, 91
Stamm, Rudolf G., 195
Stancliffe, James, 250, 251
Stancliffe, Samuel, 38, 250, 251
Steele, Richard, 89–90, 95–96, 113–115,
    116
Stephen, Leslie, 33, 87, 107, 118, 120
Strafford, Earl of, 107–108
Sutherland, James, 23, 37, 70, 91, 101
Swift, Jonathan: poetry, 33; Defoe and,
    81–87; Scriblerus Club, 88; on mar-
    riage, 153; mentioned, 93, 120, 241

Tale of a Tub, A, 81
Tate, Nahum, 34, 35, 56
Tatler, The, 89, 95–96, 116
Taverner, Jeremiah, 73
Tawney, R. H., 126
Taylor, William, 116, 122

Temple, Sir William, 33, 87, 93
Test Act (1673), 58
Theatre, The, 114
Thomas, Dalby, 48–49, 50
Tonson, Jacob, 116
Townsend, Viscount (Secretary of State),
    102
Trent, William P., 57, 73, 82, 90, 175
Trevelyan, G. M., 153, 214
True Bred Gentleman, The, 224
Tuffley, Mrs. Joan (D's mother-in-law),
    38
Tuffley, Mary, *see* Defoe, Mary
Turberville, A. S., 87
Tutchin, John, 51, 76–80, 84, 92, 241

Utrecht, Treaty of, 107, 111

Van der Gucht, Michael, 31, 74
Van Ghent, Dorothy, 142, 159
Virgil, 32

Wagner, Anthony R., 54
Waller, Edmund, 32
Walpole, Robert, 116
Ward, John, 248
Watt, Ian, 124, 147
Watts, John, 245, 250
Weber, Max, 125
Wesley, Samuel, 12
William III: Defoe serves, 29–30, 48–49,
    51–53, 55, 56–57, 99; death of, 58, 94;
    gardening, 247; mentioned, 63, 66, 67,
    76, 124
Withers, George, 91
Woolf, Virginia, 142, 157, 159
Wren, Sir Christopher, 24
Wright, Thomas, 246

Young, G. M., 23